S0-AHB-869

Office and Office Building Security

Second Edition

Office and Office Building Security

Second Edition

Ed San Luis
Louis A. Tyska
Lawrence J. Fennelly

Butterworth-Heinemann
Boston London Oxford Singapore Sydney Toronto Wellington

Copyright © 1994 by Butterworth-Heinemann
ℜ A member of the Reed Elsevier group
All rights reserved.

No part of this publication may be reproduced, stored in a retrieval
system, or transmitted, in any form or by any means, electronic,
mechanical, photocopying, recording, or otherwise, without the pri-
or written permission of the publisher.

Recognizing the importance of preserving what has been written, it
is the policy of Butterworth-Heinemann to have the books it publishes printed on acid-free paper, and we exert our best efforts to that
end.

Library of Congress Cataloging-in-Publication Data

San Luis, Ed.
    Office and office building security / by Ed San Luis, Louis
A. Tyska, Lawrence J. Fennelly. —2nd ed.
        p.   cm.
    Includes index.
    ISBN 0-7506-9487-4
    1. Offices—Security measures.   2. Office buildings—
Security measures. 3. Crime prevention. I. Tyska, Louis A.,
1934– . II. Fennelly, Lawrence J., 1940– . III. Title.
HF5547.S23   1993
658.4'73—dc20   93-32389
                                                         CIP

British Library Cataloguing-in-Publication Data
A catalogue record for this book is available from the British
Library.

Butterworth-Heinemann
313 Washington Street
Newton, MA 02158

10 9 8 7 6 5 4 3 2

Printed in the United States of America

This is offered as a tribute to E.J. "Cris" Criscouli, Jr., CPP, who over the past seventeen years has promoted and honored the professions of Asset Protection Management and private enforcement through his role as executive vice president of the American Society for Industrial Security–International. His patience and guidance, combined with exemplary management skills, have laid the foundation for future generations of leaders and entrepreneurs in our profession.

Contents

Foreword

Terrorism. Espionage. Violence. These words can strike terror into the hearts of even the most polished, competent security professional. Unexpected threats occur at any time and, as a security professional, you must be prepared for any contingency. Savvy owners of businesses and office buildings know that physical security now is inevitable and crucial to the success of any establishment.

In today's society, office building security and property managers have an increasing need to protect sensitive information, fixed assets, and the safety of persons employed in the facility. There are obstacles that industrial sites don't have—high traffic, fenced entrances, numerous visitors, and transient office workers.

The security industry constantly changes and, to be effective, persons charged with security must keep abreast of new trends in the industry and society. *Office and Office Building Security*, Second Edition, has been entirely revised and updated to cover a wealth of new information.

The specific needs of office building security managers are explained in detail in this book—a "must have" for any security professional. Burglary and robbery, access control, violence, espionage, computer security, and the threat of substance abuse in the American workplace are only a handful of the topics discussed.

As a lifelong security professional, with experience as a military and Department of Defense contractor, and presently as a supplier of a wide range of security services, I've learned that education is essential for security professionals who wish to remain effective. I urge you to learn all that you can from the highly competent experts who authored this book in an effort to provide even better security to those who count on you everyday.

Tom Walthen,
Chairman and Chief Executive Officer,
Pinkerton's Inc.

Preface

Twenty years ago Edward San Luis wrote *Office and Office Building Security*. It was then and still is a fine compilation. At the time, it addressed burgeoning loss and liability issues that most businessmen and security practitioners were only just beginning to experience and prepare safeguards against.

In those twenty years, we have witnessed scientific and technological advancements that have defied imagination and complicated and changed the way business is conducted. No one can argue that recent geographic, political, economic, and social changes have had a great impact on the international business community. Major corporations such as Bendix, RJR-Nabisco, General Motors, Norton, Revlon, and many others underwent major divestitures, hostile takeovers, and leveraged buyouts—all affecting the global economy, and the American economy in particular. Businesses that weren't directly affected by these conditions were influenced by the ensuing political upheavals.

Corporate downsizing also has had an effect on workplace integrity and ethics, as well as where, when, and how business is conducted. Office location decentralization and the delegation of authority downward to ease business decision-making have in recent years transformed and complicated the conduct of traditional business. Places of business have simultaneously become sites of extreme security effectiveness and extreme security vulnerability.

Consequently, a total rewrite of the original book to meet the needs of the 1990s was demanded. We are pleased to offer *Office and Office Building Security*, Second Edition.

Louis A. Tyska
Lawrence J. Fennelly

Acknowledgments

Among the legions of people to whom we are indebted for their contributions, directly and indirectly to this work specifically, and as an influence on our general development as security practitioners, we are especially thankful to Fuller "Bud" Brooks, August "Gus" Bequai, Dennis Devlin, Robert Hanna, Eugene Houssling, Paul Johnson, John Lombardi, Dave Neudick, Anthony Piazza, Mickey Rosenberg, Adam Thermus, and Annmarie Thomas. A special thanks to Annmarie Fennelly for her able assistance in proofreading, and to Jan Rossi, whose advice, computer, and administrative skills made sense of it all.

Louis A. Tyska
Lawrence J. Fennelly

Chapter 1

Robbery, Larceny, Burglary, and Access Control

No office or office building can conduct business while closed to the public. Clients, sales- and delivery-people, messengers, service personnel, visitors—a steady stream of outsiders is essential to the operation of almost every business. This exposure, however, is the key contributor to the vulnerability of businesses.

High levels of activity and traffic are the vehicle or cover for the criminal few who enter to victimize the office and its personnel. They may enter in any guise and, because they are familiar with modern office layouts, they are rarely identified as a risk or questioned as to their purpose. There are many serious crimes that can be attributed to these relatively few individuals:

Theft

Theft (larceny) is the most common crime committed by outsiders while businesses are open. Computers, office equipment, calculators, purses, and wallets disappear constantly, regardless of the office type, location, or number of employees present.

The great frequency of theft means this problem receives top priority in office loss prevention programs. Because the procedures which reduce theft are generally those which deter other open-hours crimes, preventive measures are discussed later in this chapter, after the entire area of vulnerability and risk has been examined.

Assault

By definition, "an attempt to commit a battery or an intentional placing of another in apprehension of receiving battery." Less common in a busy office, but far more feared, are crimes against persons, including robbery, rape, assault, and even murder. In 1992 the National Safety Council stated that between 1980 and 1985 murder was the third leading cause of death in the workplace, accounting for 13 percent of workplace deaths. (The percentage was higher for women.) In the 1990s the number of stalking murders is rising and will continue.

In many offices such crimes may seem impossible, but they do occur. Rapes have occurred in a women's restroom in the Senate Office Building, on the firestairs of a Los Angeles building, and in unlocked offices where workers were putting in overtime at night. Robberies have occurred in rest rooms, corridors, elevators, and subterranean garages. No one and no place is immune. The fear that such attacks create is infectious and every employee feels victimized. People leave employers for jobs in "safer" locales and those who remain are reluctant to work overtime. An entire office can be demoralized by an attack on one of its members. There is also the possibility that the employer or building management company may be liable for injury or damages if inadequate security and negligence can be proven. Businesses' knowledge of criminal activity in their areas has been cited by many courts in civil negligence proceedings. The following are some crimes which will affect your office security program:

Robbery

By definition, "by force and violence or by assault and putting in fear, robbing, stealing and taking from the person of another money or other property which may be the subject of larceny."

Burglary

By definition, "breaking and entering of the dwelling of another in the nighttime with the intent to commit a felony." (See Appendix I)

Larceny

By definition, "taking and carrying away the personal property of another with the intent to deprive the owner permanently of its use."

Disorderly Conduct

By definition, "that conduct which involves no lawful exercise of First Amendment rights and which by its very nature use of physical violence or any threat to use such force or violence if that threat is effectively possible of immediate execution or which is tumultuous."

Rape

By definition, "having sexual intercourse or unnatural sexual intercourse with a person and compelling such person to submit by force and against his/her will or compelling such person to submit by threat of bodily injury."

Domestic Violence

Laws vary from state to state. However these types of incidents have a moral effect on the workplace. Both building and security managers should familiarize themselves with and implement policies to deal with domestic violence.

PREPARATION FOR CRIME

Freedom of access to buildings and particular offices is very important to the criminal. It permits him or her to "case" the office for burglary or larceny potential during business hours. Taking advantage of this freedom of movement, criminals can identify the most attractive targets and plan escape routes. Hiding places to wait until closing time, such as air conditioning machinery rooms or accessible crawlspaces, can be ferreted out. Thieves can get into telephone equipment rooms where alarm connections can be identified or taps installed on the phone without the risk of approaching the targeted victim. Telephone lines might even be tapped to record incoming or outgoing data.

Criminals enjoy even more freedom of access if they appear as "pseudoservicemen." They enter as the "XYZ repairman" who has come to "pick up the machine"; or as the electrician who comes to fix Mr. Smith's desk lamp when he's away on vacation (and check his desk and files between bulb changing); or as a telephone serviceman who wanders freely from desk to desk "looking for the trouble in the phone." These predators are rarely challenged and hardly noticed by a busy office staff. Frequently, they present themselves in normal business attire and simply blend into the mainstream of activity in much the same way a "sneak thief" would (see below).

As long as thieves have freedom to roam the premises, the odds are in their favor. They will, in no time, familiarize themselves with the rooms accessible from the public corridor, find out how (or if) the doors to the firestairs are secured against reentry from the stairwell, and see whether or not there is an escape route over the roof. A great many offices are entered on the "oops, wrong office" routine—and at the same time checked for the quality and quantity of equipment and the alertness of personnel.

The key task here is to train employees to be alert to suspicious activity and to ask strangers, "May I help you?", observing their activities and calling for assistance if necessary.

SNEAK THIEVES

Sneak thieves don't break into your office—they blend in. They are friendly and say "Good morning" as they pass—or they may hide and allow you to walk by. They are professionals at what they do; 99 percent of the time after a theft occurs, no one saw a suspicious person. Your receptionist is the first line of defense in your office. Teach him or her to greet each visitor, ask for identification, and check with employees to see if they are expecting someone. Make visitors sign in and out. The key here is to not make it easy. The thief doesn't want to get caught. When he knows how good your security is he will move on to the next building—an example of the *displacement of crime theory.*

THE GEOGRAPHY OF SECURITY

Neighboring tenants, the neighborhood, and even the city where the office is located play important roles in determining security needs. If all other factors were equal, the level of office crime would vary directly with that of the city and the neighborhood in which the office is located. It doesn't work that way, however. The other factors are not equal and can materially affect the crime risk for a particular office.

These elements can include the kinds of tenants in a multiple occupancy building; the size and makeup of the working population of the building; the number and kind of outsiders legitimately present during business hours; and the amount of pedestrian traffic outside. Alone or in combination, any of these factors can be enormously important in determining the crime potential facing your office. Here is an example of the effect of just one of these factors: A downtown building in Los Angeles had the same infrequent incidence of crime as that of the general neighborhood. Subsequently, three bail bond firms moved into the building, changing the character of authorized visitor traffic significantly—and also the rate of theft.

OPEN IS NOT PUBLIC

Office building security during daylight hours is an area of protection which, in spite of its paramount importance, is all too often neglected until a serious loss or tragedy occurs. Such an event usually brings on a rash of security measures and directives, many of them effective but overdue, and most of them aimed at the control of building traffic. Your office security program should be proactive and ongoing. It should be remembered that building access is not a right—it is a privilege subject to control.

Offices and office buildings are not open to every casual visitor who happens to stroll by. If you are to hope for any degree of security, building traffic can and must be controlled. It can be regulated courteously and economically, but it must be controlled.

There are many ways to bring about access control; some involve built-in security measures; others are customized to fit specific needs and may involve equipment installation in older buildings. All methods are designed to safeguard personnel, their assets, and the office environment itself.

ANNOYING TELEPHONE CALLS

Many of us have experienced some form of annoying telephone call, at work or at home. The phone rings, and, when we answer, no one responds. Usually we just hang up and forget it. However, some annoying telephone calls are more serious. When should you be concerned? What should you do?

The Silent Caller described above *should* concern you if the call is repeated over a period of hours or days. Especially be aware of such calls just before or during a holiday period. Burglars typically use this means to find out if anyone is at home or in the office. Report your suspicions to the police without delay.

Abusive, Harassing, or Obscene Calls are more frightening. Don't stay on the line once you realize what kind of call is intended. Remember that the abusive or obscene caller, just like the silent caller, is hoping for a response—anger or fear. Don't give in—just hang up.

The Threatening Call requires immediate action. Since it's specifically directed at you or your family, it's hard not to respond to this type of call. Don't give in and talk with the caller. But hanging up is not enough—call the police *immediately*.

Any time you receive an annoying call, jot down some relevant information just in case. Note the date, time, and duration of the call, as well as a description of the caller's voice. Note any sounds you heard in the background, and also indicate who was with you at the time. If the problem persists, this information will be helpful to the police.

Taking some basic precautions can help you avoid serious problems. Never give out your name, address, or any other personal information over the phone, unless you definitely know the caller. If an unknown caller asks your name, respond by saying, "What number did you call?" or "Who are you calling?" If the caller won't tell you, don't express anger, just hang up.

Always let the caller tell you his name, don't provide him with one. It may seem obvious, but a common con game involves the caller who says, "Do you know who this is?" If you say the name of someone you know, the caller agrees, telling you he has been arrested and needs to borrow fifty dollars for bail, asking you to turn the money over to a third party. Your real friend will be very surprised when you ask him to pay back the loan!

Appendix I

Burglary Prevention

SECURITY TIPS FOR SMALL BUSINESSES, PART I

Burglary is a property crime that occurs when a business is closed. The burglar may enter though any opening (door, window, air conditioning duct, skylight) or even create one through an interior shared wall or an outside wall. Reduce your risk as much as possible. Burglary is a crime of opportunity that can be prevented.

Surveillance and Security Are Critical

- Lighting—Install bright interior and exterior lighting to make all entrances visible from both the outside and inside of the business.
- Locks and Safes—Purchase high quality door locks and use them. Grilles and storefront gates delay entry. Use an Underwriters Laboratory–listed money safe, bolted to the floor and visible from the street.
- Entry Control—Know who has keys and restrict access to the front door only. Rekey the lock if a once-trusted employee is discharged for cause. If you have a high turnover of employees, rekey locks annually. Consider an access control system rather than keys.
- Intrusion Alert—Install a good quality alarm system to detect unauthorized entry. Check with your local Chamber of Commerce and police department before you make this investment.
- Windows—Consider installing burglar-resistant glass in accessible areas. Unbreakable polycarbonate may work even better, particularly if you have high-value items in window displays.
- Environment—Keep areas around the business clean to aid visibility. Display your most valuable articles near the center of a room to force a burglar to take the longest possible escape route. Keep merchandise displays organized to allow maximum visibility and check closets and restrooms before you lock up. You don't need an unwanted visitor staying inside after closing hours.

If you practice these techniques you will certainly diminish your chances of becoming a burglar's victim.

Prepared by Robert Hanna, Crime Prevention Officer,
Quincy Police Department, Quincy, Massachusetts

Appendix II

Reduce Your Crime Vulnerability

Employers and Crime

Businesses can reduce their vulnerability to crime in many ways. Measures such as locks, alarms, and good lighting make any establishment a less attractive target for criminals. Your local police department can conduct a security survey (usually offered *free*) and give advice on alarm systems and other protection devices. Community service and involvement are some other important safeguards against crime. Customers and neighbors who view a business as a valued resource in the community will watch out for its property and employees.

Employees and Crime

Employees either can help you to be profitable or hurt you through waste, inattention to customers, or stealing. You must set the example for honesty and develop clear policies regarding security and theft.

- Develop procedures and advise all employees about inventory control. All merchandise entering and exiting your premises should be accounted for.
- Screen employees carefully before hiring them. Check their backgrounds to be sure they have not been fired for behavior you would find dangerous or unacceptable. A Polaroid photo will help police in any investigation that involves a dishonest employee.
- Train employees in proper cash handling and security measures. Set a policy regarding daily accounting procedures for cash on hand and stick to it.
- Research shows that employees steal from businesses that are impersonal and lack clear policies. Show employees you care about them and their property. Provide a clean orderly work environment with secure places for their personal property. A satisfied employee can be the first line of defense against crime in your business.

Prepared by Robert Hanna, Crime Prevention Officer,
Quincy Police Department, Quincy, Massachusetts

Chapter 2

Security for the Open Office Building

The first step in office security begins with a careful, realistic examination of the building and its environment. Even if you feel your own office is secure, there can be no security for your employees or your assets if building corridors, restrooms, elevators, and the adjacent streets are crime-ridden. You should, therefore, familiarize yourself with every aspect of your building or the building in which you are planning to lease space. The second step is to identify office vulnerabilities and to make recommendations which will reduce your crime risk.

PEDESTRIAN TRAFFIC AND INTERIOR TRAFFIC

One veteran security administrator we know visits the neighborhood of a proposed lease several times and at all hours to watch the flow of traffic and observe activity in the area. This technique, which is patterned after the police stake-out, can be a valuable tool for evaluation of a neighborhood. This is not to suggest that offices should never be located in high risk areas; rather that the risk must be weighed and both office and office building security measures structured accordingly.

Take Manhattan's subway entrances, for example. On one hand, the nearness of subway entrances to buildings increases the number of "floaters"—idlers wandering through the buildings, often looking for an opportunity to steal. To them, the subway entrance is an effective escape route. On the other hand, office personnel regard the subway entrance as an escape route. They don't feel safe on the street and look on the proximity of the subway entrance as a plus for their security. (A security officer would be a valuable asset in this situation to reduce unwanted traffic, thereby maximizing the advantage that the nearby subway entrance represents while minimizing the amount of casual traffic it offers.)

While checking a building, observing the lobby during both heavy and light traffic periods and riding the elevators will give you a good idea of the kind of population the building has.

OFF-HOURS SECURITY

If traffic is freely permitted in the building at unusual hours due to the needs of a few offices, are there means of securing uninvolved floors from traffic?

The use of a lobby security officer with a sign-in/out log will discourage the casual criminal or the eager amateur. Such a log would also serve as a continuous profile of the building's after-hours traffic pattern. The supervised off-hours lobby is more effective, of course, in conjunction with a closing-hour building check of office doors, stair doors, and unsecured areas. Where firestairs are secured against reentry at office floors, such a search is effective in flushing stowaways out of the building.

If it is illegal to lock roof and firestair doors, they can be alarmed if opened to sound locally and at a manned remote point in the building. Alternatively, the stairwells themselves can be alarmed at various levels. In either case, thought must be given to the response the alarm will receive—an unanswered alarm offers no protection.

Many buildings are choosing card access control and closed-circuit television (CCTV) as an effective means of traffic control. With card access, former employees are punched out of the system; there is no need to worry about changing locks to guard against illegal master keys.

DAY TRAFFIC CONTROL

Little can be done to regulate everyday traffic under ordinary circumstances while a building is open—building tenants require an unimpeded flow of traffic. Daytime uniformed lobby guards, unsupported by communications and backup, can in no way regulate traffic, although their presence seems to ward off less determined thieves. Guards will have no effect on the professional office thief, but they can project an image of safety and order to the general public.

Unfortunately, this image can actually be damaging to the security of the building. Far too many people think that a security guard constitutes security; they feel a sense of protection which may not be—and usually is not—justified by real circumstances. Tenants, as well as building management, are prone to believe that the presence of a lobby security officer during open hours means that the building is secured and that they can be excused from taking basic precautions dictated by good sense. No building security system, however practical and complete, can relieve tenants of their responsibility to take reasonable precautions on their own behalf.

The assumption that any security equals all security is so common that, to the security professional, "a little security is worse than none." Where there is no security at all, management can see the risk and take appropriate steps. Where there is token evidence of security, management often takes outrageous risks which are in no way provided for.

You would be wise to be constantly aware of this tendency by the public to presume more security than in actuality exists, and to guard against it in all phases of security planning and administration.

A classic, though hopefully rare, instance of the depths to which advertised security can fall is the case of a much-publicized "security building" which places a guard in the main entrance lobby, while tenants park in a subterranean garage where building access on foot or by car is not only open but unobserved. Anyone who can walk into the garage and push an elevator button may enter this "security building" at tenant floors. On the other hand, if the trespassers prefer not to go farther than the garage, they can wait for the tenants in the cul-de-sac which must be entered to reach the elevators.

Only unusually knowledgeable tenants can distinguish between real and apparent security, whether in the original evaluation or in the status review periods that are so important. These reviews can be valuable in more ways than one. It has been held in the courts that where security levels have fallen below advertised levels, lessors are guilty of a breach of the lease, even though security was not an article in the lease.

Inadequate security is frequently the result of inexperienced building operators. The natural solution for both building management and responsible tenants is to employ a qualified security person on staff, or a security consultant, or both.

BUILDING SECURITY SYSTEMS

In spite of the difficulties inherent in "open-hours" security, a growing number of high-rise office buildings have developed security systems which have proven effective in reducing problems.

The common denominator in all these systems is the presence of a guard or attendant at a lobby security station. This station, which is either the primary or a secondary security communications center, is usually centrally located and highly visible. The communications network may be simple or elaborate, depending on the needs of the building, but whatever it is, it is connected to back-up support that can be in the lobby within minutes.

Locations of backup systems are a confidential feature of any building security program. Any emergency which brings guards on the double to the lobby leaves other areas unmanned and temporarily vulnerable.

It must be emphasized that the police cannot be considered to be this kind of immediate, on-call support in any security plan. Police response will always be dependent upon police problems. Their assistance should only be requested in cases of unavoidable arrest or where the situation seems to be potentially serious. The best and the worst police response times should be calculated, and emergency planning based on the probable length of time required for police arrival.

Most lobby problems, however, can be handled by unflaggingly cheerful determination and persuasion without any need for back-up personnel. The daily role of the lobby security center is to serve as a building information and directory service. Another alternative places both a receptionist and a uniformed security officer on duty in the lobby. Many building managers feel that this public relations role is of prime importance and they stress the role of "attendant" rather than "security officer." Other building managers are convinced that the public relations role is implicit in the function and use of security officers in the belief that their presence underscores the management's intent to discourage crime in the building.

COMMUNICATIONS

Another necessary feature of a building security system is some method of communication to and from the security station. This may be a transmitter communicating with hand-held two-way radios, a telephone-to-pager system, or equivalent systems all having the ability to reach building personnel wherever they may be. Normally, this communication system includes building engineers and emergency maintenance persons, as well as security personnel and their supervisors. Personal pocket pagers are more reliable and less disturbing than public address systems, and offer the advantage of notifying only those being sought. In this age of high technology, only state-of-the-art equipment should be considered.

THE "ELECTRONIC SECURITY OFFICER"

An increasing number of high-rise office buildings are setting up closed-circuit television surveillance systems to permit full and regular inspection of key points without the necessity of employing more guards. Exterior fire doors and emergency stairwells are alarmed and flash signals at a manned television console. Particularly in newer buildings, closed-circuit television cameras provide surveillance of all stairwells, key or card access corridors, and other areas attractive to thieves. After-hours access identification and admittance are sometimes controlled remotely from television-equipped security consoles which, in these applications, are usually located away from the lobby in order to protect the confidentiality of the building security operation.

Where the lobby console is not the primary (and protected) communications console, a closed-circuit television camera can be installed to view the lobby desk area for the protection of the lobby guard. Also located at the security console or a lobby panel are inconspicuous coded lights, supplemented by audible signals, which are alarm terminals for fire, intrusion, and air conditioning failure warning systems. A considerable number of alarms can terminate in a relatively small console panel.

The "electronic security officer" doesn't have to be a full-time engineer, but he must understand the equipment in front of him and know how to operate it.

When fire and intrusion systems go off they require a specific action or procedure, even if this procedure is as simple as contacting the supervisor on duty or calling the local fire department.

ELEVATORS

Traffic indicators, emergency communications, and emergency controls for the elevators are frequently located at the lobby security station. Elevator traffic patterns may be switched for an evacuation, for example, or all elevators brought to the first floor and secured against automatic operation to make them available to firemen. Elevators can be equipped with closed-circuit television, mirrors, telephones, alarms, and card access-control systems.

SMALLER OFFICE BUILDINGS

Security systems for small one- or two-story buildings are correspondingly simpler and cheaper. Lobby security becomes the receptionist at the entrance. Fire exits are alarmed. Closed-circuit television, if used, is more likely watching the parking lot. In problem areas it may be necessary to install additional lighting and fence the employee parking area, locking it except during heavy use periods. In small buildings, good security practices substitute for a guard force and are essential to the safety of all.

SECURITY FOR THE OPEN OFFICE

The final responsibility for security rests with the individual office—it cannot be delegated. In order to arrive at an effective security program, each office must evaluate its specific problems and needs in light of its specific exposure. Office policy and procedures follow from that.

EMPLOYEE COOPERATION

Consider starting an Office Crime Watch (similar to the Neighborhood Watch concept, see Appendix I). Your three objectives should be:

1. Report crime
2. Report suspicious persons
3. Look out for each other

Cooperation by employees is, without doubt, the first essential for office security; rules are useless without it. And this cooperation must be continuous, just as any effective security procedure must be, and it must be gained by persuasion.

To threaten employees into protecting themselves, their belongings and the company's property by frightening stories would have the same effect on morale and employee retention as working in a crime-ridden environment. This is hardly the goal of security, which aims for tranquility and the safety of the office. Posters, coasters, scratch pads—security reminders with a light touch—are some of the techniques used to remind employees of their personal responsibility to reduce the potential for crime in their office.

EMPLOYEE PROPERTY

It hardly seems necessary to remind employees to exercise reasonable care of their property, yet self-protection must be a continuous campaign. Crimes of opportunity occur when property is left unattended, unsecured, and unoccupied. Purses are left habitually on top of desks or on the floor beside them, jackets containing wallets and checkbooks are hung in unoccupied offices. These are attractive targets and thieves are lured by easy pickings. Not only are they looking for carelessly left money, but also for credit cards which bring fast cash, and the checkbooks and personal identification needed to facilitate forgery.

Carelessness with purses and wallets brings thieves back again and again, until eventually they raise their sights from purses to office equipment—the single largest source of loss from offices according to insurance statistics.

THE THIEF'S EYE VIEW

What does the thief see in your office when he looks in from the corridor door? Does he see a one-desk reception area that is usually—but not always—occupied? Or is it *always* occupied by a receptionist?

The reception area is the office's first line of defense during open hours. In many offices it is the only defense. Despite this, more computers are stolen from this point than any other. One company located in a single two-story office building in a low-crime area ignored four separate open-hours thefts of new computers from the front office reception area, despite the fact that their insurance was cancelled after the second loss. At last report, they had just lost their fifth computer from that desk—along with six more—in a nighttime smash-and-grab burglary. This company's controller is aware that there are office equipment locks that will withstand a surprising amount of force. But he doesn't believe it would be "wise" to drill holes for these devices in office desks, although the company's loss in computers is now approaching $70,000. Computers today can be alarmed so easily that a wire isn't exposed. Office and security managers should explore available options.

Executive decisions such as these have everything to do with the "why" of office security. The question that is so hard to answer is, why are so many offices operated as blatant invitations to theft?

Unfortunately, the office thief or criminal tipster may be an unemployed opportunist; he may be a messenger or a deliveryman. Does he learn that what he brings will be received by an employee at the reception area, freight entrance, or freight elevator? Or will he be directed with a wave of the hand in the general direction of the department or office where he says he is going? We've met this type before and we'll meet him again. He is the most common type of impostor, one who can easily break through an office's defenses unless effective systems are established to keep him out.

Making sure that the reception area is never unattended, meeting and escorting visitors, and receiving deliveries at the entrance may seem like simple measures, but their effect on open-hours theft and burglary is substantial. Such open-hours measures can also reduce burglary by concealing attractive targets.

LOW-TRAFFIC-HOURS SECURITY

Office entrance doors should be kept locked after normal business hours, regardless of the number of employees who may still be present.

The hours immediately before and immediately after regular business hours are recognized by the thief as times of unusual opportunity. It is these hours, too—when traffic in the halls and offices are lower—that attract criminals whose specialty is robbery and assault. The presence of a receptionist in an office where the majority of workers have left for the day is no protection for the office—or for the receptionist.

The responsibility for locking entrance doors (and alarming fire exit doors, if necessary) should be primarily assigned to one person, with the responsibility for checking that it has been done assigned to another.

Where employee keys are issued for a corridor entrance, the doors should have a latching lock that can be set to automatically lock behind each arriving and departing employee, until it is put in the handle-operated latching position for business hours. This measure will reduce the human-error factor and—almost as importantly—will require fewer morale-squelching lectures on why the doors must be kept locked.

These are also the hours that employees may be least safe in corridors or unlocked rest rooms opening off halls accessible to visitors. *There is no excuse for unlocked rest rooms in today's office building.* They are not designed for use by the general public and can be extremely dangerous if they are so used. Office keys can be loaned to clients and visitors. Public facilities, if needed, are usually located on the lobby floor and are clearly marked.

For the same reason, equipment rooms should also be kept locked 24 hours a day. Necessity of access to such rooms is very low, and keeping them unlocked invites their use by stowaways or muggers (or even as a place to conceal a bomb). They should always be kept locked and/or alarmed. In addition, these rooms should have separate master keys and access should always be limited. Remember—rekeying is a simple process. Removable core cylinders are cost-effective and should be considered.

STAIRWELLS

Stairs and elevators offer opportunity for robbery and assault, a situation which all concerned regard as intolerable. Even when the building is secured at the close of business, with a lobby security officer on duty with a sign-in log, the problem remains to some degree. The loitering criminal who entered during open hours may still be in the building looking for an opportunity.

Where the building has a security force, and where floors can be secured against reentry from elevators or firestairs, a sweep-search will move loiterers out. When floors can't be secured against reentry, the sweep-search—although not as absolutely effective—may be enough to send the criminal loiterer on to another, more vulnerable building. Few employees, however conscientious, will continue to work overtime once they have had a frightening experience, even if it is only finding a stranger inside the office and no one within calling range.

OFFICE SECURITY SYSTEMS

In lieu of, and sometimes in addition to, building security systems, individual floors may be secured much in the same manner as the building by a combination of personnel and equipment.

In one such installation, doors from the elevator foyer into the office area are automatically and remotely unlocked and locked at the opening and closing of business hours. After business hours, access from the elevator lobby at each floor is activated by the employee's identification card, and each entry and exit is logged by computer. Elevators will not rise to protected floors unless activated by an authorized user, and firestair doors, already locked against reentry, are placed on alarm.

During business hours, the visitor always finds a receptionist on duty just within the doors. Out of sight at her desk is a "panic button" to use in the event she has a troublesome visitor or if strangers refuse to stop. Plainclothes security personnel quickly and quietly respond to silent alarm signals. Rest room facilities are within the protected office area, and the building's freight elevator is manned by a security officer to prevent its use for access or escape.

A second example is an installation which addresses the special needs of a Manhattan building in a manner appropriate to the occupants. Nine floors of an otherwise unsecured building are occupied by a single tenant, whose personnel use the firestairs to travel between floors. Day or night, alarms signal if an outsider gets into the protected nine-story area. Signs warning that this will happen prevent accidental entry into this area by outsiders.

Visitors leaving the elevators at any of the nine floors trigger an alert at the communications center. The floor's small elevator lobby is designed to direct a visitor toward a point where he can be seen by a closed-circuit television camera and responded to on a monitor. The operators responding are seen "on-camera" also to avoid a totally impersonal response. If the person arriving is an employee, however, he simply walks to one of two doors in the elevator lobby and punches a code which opens that door. If he is a frequent authorized visitor, or an employee from another location, he may have an identification card that he shows to the camera. The door can be released from the communications console. In other cases, the person being visited is notified by telephone of a guest's arrival and is then responsible for dispatching someone to bring the visitor in. If an attempt is made to force the door, an alarm will sound.

In planning this installation, careful consideration was given to the amount of expected authorized-visitor traffic; the electronic receptionists are on those floors having the least visitors. Where there is more traffic, or where a department head decides she would prefer a receptionist, the camera and monitor can be removed easily and replaced by a receptionist's desk.

FEW RULES AND MUCH THOUGHT

Office security during business hours is the application of a few standard rules and much thought. Each building and its traffic present different problems, and the application of original thinking to the tactful solution of security problems is probably at no time more necessary than in the protection of open buildings. Most or all of the rules discussed above will be mentioned again in other contexts—these rules are the very basics of office defense.

If an office is not a pleasant place to work, it cannot retain the best employees. Office security plays an important role in how employees feel about their work, their company, and its leadership.

Appendix I

Crime Watchers Can
Reduce Crime

By reducing opportunities for crime, looking out for your neighbors, and acting as extra eyes and ears for law enforcement as a member of a Crime Watch group, you can improve the quality of life in your community.

First, check security in your own home or office. Your police or sheriff's department may provide a free security survey. Make sure there are good locks on exterior doors and windows and use them. Don't forget to lock up when you go out, even if it's only for a few minutes. Trim shrubbery that hides doorways or windows and join Operation Identification to mark valuables. (Engraving tools can be obtained through local police departments or local hardware stores.) If you leave for a vacation, use timers on lights and radios to make your home appear lived-in and have a neighbor take in your mail and newspapers. Make an effort to know your neighbors and their daily routines and keep a block map near the telephone for emergencies. Check your neighborhood for things that might contribute to crime, like poor street lighting, abandoned cars, vacant lots littered with debris, or boarded-up buildings.

An important responsibility of Crime Watchers is to report anything suspicious to the police or sheriff's department, such as:

- Someone running from a car or home.
- Someone screaming. If you can't determine what the screams are about, call the police.
- Someone going door-to-door in the neighborhood looking into windows and parked cars.
- A person who seems to have no purpose wandering in the neighborhood.
- Any unusual or suspicious noise that you can't explain, such as breaking glass or pounding.
- Vehicles moving slowly, without lights, or with no apparent destination.
- Business transactions conducted from a vehicle. This could involve the sale of drugs or stolen goods.
- Offers of merchandise at ridiculously low prices—they're probably stolen.
- Property carried by persons on foot at an unusual hour or place, especially if the person is running.
- Property being removed from closed businesses or residences known to be unoccupied.

18

- A stranger in a car stopping to talk to a child.
- A child resisting the advances of an adult.

How to Make a Police Report

The police need to have accurate information as quickly as possible about a suspicious activity or crime in progress.

- Give your name and identify yourself as a member of a Crime Watch group.
- Describe the event as briefly as possible: where, when, how, and who did it.
- Tell if the crime is still in progress.
- Describe the suspect—sex, race, age, height, weight, hair color, clothing, accent, beard or mustache, and distinctive characteristics.
- Describe the vehicle if one was involved—color, make, model, year, license plate, special markings, dents, the direction it went.

Prepared by Robert Hanna, Crime Prevention Officer,
Quincy Police Department, Quincy, Massachusetts

Appendix II

How to Avoid Becoming the Victim of an Attacker

When you start an awareness program for your employees, feel free to use the following material either as part of your presentation or as a handout.

1. Stay alert for the unexpected at all times.
   - While you are walking, keep your mind on what is going on around you.
2. Don't take unnecessary chances.
   - Walk confidently, know where you are going.
   - Whenever possible, walk with another person.
   - Stay near people. Walking in deserted areas only invites trouble.
   - Stay in well-lit areas.
   - Avoid shortcuts.
3. If you are followed:
   - Cross the street.
   - Reverse direction.

   If you are still followed:
   - Go to a business that is open and ask for help.
   - In a residential area, go to a home and ask for help.
   - Attract attention. Yell, scream, flag down a passing car. You can also carry a whistle and blow it to attract attention.
   - Act suspicious. Keep looking back at the person following you to let that person know you can't be taken by surprise.
4. If you are attacked:
   - Yell and scream to attract attention and scare your attacker off.
   - Swing an umbrella or briefcase, or anything you have in your hand, at the attacker's head.
   - Make a scene. Take your attacker by surprise.
   - Jab the attacker with your elbow.
   - Twist your body to break free from the attacker's hold.
   - Bite hard.
   - Scratch at his face with your fingernails.
   - Bend the attacker's fingers back.
   - Kick the attacker with the toe of your shoe.

- Punch him in unprotected areas.
- Get away from the attacker.
5. Get a description of your attacker. Try to remember such things as:
   - Height, weight, age, skin tone, hair color, eye color, color and type of clothes, and type of jewelry the attacker was wearing.
   - Any scars, tattoos, or disabilities he may have had.
   - Any odor you detected, such as alcohol, drugs, or cologne.
   - Anything you were suspicious of prior to the attack: a motor vehicle that may have passed you several times, or someone who was watching you.
   - Anything that the attacker said to you and if he had an accent.
   - A description of any weapon used.

A question frequently asked is, "Should I carry a weapon?" I do not believe that you should carry a weapon unless you are thoroughly trained in its use and licensed to carry it. Anything you use as a weapon can also be taken from you and used against you. You would be better off using the time that it takes to get the weapon out to escape the situation or attract attention. An umbrella is an example of a good weapon that you could have in your hand ready to use in case of attack.

Another question asked is, "What about self-defense?" Karate, judo, and other martial arts can improve your self-defense skills, but you must remember that it takes years of practice to become good enough at these skills to ward off an attacker.

Above all, report anything suspicious to your police department immediately. If you follow these suggestions you will diminish your chances of becoming an attacker's victim.

Prepared by Robert Hanna, Crime Prevention Officer,
Quincy Police Department, Quincy, Massachusetts

Chapter 3

After-Hours Burglary

As offices became equipped with more portable and readily resalable office equipment, house burglars turned their professional attentions to the office. Today, some theft operations are so well organized and selective that offices are burglarized for "pre-ordered" merchandise!

The obvious goal of the ordinary office burglar are those items having the highest demand, the best resale value, and—to facilitate the theft—the least weight or bulk. Modern office equipment is accommodating in every detail.

In addition to the more obvious examples of office equipment, postage meters and check protectors also attract burglars, as do fax machines, laptop computers, and answering machines.

WHAT IS RISK?

There is little chance the office burglar will run into deterrent security measures—and even less chance of being detected while in the act. Burglars will usually go to great pains to avoid running into an overtime worker. Unfortunately, "usually" is not "always," and cornered burglars have been known to make vicious attacks. But except for accidental discovery—which is rare—most office burglaries are a thief's dream of ease and safety.

WHAT IS BURGLARY?

Under old English common law, burglary was "the breaking and entering of a dwelling place in the nighttime." But burglary today is more correctly defined as occurring when a person "knowingly enters, or without authority remains within" premises "with intent to commit a felony or a theft therein."[1]

This modern definition extends to sneak thieves who enter the office to steal during the regular working day—a far cry from the traditional idea of the burglar with mask and bull's-eye lantern entering in the dead of night. In this chapter, however, we are concerned with the aspect of the legal definition that says, "without authority, entering, or *remaining within.*"

The hide-in burglar is an example of remaining within. It is a technique growing in popularity that has, therefore, been recognized in the broader scope of the law. This hide-in burglar steals—and then breaks *out* with his loot.

Fortunately, however, perhaps due to the success of available and appropriate security precautions, most office burglaries are still committed by breaking *in*.

ASSESSING THE RISK OF BURGLARY

The most effective approach to burglary prevention begins with the recognition that each office *building*—and virtually every *office* in the building—is different in operation, construction, exposure, and ease of access. Each occupancy presents a different problem and a different risk.

One office may be small, well-insured, without irreplaceable equipment or information, and no cash on hand. It may be housed in a low-rise building, and located in a low-crime area frequently patrolled by police. Another office may be located in a high-rise building in Chicago, and accessible to building visitors around the clock. This particular office may have negotiable securities on hand, or vital confidential material and trade secrets in its files.

From a security point of view, the only common ground between these examples is that both are offices. Beyond that similarity, even though both might be offices of the same company, their security needs are totally different. The security measures adequate for the former would be completely insufficient for the latter.

In determining our defense against burglary then, we must ask, *What* should we defend? *Where* (or how) shall we defend it? And *what* should we defend it *against?*

Any office can be burglarized. Indeed, burglary occurs on military bases and in prisons, even though both are considered to be under heavy guard and constant surveillance. An absolutely burglar-proof office is possible, but the cost would be prohibitive—and cost is an essential consideration in security planning.

Furthermore, the ultimate burglary-proof office would have to be built in such a way as to compromise its occupants in the event of fire—anti-crime measures must always yield to human safety whenever the two conflict.

COSTS AND CONSEQUENCES

Many companies regard a burglary as a nuisance; a matter of no great concern. This attitude is more common in offices that have so far been spared. Managers with this attitude are aware that a burglary will cause insurance premiums to go up, but they overlook the fact that repairing the damage caused by forced entry may prove a greater cost and nuisance than the theft itself. Under almost every standard lease the tenant is liable for all such repair work and the building has no responsibility in the matter.

Arson, often used to cover up a burglary, can inflict a far greater loss. In addition, if the burglar has turned over desks and files in his search for valuables, the interruption suffered by the business while files are reorganized or duplicated may, as in the case of fire, represent a serious business interruption.

Offices holding negotiable securities or jewels, or those that have a considerable amount of cash on hand, are obvious targets. Such offices present substantial risks—both from the consequences of a successful burglary and from the higher probability of attack by experienced and skilled professional burglars.

INSURANCE

Office buildings are subject to all of the usual property and liability risks to which other enterprises, like shopping malls and movie theaters, are exposed. Losses can occur from fire, smoke, explosion, water, and theft. Additional costs can be incurred such as rent for an alternative site as well as loss of profits while the property is undergoing repairs. An all-risk property policy will cover the building and endorsements can be added to cover equipment, HVAC systems, loss of income, and other additional expenses. Since insurance policies differ and pricing varies depending on building value, deductibles, type of construction, and other factors, an insurance broker or agent should be consulted.

Another risk to building owners is claims or suits for personal injury and damage. Many claims can also involve the loss of future earnings, mental anguish, emotional distress, or loss of reputation. Liability risks can represent the greatest cost potential for a building owner.

Liability policies can be purchased to provide coverage for these types of risks; limits vary from a low of $100,000 per claim to $100 million. In today's litigious society it is important to maintain adequate liability limits because attorneys' fees in defending a suit can sometimes exceed the amount paid to the injured party. Besides talking to your agent or broker, it might be helpful to talk to other property owners to ascertain the limits they carry. Your attorney might be able to give you an idea of recent jury awards in your area.

Workers compensation and automobile insurance are usually required by law, but if not, businesses should never neglect these coverages since uncovered losses could be the responsibility of the firm and the financial impact could be disastrous.

Finally, building owners should require in the lease agreement that their tenants have insurance to protect the tenant's property, employees, and against liability claims. The lease should also specify that the tenant deliver certificates of insurance proving such coverage to the owner prior to the inception of the lease and that the owner be named as a certificate holder—guaranteeing that the owner will be notified if the tenant's insurance is cancelled. Consult your attorney to make sure your leases contain these provisions. If the tenant doesn't have insurance, the landlord-owner may find that he's being looked at to pay for losses on the tenant's property.

INSURANCE RECOVERY

Many office managers sleep soundly—secure in the knowledge that they are insured against burglary. But often this sense of security is not justified. Insurance policies state very clearly what is covered and what is specifically exempt. All too frequently, management overlooks the exceptions, for example:

- It is usually stipulated that *proof* of burglary must appear. This generally requires visible evidence of forced entry or forced exit.
- If a loss occurs through negligence, such as an unlocked door, or by key— even if the key was in the hands of an unauthorized person—most burglary insurance policies will not pay.
- There must be proof of the nature and amount of the stolen property.
- If the means by which the theft occurred are unknown, nonpayment for losses is almost certain under standard policies.

It is as important to understand the definitions that govern insurance recovery and the provisions of the specific policies in force, as it is to understand the principles of loss prevention.

THE PROTECTION "EQUATION"

In setting up appropriate security programs to counter the burglar's attack, it is vital to begin by considering how the thief *could* steal. Each countermeasure considered must be evaluated in terms of cost, feasibility, protection offered, and convenience lost.

No preventive security arrangement can be absolutely secure. The best security protection will always be a special case; that is, the most appropriate measures feasible for that specific risk in that specific environment. Beyond that level of security, insurance is the means by which management completes its protection duties and safeguards against the improbable and unavoidable.

FROM THE OUTSIDE IN

Security planning against burglary begins with the first-line defenses—the perimeter of the premises to be protected. In an office building the perimeter is the *complete* exterior of the building, since entry is possible at virtually any point.

Entrance Security

The central entry point of any building is, of course, its main entrance. Today most of these entrances are made of aluminum-framed glass set into plate-glass facades. Ordinary quarter-inch plate glass can be easily broken; in practice, however, these entrance facades are rarely attacked. Main entrances are usually well-lighted, and they are generally located on well-traveled streets. Such an exposed location is unattractive to the burglar seeking an unobtrusive entrance.

Plate glass is shattered from time to time, but—except for vandalism—this is done almost exclusively for smash-and-grab burglaries where valuable merchandise is scooped up and carried away faster than any response can be implemented.

"Burglar-Stopping" Glass

While many new office buildings have no glass at street level except at the main entrance, there are enough exceptions—and certainly enough older buildings with easily accessible windows—to justify consideration of the security offered by the use of UL-listed burglary-resistant glass or plastic glazing materials.

Unlike tempered glass, safety glass is designed to protect people from dagger-like shards of broken glass. Laminated UL-listed burglary-resistant glass withstands heat, flame, extreme cold, hammers, picks, and axes. Only the most determined criminal, working under highly unusual circumstances, could make a human-sized opening in this type of glass. Practically speaking, it can't be done.

Considerably more expensive than plate glass, however, UL-listed burglary-resistant glass is generally used only in situations where an attack through glass is likely, or where the risk (or insurance premium reduction offered) is enough as to justify the added expense.

UL-listed burglary-resistant polycarbonate or acrylic plastic glazing materials also resist blows that would shatter plate glass and destroy tempered glass. These plastics are less expensive and lighter than glass laminates, but are more readily defaced and scratched. These plastics are useful above the street level in areas where vandalism, such as rock-throwing, is a problem.

If you are planning exterior metal gates across an entrance you instead might want to consider burglary-resistant glazing. It is more expensive, but the added security—and better aesthetic appearance—might offset the difference in cost.

Entry by Lock

As a security device, the average lock only insures privacy. "It keeps honest people out" is the common saying. Well-chosen locks *can*, however, defeat most amateur burglars and force even the skilled professional to make some effort to gain entrance, resulting in the visible signs of forced entry required to satisfy insurance requirements. There are many ways to attack a lock, its cylinder, and its casing. The experienced professional can accomplish them with astonishing speed.

FORCIBLE ATTACKS

When a door is locked, a metal bolt extends from the door into the door frame. If this bolt can be disengaged from the door frame by any means, the door is open and the thief can gain entrance.

If the lock has a short bolt and the unreinforced jamb is lightweight and flexible, as is the case in some modern construction, it may be possible to pop the door open. Unfortunately, this can be done in such a way as to leave no sign of forced entry. If the jamb is a little stronger or the bolt a little longer, the jamb must be pried away to release the bolt. Even where the lock is properly equipped with a long-throw bolt, if the soft aluminum jambs are unreinforced they can be "peeled"—which is the accurately descriptive word for the way that the aluminum frame around the jamb is ripped away from the bolt. Peeling can be prevented by installing a reinforcing section within the door jamb.

Sawing through the bolt is a less common but effective method used to force entry. This method is used in low-traffic locations where the burglar has plenty of time and little fear of being heard. Entry by sawing can be prevented by using locks with special ceramic inserts in the bolts.

"Pulling" is the technique whereby the lock cylinder is ripped from the door so the lock then can be operated through the opening left in the face of the door. Special hardened-steel cylinder guards prevent this type of attack.

ENTRY BY KEY

The most efficient burglar tool, of course, is the key that fits the lock the burglar wishes to open. This can be a stolen key, a loaned key, an unauthorized duplicate key—even an authorized key in the hands of the keyholder.

Entry by key is doubly harmful because not only do burglars make off with your property, they leave no evidence of forced entry. However much "evidence" of burglary they may leave within the office, entrance by key prevents you from recovering your loss through insurance.

The risk of key misuse is enormous, necessitating the most careful consideration in selecting the basic keying system and requiring vigorous and continual supervision of a well-planned key control system.

Both of these aspects of security are illustrated in the following example. The master key for an 18-story office building was reported stolen, and rekeying was considered. An estimate of $20,000 was received to rekey all the locks operated by that master key. As a result, the locks have never been rekeyed. None of the tenants are aware of their vulnerability.

Any master key system is vulnerable. And any system where one key can open every lock in a building is unjustifiably insecure, particularly against lockpicking and unauthorized key duplication. For a related reason, tenant office keys should not be able to open main entrances to a building.

Depending upon building hours and access policies, separate entrance keys should be issued upon tenant authorization. More desirably, no entrance keys should be issued to tenants, with entry before and after hours controlled by a building employee or guard. Where entrance keys must be issued to tenants, the lock cylinder in the entrance should be changed and new keys issued to authorized tenant personnel every few months and whenever an entrance key is reported lost for any reason.

KEYS FOR MAINTENANCE STAFF

Due to their high rate of personnel turnover, cleaning personnel should be admitted by building employees; avoid issuing exterior entrance keys to them. Appropriate interior keys should be passed out to each shift upon arrival and returned to the building representative before the cleaning personnel leave the premises at any time. This reduces the possibility of unauthorized duplication.

THE WATCHED DOOR

Although, as we have pointed out, attacks on building entrances are not common, they have occurred. In many instances, some kind of entrance surveillance is necessary or desirable, whether supplied by a guard, a closed-circuit TV camera observed from a nearby point, or even by alarms that bring a fast response.

A lobby guard with a sign-in/out log for after-hours traffic is the most common and most economical positive protection, particularly in existing buildings. Some new office buildings under construction, however, are incorporating alarms and closed-circuit TV to protect sensitive areas.

ROOFS

Sloping roofs (of whatever style) are unattractive to intruders because anyone on a sloping roof is usually visible from ground level. The slope itself poses a risk of falling, and the necessary break-in tools must be held in place while not being used. Sloping roofs should be analyzed, however, with respect to ventilating ducts, skylights, or other possible access points.

The flat roofs most often found on commercial buildings, on the other hand, are very attractive to intruders. Because walls on many commercial buildings extend a few feet above the roof line, they provide excellent concealment for any intruder attempting to penetrate by the roof. Large, sophisticated tools can be used for extended periods of time, and a considerable amount of noise can be made if the building is unoccupied. Given such favorable conditions, no flat roof except one made out of thick, reinforced concrete offers any real resistance to burglars. However, penetration of the roof itself is seldom required, because the typical flat commercial roof has numerous skylights, ventilation openings, trap doors, and other maintenance accessways that are more convenient points of penetration. These accessways should be strengthened to the point of being as penetration-resistant as the rest of the roof.[2]

WALLS

Wood frame and masonry are the two basic materials used in most wall construction. Most single-family residences have wood-frame exterior walls, with or without a surface layer of masonry. The rest have solid masonry walls. For commercial structures, masonry or concrete is usually the material of choice because of its durability and resistance to fire.

Wood-frame walls are relatively inexpensive, easy to build, durable, and provide good insulation against noise, weather, and heat loss. But they do not provide much penetration resistance unless additional protective measures are taken to strengthen them. Even frame walls, however, can deter impulsive intruders. Their points of attack will most always be doors, windows, and other accessways, and if these are secure they will move on to easier targets unless there are high-value items inside the structure. Because a determined intruder can break through an ordinary frame structure in just a few minutes, a frame wall is insufficient protection for high-value property, unless coupled with an intrusion detection system.

Masonry and concrete walls, more expensive than frame walls, are used especially in commercial and institutional structures because of their durability, fire resistance, and insulation against weather, noise, and heat loss. They usually consist of either poured concrete or concrete block. As stated previously, poured concrete walls are relatively difficult to penetrate. Concrete block walls that have not been filled with concrete or reinforced with steel, however, can be as vulnerable to attack as wood-frame walls. On the other hand, any masonry walls can be penetrated by a determined attacker.[3]

EXTERIOR SECURITY

The modern high-rise office building offers the ultimate in security when we think of traditional kinds of forced entry.

Air conditioning alone has served to virtually button up buildings. In modern construction, street-level windows are omitted, other windows let in light but cannot be opened, and the enclosed firestairs terminate in steel doors with heavy-duty latch locks. It is common for these new buildings to be separated from their neighbors, thus avoiding the danger of common walls and forgotten connecting doors. Delivery of merchandise and supplies and refuse removal is handled at supervised loading docks.

There can be no question but that such buildings are more secure from direct assault. But they are jam-packed with the desirable, resalable goods so dear to the heart of the burglar. So the very security that protects the modern office from forcible perimeter entry makes surreptitious entry from keys, lock-picking, and hide-ins more likely.

OLDER CONSTRUCTION

Older office buildings present different and more difficult problems. Exterior fire escapes, operable windows, older (and worn) locks, common walls, unused and forgotten connecting doors and windows, and windows at street and basement levels all increase the exposure of the building perimeter to burglary.

In crowded urban areas, fire escapes can be accessed from adjacent buildings and streets for entry at any level. In such cases, accessible windows can be protected by burglary-resistant glazing if they are properly locked; or they can be barred. In either case, fire safety must be a primary consideration. You must check your local fire codes before taking any step that would eliminate or obstruct any openings that might be thought of as emergency exits—whether so designated or not.

Window air conditioners are frequently used in older buildings and entry can often be gained by removing the unsecured unit. Such windows should be alarmed when they are accessible from ground level, exterior fire escapes, or adjacent windows. Other accessible windows should be barred, alarmed, or secured in position so that they cannot be opened far enough to permit entry.

Remember, in older buildings you have old hardware which may be a vulnerability in your security program.

COMMERCIAL BUILDINGS

Many smaller offices are located in one-story buildings, either connected or free-standing. These buildings normally have the characteristic glass entrance, a single rear exit, and one or more accessible rear windows. It is important that the rear door be solid, steel-framed, and secured with heavy-duty locks, and that rear windows be treated as suggested above—again in compliance with local fire laws and good safety practices.

A very common method of entry into adjoining offices is through a common crawlspace above the ceiling, or through common walls. The freestanding single-story building is vulnerable to attack through the roof. Roofs can be easily chopped open, an activity rarely detected by passersby or patrols. A roof entry also bypasses perimeter (door and window) alarm systems. Obviously, breaking through a common wall is performed from an office or store having little to lose (and hence, poorly secured) into a high-risk occupancy that is otherwise protected against direct access.

If the risk factor is significant, you have two countermeasures that can be used singly or together, depending on your assessment of the situation: You can secure your negotiables, records, or goods within the premises in burglary-resistant safes or vaults; or you can alarm the interior in whole or in part with an intruder alert system. Obviously, the high-risk office should use both measures, and might well consider others.

SUMMARY OF PERIMETER PROTECTION

Clearly, some precautions should be common to all buildings, particularly heavy-duty tamper-resistant locks, strongly-framed doors, good key control, and secure windows. In many instances alarms are invaluable, and certainly alarm, guard, or closed-circuit TV surveillance of vulnerable and high-risk areas can be important in your defense against burglary and other crimes.

Much more can be done—and in many cases should be—depending on your situation. But office buildings aren't fortresses and can't be as long as you continue to conduct business in them. Nevertheless, you can prevent casual, unskilled burglary—the crime of opportunity—by a careful evaluation of your situation and the application of a reasonable and practical physical security program. Remember the perimeter of your complex is your first line of defense.

ELEVATOR SECURITY

Another measure available to complement interior security is the incorporation of lock-out features on the elevator. Stairways are (or should be) locked against entry from the stairwells, leaving the elevators as the only ready means of access to the upper floors. Elevators, however, can be programmed to lock out all but authorized personnel after hours. An elevator control panel can be installed that has locks for each floor. Once the floor is locked off for the day or weekend, the elevator will not stop there unless a keyholder arrives and uses a key to enter the secured floor.

Another form of elevator control is badge or card access control. In this method, like other smart-card access systems, a badgeholder inserts a badge into a card reader at the lobby level. The elevator will then travel to the floor authorized for that badge. Coupled with a computer, this reader can also record the time and identify the employee. However, this system is only as secure as the holder's control of the activating badge, unless other controls are incorporated in the system.

PORTABLE ITEMS

A simple and generally desirable method of reducing the attractiveness of office equipment, both to the after-hours burglar and the open-hours thief, is to secure valuable office equipment with one of many types of locking devices. Property also can be engraved under the guidelines of your Operation Identification program.

THE INTERIOR OFFICE

The second line of defense against burglary is the suite or floor of offices within the building. Modern interior office construction is standardized. The decor varies, but the construction is much the same everywhere. Fire codes spell out the requirements for corridors and the doors that open from them. Corridor ceilings are fixed, and fire resistance requirements for corridor doors ensure that these doors will resist most prying if locked with adequate hardware.

On the other hand, the modern office itself is essentially an open-top box. It is walled, has a relatively solid door hung in a steel frame, and a concrete floor— but nothing on top. What appears to be a solid ceiling is, in fact, tiles lying loose on suspended runners at the top of partition walls, which end well below the concrete slab of the floor above. In the space between the ceiling and the next floor run power and telephone lines and air conditioning ducts.

The net effect is that virtually every room and every office is accessible through the ceiling from any other office on that floor, particularly adjacent ones. It is possible to extend the office walls up to the slab above, but this is merely drywall construction and the passage of utilities must still be allowed for. Such wall extensions are effective as soundproofing, but are expensive and offer no total security; drywall construction can be broken through easily.

Older buildings have a distinct security advantage in that heavy, permanent, floor-to-ceiling walls cannot readily be breached. Unfortunately, this advantage is usually offset by older, less adequate locks, worn cylinders, and the many, many unrecovered building and office keys floating around, "out there somewhere."

WINDOWS AND GLAZING

Windows have always been a particularly difficult problem in building security. Their primary functions are to provide light and ventilation and to serve as a barrier to weather. Windows are not ordinarily intended to provide a substantial barrier to intrusion, and it is often difficult, expensive, and unsightly to increase their security levels without destroying their primary functions.

WINDOW LOCKS

Intruders are reluctant to break glass, because it creates a distinctive sound which invites investigation. Therefore, simply locking windows can provide a degree of security. Existing latches on most windows, however, cannot resist a strong jimmying or prying attack and can be opened once the glass has been broken. Minimum locking protection requires a device that will resist prying and manipulation.

The only type of window that cannot be easily secured from the inside is the jalousie-style window—always a poor security risk that should be either replaced or covered with bars or grillwork.

SECURITY GRILLS AND BARS

If the risk that an intruder will break the glass is high, sturdy metal bars, wire grills or expanded mesh placed over vulnerable windows can usually provide the security needed. It should be applied to all windows closer than 8 feet to the ground, or to any window higher than 8 feet which borders a roof line or is otherwise accessible. Grills and bars should usually be attached to the inside of windows. In residential applications, if the window is to be used as an exit in the case of fire, emergency releases should open the bars instantly.

GLAZING MATERIAL

Glass is by far the most common glazing material. It is found in both single- and double-strength single panes, in dual panes for insulating purposes, in tempered form two to five times stronger than ordinary plate glass, and in various laminated forms. Laminated glass is made by bonding alternate layers of transparent plastic and glass. If sufficiently thick, it can provide a significant barrier to penetration. This glass, however, can be broken if given enough time. (Glass with wire imbedded in it was designed exclusively for fire protection and is not considered as security glazing.)

The two most popular plastic glazing materials are acrylic and polycarbonate. Both come in various patterns and in transparent, translucent, and opaque colors. Acrylic is clearer than polycarbonate, but polycarbonate is much stronger against impacts.

Acrylic comes in a wide range of thicknesses, and is much more impact-resistant than ordinary window glass (17 times more resistant in 1/8- to 1/4-inch sheets). Acrylic shatters and burns, although it will withstand a wide range of climate extremes for many years without deterioration.

Polycarbonate, like acrylic, weighs 50 percent less than glass of equal thickness. It has 300 times the impact resistance of glass, however, and 20 to 30 times the impact strength of acrylic. It is less translucent and also somewhat less weather resistant than glass or acrylic, but it still can provide service for a period of years and will not burn or shatter.

The cost of either acrylic or polycarbonate is about four times that of glass. In situations where frequent glass breakage occurs due to vandalism or other factors, plastic glazing material can pay for itself. For intrusion resistance purposes, polycarbonate is superior to acrylic. Properly installed polycarbonate glazing provides approximately the same degree of window security as bars and grills—provided that adequate locking devices are used on the windows. Proper installation is quite important with either plastic, however, because unlike glass, it is subject to significant shrinkage and expansion with temperature and humidity. Polycarbonate also has a significant degree of flexibility, enough that a determined burglar could force it out of its frame. A deeper frame is therefore needed for polycarbonate.

OTHER ACCESS OPENINGS

Permanently installed (or hinged and lockable) bars or expanded metal grill-work can be used to secure access points such as ventilation ducts, utility tunnels, skylights, and other small openings used for wires, pipes, air, or light. Other specialized building surface openings include very large vehicular openings for garages and commercial and industrial structures. Unusually large openings such as these can be secured following the same general principles discussed above for door systems but may require special security hardware and materials because of their size, shape, or method of operation.[4]

INTERNAL BARRIERS

Within the structure itself, a variety of barrier arrangements may be set up to protect specific targets from criminal attack. Internal barriers must not only provide specific security against intruders for high-value items, they must also provide security against criminal activities by those who may have legitimate reason to be inside (for example, visitors, customers, clients, patients, or employees). Perimeter barrier systems and building surface barrier systems are of no value whatsoever in preventing theft by persons who are entitled to enter— and remain inside—the facility.

Internal barriers generally serve to control movement and limit access in such a way as to reduce the likelihood for criminal attack to an acceptable level, while not interfering with normal activity within the building. They consist of both low-security structures (such as interior walls, privacy doors, display cases, counters, racks of merchandise, light steel mesh screening, glazing materials, even ropes and chains) and high-security structures (such as safes and vaults).[5]

FILES, SAFES, AND VAULTS[6]

The final line of defense at any facility is in the high-security storage areas where papers, records, plans, cash, precious metals, or other especially valuable assets are protected. These security containers should be of a size and quantity that the nature of the business dictates.

Every facility will have its own particular needs, but certain general observations apply. The choice of the proper security container for specific applications is influenced largely by the value and the vulnerability of the items stored inside. Irreplaceable papers or original documents may not have any intrinsic or marketable value so they may not be a likely target for a thief, but since they do have great value to the owners, they must be protected against fire. On the other hand, uncut precious stones or recorded negotiable papers that can be replaced may not be in danger from fire, but they would surely be attractive to a thief.

In protecting property, it is essential to recognize that generally speaking protective containers are designed to secure against burglary or fire. Each type of equipment has a specialized function and provides only minimal protection against the other risk. There are containers designed with a burglary-resistant chest within a fire-resistant container that are useful in many instances, but each must be evaluated in terms of their purpose.

Whatever the equipment, staff must be educated and reminded of the different roles played by the two types of containers. It is all too common for company personnel to assume that a fire-resistant safe is also burglary-resistant and vice versa.

Files

Burglary-resistant files are secure against most surreptitious attacks. On the other hand, they can be pried open in less than half an hour if the burglar is working undisturbed and is not concerned with the noise created in the operation. Such files are suitable for nonnegotiable papers or even proprietary information since these files are normally only targeted by surreptitious assault. Filing cabinets with a fire rating of one hour and further fitted with a combination lock will probably be suitable for all uses but the storage of classified government documents.

Safes

Safes are expensive, but if they are selected wisely, they can be very important security investments. Emphatically, safes are each designed to perform a particular job to a particular level of protection. The two types of safes of most interest to the security professional are the fire-resistant record safe and the burglary-resistant money safe. To use fire-resistant safes for the storage of valuables—an all too common practice—is to invite disaster. At the same time, it would be equally careless to use a burglary-resistant safe for the storage of valuable papers or records since, if a fire were to occur, the contents of such a safe would be reduced to ashes.

Safes are rated to describe the degree of protection they afford. Naturally, the more protection provided, the more expensive the safe will be. In selecting the best one for your requirements, a number of questions must be considered: How great is the threat of fire or burglary? What is the value of the safe's contents? How much protection time is required in the event of a fire or of a burglary attempt? Only after these questions have been answered can a reasonable, permissible capital outlay for their purchase be determined.

Record Safes

Fire-resistant containers are classified according to the maximum interior temperature permitted after exposure to heat for varying periods of time. A record safe with a UL rating of 350-4 (formerly designated "A") can withstand exterior temperatures to 2000°F for four hours without permitting the interior temperature to rise above 350°F.

The UL tests that result in the classifications are conducted to simulate a major fire with a gradual heat build-up to 2000°F, including circumstances where a safe might fall several stories through a fire-damaged building. In addition, an explosion test simulates a cold safe dropping into a fire that has already reached 2000°F.

The actual test for a 350-4 rating places the safe for four hours in a 2000°F furnace. The furnace is turned off after four hours but the safe remains inside until it is cool. The interior temperature must remain below 350°F during heating and cooling-off periods. Interior temperature is determined by sensors sealed inside the safe in six specified locations to provide a continuous record of the temperatures during the test. Papers are also placed in the safe to simulate records. The explosion impact test is conducted with the same model safe placed for a half hour in a furnace preheated to 2000°F. If no explosion occurs, the furnace is set at 1550°F and raised to 1700°F over a half-hour period. After this hour in the explosion test, the safe is removed and dropped 30 feet onto rubble. The safe is then returned to the furnace and reheated for one hour at 1700°F. The furnace and safe then are allowed to cool after which the papers inside must be legible and uncharred.

Computer media storage classifications are for containers that do not allow the internal temperature to go above 150°F. This is critical since computer media and diskettes begin to distort at 150°F and 125°F, respectively.

Insulated vault-door classifications are much the same as they are for safes except that vault doors are not subject to explosion/impact tests.

In some businesses, a combination fire-resistant/burglary-resistant safe may serve as a double protection for different kinds of assets, but in no event must the purpose of these two kinds of safes be confused if there is one of each on the premises. Most record safes have combination locks, relocking devices, and hardened steel lockplates to provide a measure of burglar resistance. It must be reemphasized that record safes are designed to protect documents and other similar flammables against destruction by fire. They provide only slight deterrence to attack from even unskilled burglars. Similarly, the protection provided by burglary-resistant safes is useless against a fire of any significance.

MONEY SAFES

Burglary-resistant safes are nothing more than very heavy metal boxes without wheels, offering varying degrees of protection against many forms of attack. A safe with a UL rating of TL-15, for instance, weighs at least 750 pounds and its front face can resist assault by common hand and electric tools for at least 15 minutes. Other safes resist attack from tools, torches, and explosives concurrently.

Since burglary-resistant safes have a limited holding capacity, it is always advisable to know the volume of items to be secured. If the volume is sufficiently large, it might be advisable to consider installing a burglary-resistant vault, which, although considerably more expensive, can have an enormous holding capacity.

Securing the Safe

Whatever safe you select must be securely fastened to the structure of its surroundings. Police reports are filled with cases where unattached safes, some as heavy as a ton, were stolen in their entirety. A study of safe burglars in California showed that the largest group (37.3 percent) removed safes from the premises to be opened elsewhere.

A convicted criminal once told investigators how he and an accomplice watched a supermarket to determine the cash flow and the manager's banking habits. They noted that he accumulated cash in a small, wheeled safe until Saturday morning when he deposited it. Presumably, he felt secure in this practice because he lived in an apartment above the store and perhaps felt that he was very much on top of the situation. One Friday night, the thief and his friend rolled the safe into their station wagon and pried it open at their leisure to get the $15,000 inside. Pleased with their success, the thieves were even more pleased when they found that the manager replaced the stolen safe with one exactly like it and continued with the same banking routine. Two weeks later, our man went back alone and picked up another $12,000 in exactly the same way.

It is becoming a common practice to install the safe in a concrete floor where it is greatly protected from attack. In this kind of installation, only the door and combination lock are exposed. Since the door is the strongest part of a modern safe, the chances of successful robbery are considerably reduced.

Vaults

Vaults are essentially large safes. As such, they are subject to the same kinds of attack and fall under the same basic principles of protection.

Since it would be prohibitively expensive to build a vault out of shaped, welded steel and special alloys, the construction, except for the door, is usually of high-quality, reinforced concrete. There are many ways that a vault can be constructed, but however it is done, it will always be extremely heavy and at best a difficult architectural issue.

Vaults typically are situated at or below ground level so they do not increase the stresses on the structure housing them. If a vault must be built on the upper stories of a building, it must be supported by independent beams that do not support other parts of the building. the vault also must be strong enough to withstand the weight imposed on it if the building collapsed as the result of fire or explosion.

The doors of such vaults are normally 6-inches-thick, and they may be as much as 24-inches-thick in the largest installation. Since these doors present a formidable obstacle to any criminal, an attack will usually be directed at the walls, ceiling, or floor, which for that reason must match the strength of the door. As a rule, these surfaces should be twice as thick as the door and never less than 12-inches-thick.

If at all possible, a vault should be surrounded by narrow corridors that permit inspection of the exterior but are sufficiently confined to discourage the use of heavy drilling or cutting equipment. No power outlets should be available anywhere in the vicinity of the vault; such outlets could provide criminals with energy to drive their tools.

CONTAINER PROTECTION

Since no container can resist assault indefinitely, it must be supported by alarm systems and frequent inspections. Capacitance and vibration alarms are the types most generally used to protect safes and file cabinets. Ideally, any container should be inspected at least once within the period of its rated resistance. Closed-circuit TV surveillance can, of course, provide constant inspection and, if the expense is warranted, is highly recommended.

CONTINUING EVALUATION

Security containers are the last line of defense, but in many situations, they should be the first choice in establishing a sound security system. The containers must be selected with care after an exhaustive evaluation of the needs of the facility under examination. They must also be reviewed regularly for their suitability to the job they are to perform.

Just as safe manufacturers are continually improving the design, construction, and materials used in safes, so is the criminal world improving its technology and techniques of successful attack. Because of the considerable capital outlay involved in purchasing adequate security containers, many businesspeople are reluctant to entertain the notion that these containers may someday become outmoded—not because they wear out or cease to function, but rather because new tools and techniques have nullified their effectiveness. In 1990, a series of attacks on financial institutions in a major west coast city had burglars using drainage tunnels to enter vaults from beneath the buildings and proving that vaults are not impregnable.

In selecting security containers, it is important that the equipment conforms to the needs of the risk, is regularly reevaluated, and if necessary, brought up to date however unwelcome the additional capital outlay may be.

INSPECTIONS

In spite of all defensive devices, the possibility of an intrusion always exists. The highest fence can be scaled, and the stoutest lock can be compromised. Even highly sophisticated alarm systems can be contravened by a knowledgeable professional. The most efficient system of physical protection can eventually be foiled.

ENDNOTES

1. Massachusetts General Law C.266 S.15
2. National Crime Prevention Institute, *Understanding Crime Prevention*, (Stoneham, Mass.: Butterworth-Heinemann, 1986), p. 63.
3. Ibid.
4. Ibid., pp. 76–77.
5. Ibid, p. 78.
6. Robert J. Fischer and Gion Green, *Introduction to Security*, (Stoneham, Mass.: Butterworth-Heinemann, 1992), pp. 239–44.

Appendix I

Methods of Attacking a Safe

ATTACKS

Before a skilled burglar attacks a safe, she studies the methods used to protect it. Inside information (e.g., a safe's combination) is valuable, and scores of employees and ex-employees of attacked firms have been implicated in burglaries. Listed below are two major attack techniques: with force and without force.

With Force

Rip or peel. Most commonly used on fire-resistant safes that have lightweight metal. Like opening a can of sardines, the metal is ripped from a corner. The peel technique requires an offender to pry along the edge of the door to reach the lock.

Punch. The combination dial is broken off with a hammer. A punch is placed on the exposed spindle which is then hammered back to enable breakage of the lock box. The handle is then used to open the door. Effective against older safes.

Chop. Attack on a fire-resistant safe from underneath. The safe is tipped over and hit with an axe or hammer to create a hole.

Drill. A skilled burglar drills into the door to expose the lock mechanism; the lock tumblers are aligned manually to open the door.

Torch. Used against burglar-resistant safes, an oxygen-acetylene cutting torch literally melts the steel. The equipment is brought to the safe or the offender uses equipment at the scene.

Carry away. The offender removes the safe from the premises and attacks it in a convenient place.

Other techniques that are variations of the above are also used by offenders. Explosives such as nitroglycerin are rarely used because of the noise involved.

Without Force

Office search. The offender simply finds the safe combination in a hiding place (e.g., taped under a desk drawer).

Manipulation. Opening a safe without knowing the combination by using sight, sound, and touch. A rare skill. Sometimes the thief is lucky and opens a safe by using numbers similar to an owner's birthdate, home address, or telephone number.

Observation. Viewing the opening of a safe from across the street with the assistance of binoculars or a telescope. To avert this, the numbers should be on the top edge of the dial, rather than on the face of the dial.

Day combination. For convenience, during the day the dial is not completely turned each time an employee finishes using the safe. This facilitates an opportunity for quick access. An offender often manipulates the dial in case the day combination is still in effect.

X-ray equipment. Metallurgical X-ray equipment is used to photograph the combination of the safe. White spots appear on the picture which help to identify the numerical combination. The equipment is cumbersome and the technique is rare.

The following measures are recommended to fortify the security of safes and other containers:

1. Utilize alarms (e.g., capacitance and vibration), closed-circuit TV, and adequate lighting.
2. Place the safe in a well-lighted spot near a window where police or pedestrians can see it. Hiding the safe gives the burglar better working conditions.
3. Secure the safe to the building so it is not stolen. (This also applies to cash registers that may be stolen in broad daylight.) Bolt the safe to the foundation or secure it in a cement floor. Remove any wheels or casters.
4. Do not give the burglar an opportunity to use any tools on the premises; hide or secure them.
5. A time lock permits the safe to be opened only at preselected times. This hinders access even if the combination is known. A delayed-action lock provides an automatic waiting period (e.g., 15 minutes) from combination use to the time the lock mechanism activates. A silent signal lock triggers an alarm when a special combination is used to open a safe.
6. At the end of the day, turn the dial several times in the same direction.
7. A combination written down is risky. Change the factory combination as soon as possible. When an employee leaves who knows the combination, change it.
8. Maintain limited valuables in the safe through frequent banking.
9. Select a safe with a UL rating on the inside. If a burglar identifies the rating on the outside, the attack is easier.

Reprinted with permission from Philip P. Purpura, Security and Loss Prevention, *(Stoneham, Mass.: Butterworth-Heinemann, 1984), pp. 160–63.*

Chapter 4

Key Control

A HEADACHE OR A NIGHTMARE?

A key is defined in Webster's Dictionary as "an instrument for opening and closing a lock." Your building is fifteen floors, a million square feet, three years old and you just received a report that the grand master key was stolen or misplaced last night. Here you have both a headache and a nightmare for any building manager.

Before an effective key control system can be established, every key to every lock that is being used in the protection of the facility and property must be accounted for. Chances are good that it will not be possible to account for even the most critical keys or to be certain that they have not been copied or compromised. If this is the case, there is only one alternative—rekey the entire facility.

Once an effective locking system has been installed, positive control of all keys must be gained and maintained. This can be accomplished only if an effective key record is kept. When not issued or used, keys must be adequately secured. A good, effective key control system is simple to initiate, particularly if it is established in conjunction with the installation of new locking devices. Some of the methods that can be used to gain and maintain effective key control are listed below:

Key cabinet

A well-constructed cabinet will have to be procured and be large enough to hold the original key to every lock in the system. It should also be capable of holding any additional keys which are in use in the facility but which are not a part of the security locking system. The cabinet should be installed in such a manner so as to be difficult, if not impossible, to remove from the property. It should be secured at all times when the person designated to control the keys is not actually issuing or replacing a key. The key to the key cabinet must receive special handling, and when not in use it should be kept in a locked compartment inside a combination-type safe.

Key record

Some administrative means must be set up to record key code numbers and indicate to whom specific keys have been issued. This record can take the form of a ledger book or card file.

Key blanks

Blanks that are to be used to cut keys to issue to authorized personnel must be distinctively marked for identification to insure that no employees have cut their own keys. Blanks should be kept within a combination-type safe and issued only to the person authorized to cut keys and then only in the amount that has been authorized by the person responsible for key control. Such authorization should always be in writing, and records should be maintained on each issue that will be matched with the returned key. Keys which are damaged in the cutting process must be returned for accountability.

Inventories

Periodic inventories will have to be made of all key blanks, original keys, and all duplicate keys in the hands of the employees to whom they have been issued. This does not mean making a phone call to an employee, supervisor, or executive asking if they still have their key. It must be a personal inspection of each key made by the person who has been assigned responsibility for key control.

Audits

In addition to periodic inventories, an unannounced audit should be made of all key control records and procedures by a member of management. During the course of these audits a joint inventory of all keys should be conducted.

Daily report

A daily report should be made to the person responsible for key control from the personnel department indicating all persons who have left or will be leaving the employ of the company in the near future. A check should be made, upon receipt of this report, to determine if the person named has been issued a key to any lock in the system. In the event a key has been issued, steps should be initiated to insure that the key is recovered.

Security force personnel are normally issued master keys, when such a system is in effect, or they are issued a ring of keys permitting them to enter any part of the guarded facility. Keys issued to the security force should never be permitted to leave the facility. They should be passed from shift to shift and signed for each time they change hands. Supervisors must insure that all security personnel understand the importance of not permitting keys to be compromised. A lost master key compromises the entire system and results in the breakdown of the security screen. Such a compromise will necessitate the rekeying of the entire complex, sometimes at a cost of thousands of dollars.

If rekeying becomes necessary, it can be done economically by installing new locking devices in the most critical points of the system and moving the locks removed from these points to less sensitive areas. Of course, it will be necessary to eventually replace all the locks in the system, but by using the manner just described the cost can be spread out over several budgeting periods.

ATTACKS AND COUNTERMEASURES

There are two basic methods of attacking locks themselves: surreptitious techniques and force. There are also a number of ways of circumventing a lock by assaulting the objects to which it is attached. This chapter is concerned only with techniques used to break locks themselves and the measures that can forestall those techniques.

No lock is completely invulnerable to attack. A lock's effectiveness is determined by how long it will resist the best effort of an intruder. An expert can pick an average pin tumbler cylinder in seconds, and no lock can survive strong force applied for a sufficient length of time. The sole objective of any lock is to *delay* an intruder. A good lock makes entry riskier or more trouble than it's worth. Fortunately, most intruders are not experts, therefore most moderately secure locks can survive for a reasonable amount of time against common attack techniques.

The proper use of countermeasures will significantly reduce a locking system's vulnerability to intrusion by unauthorized persons. Not all of the countermeasures suggested in the following sections will be appropriate for every application, however. There is always the necessity of striking a suitable compromise position between the expense and inconvenience of a locking system and the value of the items it is designed to protect. Complex and expensive high-security systems are simply not appropriate for most residential applications. On the other hand, a cheap padlock on a warehouse containing valuable merchandise is an open invitation for someone to break in and steal. The objective should always be to ensure reasonable protection in the circumstances surrounding a particular application. With locks, overprotection is often more harmful than insufficient protection. If the user is faced with a more complex security system than really necessary, she or he simply won't use it. A great many unlawful entries are still made through unlocked doors and windows. The temptation to avoid the inconvenience of constantly locking and unlocking a barrier seems to be insurmountable in some people. Contributing to this temptation by insisting on more protection than the user actually needs simply aggravates the problem.

SURREPTITIOUS ATTACKS

Four basic surreptitious approaches are used to breach locking devices: illicit keys, circumvention of the internal barriers of the lock, manipulation of the internal barriers, and shimming. The susceptibility of any locking device to these approaches cannot be eliminated but can be minimized through the use of common-sense countermeasures.

Illicit Keys

The easiest way to gain entry through any lock is to use the proper key for that lock. Thousands of keys are lost and stolen every year. A potential intruder who can determine which lock a lost or stolen key fits has a simple and quick means of illicit entry. If an intruder can't get the owner's key, quite often he or she can make a duplicate. The casual habit of leaving house keys on the key-ring when a car is left in a commercial parking lot or for servicing provides a potential intruder with a golden opportunity to duplicate the house keys for later use. One can also find out the owner's address very quickly by examining the repair bill or tracing the automobile license number. The risk of lost, stolen, or duplicated keys cannot be eliminated entirely, but certain steps can be taken to minimize it.

Maintain Reasonable Key Security

- If leaving the ignition key with a valet-parked car or one to be serviced, all other keys should be removed from the key ring.
- When keys are being duplicated, the owner should ensure that no extra duplicates are made.
- Many locks, particularly older locks, have their key code stamped on the front of the case or cylinder. This permits anyone to look up the code in a locksmith's manual and find the proper combination for that lock. Code-books are readily available for most brands and makes, so if the code appears anywhere on the lock where it can be read it should be removed by grinding or overstamping. If removal is not possible, the lock or its combination should be changed.
- Managers and owners of commercial enterprises should maintain strict control over master keys and control keys for removable core cylinders. The loss of these keys can compromise the entire system, necessitating an extensive and expensive, system-wide recombination. Too often in large institutions, just about everyone can justify a need for a master key. This is nothing more than a demand for convenience that subverts the requirements of good security. The distribution of master keys should be restricted to those who literally cannot function without them. Since it is impossible to prevent people from losing keys no matter how careful they are, the next precaution is to ensure that the lost key cannot be traced to the lock it operates.
- The owner's name, address, telephone number, or car license number should never appear anywhere on a key ring. This has become common practice to ensure the return of lost keys, but if they fall into the wrong hands, the address provides a quick link between the keys and the locks they fit. The proper protection against lost keys is to always have a duplicate set in a secure place.
- For the same reasons, keys which are stamped with information that identifies the location of the lock should not be carried around. This used to be a common practice on locker keys, safety deposit box keys, and some apartment

building keys. It is no longer as common as it once was, but it still exists. If the keys must be carried, all identifying information should be obliterated, or they should be duplicated on a clean, unmarked key blank.

- Purchase a large key cabinet to store and control the many keys that are in your possession.
- Two sets of key tags should be furnished with the new key cabinet. One tag should read "file-key—must not be loaned out." The second tag should read "Duplicate." The key cabinet also should be equipped with loan tags which will identify the person to whom a key is loaned. This tag is then hung in the numbered peg corresponding to the key that was used.
- Establish accurate records and files, listing the key codes, date each key was issued, and who received it.
- Have each employee sign a receipt when a key is given out.
- All alarm keys should be marked and coded.
- A check should be made of what keys are in the possession of watchmen and staff.
- Only one person should order and issue keys for the complex.
- Change the key cylinder when an authorized key holder is discharged for cause. Furthermore, terminated or retired employees should return keys at the time of termination.
- Periodic inspections should be made to assure that possession of keys conforms to the record of issuance. These periodic inspections should be held to remind key holders that they should immediately notify security about any key loss.
- The original keys and subsequent copies should be coded in a way that their corresponding lock cannot be easily identified.

Parts of this chapter are excerpted from Eugene D. Finneran's "A Handbook for Supervisors and Managers," as it appeared in Handbook of Loss Prevention and Crime Prevention, Second Edition, ed. Lawrence J. Fennelly *(Stoneham, Mass.: Butterworth-Heinemann, 1989), pp. 254–55.*

Appendix I

Key Control and Lock Security Checklist

1. Has a key control officer been appointed?
2. Are locks and keys to all buildings and entrances supervised and controlled by the key control officer?
3. Does the key control officer have overall authority and responsibility for issuance and replacement of locks and keys?
4. What is the business rationale for the issuance of keys, especially master keys?
5. Are keys issued only to authorized personnel? Who determines who is authorized? Is the authorization in writing?
6. Are keys issued to others besides office personnel? If so, on what basis? Is it out of necessity or merely for convenience?
7. Are keys not in use secured in a locked, fireproof cabinet? Are these keys tagged and accounted for?
8. Is the key cabinet for duplicate keys regarded as an area of high security?
9. Is the key or combination to this cabinet maintained under appropriate security or secrecy? If the combination is recorded, is it secured?
10. Are the key locker and record files in order and current?
11. Are issued keys cross-referenced?
12. Are current records maintained indicating:
    *   Building and/or entrances for which keys are issued?
    *   Number and identification of keys issued?
    *   Location and number of master keys?
    *   Location and number of duplicate keys?
    *   Issue and turn-in date of keys?
    *   Location of locks and keys held in reverse?
13. Is a key audit ever made, asking holders to actually produce keys to ensure that they have not been loaned or lost?
14. Who is responsible for ascertaining the possession of keys?
15. Is a current key control directive in effect?
16. Are inventories and inspections conducted by the key control officer to ensure compliance with directives? How often?
17. Are keys turned in during vacation periods?

18. Are keys turned in when employees are transferred, fired, or resign?
19. Is the removal of keys from the premises prohibited?
20. Are locks and combinations changed immediately upon key loss, theft, or employee transfer or resignation?
21. Are locks changed or rotated within the installation at least annually, regardless of transfers or known key security violations?
22. Are current records kept of safe combinations and the dates when these combinations are changed? Are these records adequately protected?
23. Has a system been set up to provide submasters to supervisors and officials on an as-needed basis, with different zones or areas assigned to each individual?
24. If master keys are used, are they devoid of any markings identifying them as master keys?
25. Are master keys controlled more closely than change keys?
26. Must all requests for key reproduction or duplication be approved by the key control officer?
27. Are key holders ever allowed to duplicate keys? If so, under what circumstances?
28. Where the manufacturer's serial number on combination locks and padlocks is visible to unauthorized persons, has this number been recorded and then removed or sanded off the lock?
29. Are locks on inactive gates and storage facilities under seal? Are seals checked regularly by supervisory or key control personnel?
30. Are measures in effect to prevent the unauthorized removal of locks on open cabinets, gates, or buildings?
31. Are key and padlock losses or thefts promptly reported by personnel and promptly investigated by key control personnel?
32. If the building was recently constructed, did the contractor retain keys during the period when construction was being completed? Were locks changed since that time? Did the contractor relinquish all keys after the building was completed?
33. If removable-core locks are in use, are unused cores and core change keys given maximum security against theft, loss, or inspection?
34. Are combination lock, key, and key control records safeguarded separately (i.e., in a separate safe or file) from keys, locks, cores, and other lock hardware?
35. Are all locks of a type which offer adequate protection for the purpose for which they are used?

From John E. Hunter's "The Use of Locks in Physical Crime Prevention," Handbook of Loss Prevention and Crime Prevention, Second Edition, *ed. Lawrence J. Fennelly, (Stoneham, Mass.: Butterworth-Heinemann, 1989), p. 244.*

Chapter 5

Intrusion Alarms

Burglary is a big business. The latest crime figures available from the FBI show that four burglaries occur every minute of every day. Moreover, crime figures show a staggering rate of increase for burglaries of private homes. It is no wonder then that many homeowners and businesspeople are giving serious consideration to electronic alarm protection. Unfortunately, some people in the burglar alarm industry are out to take advantage of the anxious buyer. These operators are in the market to make a fast dollar and the unwary customer who buys what seems to be a bargain too often ends up being cheated.

Selection of a proper alarm system is not a simple matter—the needs of each individual homeowner or businessperson are different. Some questions and issues to consider when selecting an alarm system include:

- Your threat or risk—what is the system protecting you from?
- The type of sensors needed—what will be protected?
- What methods are available to provide the level of protection you need?
- The method of alarm signal transmission—how is the signal sent and who will respond?

Most of the confusion regarding intrusion detection systems is a result of the number of methods available (ranging into the thousands) to accomplish the proper protection needed. An intrusion detection system may deter a would-be intruder, but its primary function is to signal the presence of an intruder. An intrusion detection system can be just a portion of the overall protection needed. Many large businesses supplement alarm systems with security guards and other security personnel. The successful operation of any alarm system depends upon its proper installation and maintenance by the installing company and the proper use of the system by the user.

COMPONENTS OF ALARM SYSTEMS

Sensing devices are used in the actual detection of an intruder. They each have a specific purpose and can be divided into three categories: perimeter protection, area/space protection, and object/spot protection.

PERIMETER PROTECTION

Perimeter protection is the first line in intruder detection. The most common points equipped with sensing devices for perimeter protection are doors, windows, vents, skylights, or any opening to a business or home. Since over 80 percent of all break-ins occur through these openings, most alarm systems provide this type of protection. The major advantage of perimeter protection is its simple design; the major disadvantage is that they only protect openings. If the burglar bursts through a wall, comes through the ventilation system, or stays behind after closing, perimeter protection is useless.

1. Door switches (contacts). These devices are usually magnet-operated switches. They are installed on a door or window in such a way that opening the door or window causes the magnet to move away from the contact which activates the alarm. They can be surface-mounted or recessed into the door and frame. A variety of switch types are manufactured for all kinds of doors or windows.
2. Metallic foil (window tape). This method is widely used to detect glass breakage in show windows, doors, and transoms. When the glass cracks and breaks the foil, it interrupts a low-voltage electrical circuit and activates the alarm.
3. Glass breakage detectors (window bugs). These detectors are shock-sensing devices attached to the glass that sense the breakage of glass by shock or sound.
4. Wooden screens. These devices are made of wooden dowel sticks assembled in a cage-like fashion no more than four inches apart. A very fine, brittle wire runs in the wooden dowels and frame. The burglar must break the dowel to gain entry and therefore break the low voltage electrical circuit, causing the alarm to sound. These devices are primarily used in commercial applications.
5. Window screens. These devices are similar to regular wire window screens in a home, except that a fine, coated wire is a part of the screen and when the burglar cuts the screen to gain entry, the flow of low voltage electricity is interrupted and causes an alarm. These devices are used primarily in residential applications.
6. Lace and paneling. The surfaces of door panels and safes are protected against entry by installing a close, lace-like pattern of metallic foil or fine brittle wire on the surface. Entry is not possible without first breaking the foil or wire, thus activating the alarm. A panel of wood is placed over the lacing to protect it.

Area/Space Protection

These devices protect interior spaces in a business or home against intrusion whether or not perimeter protection is violated. Particularly effective against a stay-behind intruder or the burglar who cuts through the roof or bursts a block wall, space protection devices are only a part of the complete alarm system. They should always be supplemented with perimeter protection. The major advantage of space protection devices is that they provide a highly sensitive, invisible means of detection. The major disadvantage is that improper application and installation by the alarm company can result in frequent false alarms. The types of area/space protection are:

1. Photoelectric eyes (beams). These devices transmit a beam across a protected area. When an intruder interrupts the beam, the beam circuit is disrupted and the alarm sounds. Photoelectric devices use a pulsed infrared beam that is invisible to the naked eye. Some units have a range of over 1,000 feet and can be used outdoors.
2. Ultrasonic detectors. Intruder movement in a protected area disrupts a high-pitched sound (ultrasonic) wave pattern that, in turn, activates the alarm signal. Ultrasonic motion sensors generate signals in the range between 19 and 40 kHz, which is above the frequencies that the average human can hear. Ultrasonic energy is contained completely in the area it is operating. It will not penetrate walls or windows but is absorbed by carpet, draperies, and acoustical tile. Obstructions within a room will reflect the ultrasonic energy and distort its shape pattern. A typical detection range of ultrasonic units is 20 feet wide by 30 feet long in a room with a ceiling up to 12 feet high. More complex ultrasonic systems can detect movement anywhere within the protected area. Ultrasonic devices can be mounted on either the ceiling or the wall but can be prone to false alarms due to excessive air currents and other extraneous ultrasonic noises. Proper application and installation of the equipment is important.
3. Microwave detectors. These detectors use high-frequency radio waves (microwaves) to detect movement. The most commonly used frequencies range between 915 and 10.525 MHz. Microwave energy will penetrate and pass through all building construction materials (wood, sheet rock, cinder block, plastic, glass, and brick) and is reflected by metal. Because microwave energy will penetrate, application and installation are critical. Microwave detectors have a much greater range than ultrasonic and can be used outdoors.
4. Infrared detectors. These detectors are passive sensors, because they do not transmit a signal for an intruder to disturb. Rather, a source of moving infrared radiation (the intruder) is detected against the normal radiation/temperature environment of the room. They sense the radiation from a human body moving through the optical field of view of the detector.
5. Pressure mats. These mats are basically mechanical switches. Pressure mats are most frequently used as a back-up system to perimeter protection. When used as traps they can be hidden under the carpet in front of a likely target or in hallways where an intruder would travel.
6. Sound sensors. Sound sensors detect intrusion by picking up the noise created by the burglar during a break-in attempt. These sensors consist of a mi-

crophone and an electronic amplifier/processor. When the sound level increases beyond the limit normally encountered, the unit signals an alarm. Some units have a pulse-counting and time-interval feature. Other types can actually listen to the protected premises from a central monitoring station.

Object/Spot Detection

Object/spot detection is used to detect the action or presence of an intruder at a single location. It provides direct security for individual items. Such detection methods are the final stage of an in-depth protection system. The objects that are most frequently protected include safes, filing cabinets, desks, art objects, models, statues, and expensive equipment. The types of object/spot protection are:

1. Capacitance/proximity detectors. The object being protected becomes an antenna, electronically linked to the alarm control. When an intruder approaches or touches the object-antenna, an electrostatic field becomes unbalanced and the alarm is initiated. Only metal objects can be protected in this manner.
2. Vibration detectors. These devices utilize a highly sensitive and specialized microphone called an electronic vibration detector (EVD). The EVD is attached directly to the object to be protected. They can be fine-tuned to detect a sledgehammer attack on a concrete wall or a delicate penetration of a glass surface. The alarm goes off only when the object is moved, whereas capacitance devices will detect when the intruder is close to the protected object. Other types of vibration detectors are similar to tilt switches used in pinball machines.

ALARM CONTROLS

All sensing devices are wired into the alarm control panel that receives the signals and processes them. Some of the most severe burglary losses are caused not by equipment failure, but because someone simply turned off the alarm. The type of control panel needed depends upon the sophistication of the overall intrusion alarm system. Some control panels provide zoning capabilities for separate annunciation of the sensing devices. They may also serve as a low-voltage electrical power source for the sensing devices.

Included in the control panel is the battery backup or standby power in the event of an electrical power failure. Some equipment uses rechargeable batteries, whereby the control panel has a low-power charging unit—a trickle charger—that maintains the batteries in a fully-charged condition.

The alarm control unit will normally incorporate a key-operated switch to turn the system on or off. Some control panels will accept a remote on-off switch so that the system can be turned on and off at more than one location.

If the alarm control panel is connected to a central monitor station, the times that the system is turned on and off are recorded and logged. When the owner enters the building in the morning, the alarm is activated. If this happens at a time that has been prearranged with the central station, it is considered a normal opening. If it happens at any other time, the police are dispatched.

It is possible for the owner or other authorized persons to enter the building during the closed times. The person entering must first call the central station and identify himself by a special coding procedure. Records are kept at the central station company for these irregular openings and closings.

Tamper protection is a feature that allows an alarm signal to be generated when the system is compromised in any way. Tamper protection can be designed into any or all portions of the alarm system (control panel, sensing devices, loop wiring, and alarm transmission facilities).

ALARM TRANSMISSION/SIGNALING

The type of alarm transmission/signaling system used in a particular application depends upon the location of the business or residence, the frequency of police patrols, and the financial resources of the customer. Remember that, after deterrence, the purpose of an alarm is to summon the proper authorities to stop a crime during the act or lead to the apprehension of the intruder. It is important that the response by proper authorities to the alarm comes in the shortest possible time. There are several types of alarm signaling systems in general use:

1. Local alarm
2. Central station system
3. Direct wire
4. Multiplex systems
5. Digital communicators
6. Telephone dialers
7. Radio signal transmission

From Lawrence J. Fennelly, Effective Physical Security *(Stoneham, Mass.: Butterworth-Heinemann, 1992), pp. 150–57.*

Chapter 6

Lighting

TRANSITIONAL LIGHTING

Good lighting is the single most cost-effective deterrent to crime, but what is *good* lighting? Ideally, a good lighting system would be reproduced daylight. Realistically, however, the system must supply a high level of visibility and at the same time a low level of glare. One of the most critical problems to consider is that the evenness of outdoor light is more important than an absolute level. Too much lighting can actually be a hazard in itself. Outdoor evening activity areas, such as tennis courts or playgrounds, can be dangerous because of the difficulty of seeing clearly into the surrounding area. When an individual leaves a brightly lighted area and walks into a dark area, vision is momentarily reduced and vulnerability is increased. The opportunity for criminal attack is more likely when a situation like this exists.

Transitional lighting can be used effectively to minimize this hazard. Transitional lighting merely provides a gradual light level change from a brightly lighted area to a dark area. A lower light level can be employed adjacent to the bright area and would help provide a safe transition.

UNDERSTANDING LIGHTING TECHNOLOGY: A DEFINITION OF TERMS

Lighting technology requires the understanding of a whole new language. Generally, the terms, definitions, and discussions that appear in most texts are designed for the lighting engineer who has a strong foundation in the jargon and specifics of the subject. The terms presented below will give you a better understanding of lighting and some of the basic terms that a crime prevention officer should be familiar with:

- Watt. A term used to measure the amount of electrical energy consumed.
- Lumen. The lamps (light bulbs) used in various lighting equipment are rated in lumens. *Lumen* is frequently used as a term to express the output of a light source.
- Foot Candle. This is another unit of illumination. It is defined as the uniform illumination of one lumen on a surface 1 square foot in area.

- Coverage Factor. The coverage factor is the minimum number of directions from which a point or area should be lighted, depending upon the use of the area. For example, a coverage factor of two is required for parking areas and for protective lighting to reduce the effect of shadows between automobiles, piles of materials, and similar bulky objects.
- Quality of Lighting. This term refers to the distribution of brightness and color rendition in a particular area. The term is generally used to describe how light can favorably contribute to visual performance, visual comfort, ease of scene, safety, and aesthetics.
- Reflector. A device used to redirect the light by the process of reflection.
- Refractor. A glass band, globe, or bowl designed to control the direction of the light by the use of prisms.
- Luminaire. A complete lighting device consisting of a light source, its globe, reflector, refractor, and housing. The pole, post, or bracket is not considered a part of the luminaire.
- Visibility. This term refers to the ability to be seen, facilitate seeing, or the distinctness with which objects may be observed. There are four visual factors that must be considered in planning effective security lighting—size, brightness, contrast, and time. Size is an important consideration because larger objects reflect a greater amount of light. The comparative brightness of objects is important because brightly polished silver reflects a greater intensity of light to an area than tarnished silver with the same lighting source. Contrast is important, too—an object placed against a strongly contrasting background will appear to reflect more light to the eye than an object similar in color to the background area. Time is critical because it requires less time to see accurately under good lighting than it does with poor lighting.

GENERAL TYPES OF
OUTDOOR SECURITY LIGHTING

There are four general types of outdoor security lighting: continuous lighting, standby lighting, movable lighting, and emergency lighting.

Continuous Lighting

The most familiar type of outdoor security lighting, continuous lighting can be designed to provide two specific results: glare projection or controlled lighting. The glare method of continuous lighting originated in prisons and correctional institutions where it is still used to illuminate walls and outside barriers. It has been described by some security experts as a *barrier of light* and is particularly effective for lighting boundaries around a facility and approaches to the site. This technique is normally used when the glare of lights directed across an area will not annoy or interfere with neighboring properties. The theory behind this method is that a potential intruder has difficulty seeing inside an area protected by such a barrier; therefore, the lighting method creates a strong visual and psychological deterrent. The guard, on the other hand, is able to observe the intruder, even at a considerable distance. Generally, flood lights are used in this way because the beam, although easy to direct, produces a great deal of glare that a possible intruder must face.

Another type of continuous lighting, controlled lighting, is generally used in situations where the light needs to be more precisely focused due to surrounding property owners, nearby highways, or other limitations. For example, the controlled lighting method could be used when the width of the lighted strip outside of an area must be controlled and adjusted to fit a particular need, such as illuminating a wide strip inside a fence and a narrow strip outside, or the lighting of a wall or roof. One of the most popular methods of controlled lighting for industrial and commercial use is the *surface method*. This method provides for the complete illumination of a particular area or structure within a defined site, not only the perimeters of the property, but also the parking areas, storage lots, and other locations that require improved security. Another advantage of the surface method is that the lighting units are directed at the building rather than away from it so that its appearance is enhanced at night. This same method is used in some locations to illuminate the front and surroundings of residential sites.

Standby Lighting

A second type of outdoor security lighting is standby lighting. Standby lighting systems generally consist of continuous systems, but are designed for reserve or standby use, or to supplement continuous systems. These systems are engaged, either automatically or manually, when the continuous system is inoperative or the need for additional lighting arises. A standby system is useful to selectively light a particular portion of a site should prowlers or intruders be suspected, or to light an area merely for occasional use.

Movable or Portable Lighting

A third type of system uses movable lighting hardware. It is manually operated and usually comprised of movable search or flood lights that can be put in locations that will require lighting only temporarily. The movable system can also be used to supplement continuous or standby lighting and is particularly useful at construction sites.

Emergency Lighting

The fourth system is emergency lighting. Emergency lights may duplicate any of the other three types of lighting and are generally used during power failures or other emergencies when the other systems are inoperative. The unique feature of the emergency system is that it is based on an alternative power source, such as gas generators or batteries.

GENERAL TYPES OF LIGHTING SOURCES

Listed below are the general lighting sources that are mostly used in indoor or outdoor lighting: incandescent, mercury vapor, fluorescent, metal halide, and sodium vapor.

Incandescent

Incandescent lighting systems have low initial costs and provide good color rendition. However, incandescent lamps are relatively short in rated life (500–4,000 hours) and low in lamp efficiency (17–22 LPW, or lumens per watt) when compared to other lighting sources.

Mercury Vapor

Mercury vapor lamps emit a purplish-white color, caused by an electric current passing through a tube of mercury gas. This type of light is generally considered more efficient than the incandescent lamp and is widespread in exterior lighting. Approximately 75 percent of all street lighting is mercury vapor. Because mercury lamps have a long life (24,000+ hours) and good lumen maintenance characteristics, they are widely used in applications where long burning hours are customary. Good color rendition is provided with an average 31–63 LPW range. However, it should be noted that mercury vapor lamps now are being replaced because of their energy inefficiency and consumption levels.

Metal Halide

Metal halide is similar in physical appearance to mercury vapor lighting, but provides a more luminous and efficient light source and better color rendition. The rated life of 6,000 hours is short when compared to mercury lamps, but it is used in applications where color rendition is of primary importance and the burning hours per year are low. Rated at 80–115 LPW.

Fluorescent

Fluorescent lights provide good color rendition, high lamp efficiency (67–100 LPW) and long rated lives (9,000–17,000 hours). However, their long length, relative to their small diameter means that fluorescent bulbs have very wide horizontal beam spreads. Fluorescent lamps are temperature sensitive and low ambient temperatures can decrease their efficiency. Fluorescent lights cannot project light over long distances and therefore are not desirable as flood type lights.

High-Pressure Sodium Vapor

Introduced in 1965, high-pressure sodium vapor lighting has gained acceptance for exterior lighting of parking areas, roadways, buildings, and industrial and commercial interiors. Designed on the same principle as mercury vapor lamps, they emit a golden-white to light pink color. High-pressure sodium vapor lamps provide high lumen efficiency (80–140 LPW) and relatively good light rendition. Expected lamp life is up to 24,000 hours. Maintenance-of-light output is good and averages about 90 percent throughout its rated life.

Low-Pressure Sodium Vapor

This light source has similar principles of operation as other types of vapor lights but provides much brighter lighting (135–180 LPW). The color produced is yellow within a very narrow band of yellow wavelength. For this reason, very poor color rendition is provided. Low-pressure sodium vapor (LPSV) lights have about a 95 percent lifetime lumen maintenance rating. Higher wattage LPSV lamps are about 40 inches long and therefore reduce optical control. LPSV lamps will normally restrike within a few seconds after momentary power losses.[1]

ENDNOTE

1. Lawrence Fennelly, *Effective Physical Security*, (Stoneham, Mass.: Butterworth-Heinemann, 1992), pp. 136–39.

Chapter 7

The Threat
of Fire

ARSON

Arson is defined as "the willful and malicious burning of property." Note the words "willful" and "malicious," both denoting intent, an important consideration. The fire resulting from arson can cause the most terrible damage within minutes. Irreplaceable records can be destroyed and your business brought to a complete halt until order can be restored. In the meantime, chaos rules.

This, of course, is true of any office fire, but arson is perhaps even more of a risk than most figures indicate. Felony crime has increased substantially over the past five years and so has the incidence of arson to hide evidence of burglary. Incendiary bombs have been used in terrorist attacks against offices throughout the country. Arson law varies from state to state. A review of those statutes governing arson in your own locality is advisable.

Motives

Motives for arson are numerous, but the great majority are due to the following:

- The property may be heavily insured and the owner seeks to collect for financial gain.
- A competitor decides to burn out a fellow businessman. Normally employing a professional arsonist or "torch," the competitor hopes to increase his business or perhaps even buy out his victim, who may be forced to liquidate due to the fire. Arson is also used by "protection" racketeers.
- A handy red herring or cloak to hide thefts, shortages, embezzlement, tax evasion, or other crimes.
- Revenge or satisfaction of a real or imagined grudge.
- Psychotics who get gratification from watching fires. Since there is no obvious motive, these fire setters are hard to trace. When a fire is clearly incendiary and no motive can be found, a "fire bug" may be the cause.
- Political terrorism.

Setting the Fire

To destroy a building, the arsonist must get inside with the incendiary device; fires started outside solid construction are extinguished with little danger.

Since arsonists want the fire to get a good start with as little interference as possible, they will frequently take the precaution of disabling your fire-fighting apparatus. Sprinkler valves may be shut off, fire doors blocked, fire hoses cut, and fire extinguishers removed. Windows and doors also may be opened to provide ventilation to fan the flames.

Perhaps most important to an arsonist's success is the target area. In choosing a site he or she will, if possible, be very selective—although, once again, experience may determine how wisely a site is chosen.

The Site

Basement. In most buildings, the maintenance department stores its paint, cleaning fluid, and other flammable chemicals in the basement, making it a prime area for arson. Trash often accumulates and records are often stored in or near the basement. In addition, there is the boiler room and its fuel systems.

Stockroom. Each tenant in the building usually has a room or area where office supplies are stocked. With such combustibles concentrated in one place, it becomes an excellent target area. On the same level, file rooms and mail rooms can be included.

Duplicating room. This area with its supply of paper, chemicals, inks, and rags is perfect for a fire.

Utility closets. These closets with rags, cleaning fluids, mops, and unemptied trash are good fire areas.

The roof and upper floor. The roof and the upper floor of an office building are not ordinarily prime target areas. Since flames tend to rise, such a fire would be easy to control because it moves downward slowly and with difficulty. If the target is the firm's executive offices, however, the arsonist will not be deterred by such considerations.

In surveying your building or office for possible sites to start a fire, you must consider what you see before you. We have touched on areas common to most offices that are probably prime areas of concern. You will undoubtedly have spaces peculiar to your building that also demand attention. First-floor glass exposures are, of course, vulnerable to fire attack from outside the building.

PREVENTION

Arson prevention starts with basic security. With effective traffic control, package checking, secured equipment rooms, and controlled-access systems, security protects the company against many kinds of attackers, including arsonists.

Prevention also requires good housekeeping—part of the overall fire prevention plan that includes regular inspection of all office and building areas for fire violations and potential hazards. Where fire-loading is heavy, material accumulations should if possible, be dispersed or fireproofed.

Also important in fire plans is the distribution of adequate firefighting and fire-detection equipment. Smoke, heat, and flame detectors are of great value throughout buildings, especially in areas not readily observed. In summary, the best protection against arson is found in the effective operation of your total security program.

Investigation

Although it is important to investigate every crime committed against the office, this is especially true in the case of fire. Detailed confessions of arsonists indicate that if they fail to set a big fire on their first try, they often will return again and again until eventually they set a fire that suits their purpose. This is the pattern of incendiarists, whatever their motives. Make it a rule to investigate every fire, no matter how small.

Remember that an overworked city fire department is usually unable to investigate small fires unless they are clearly the work of an arsonist. All too often the cause of fire is listed as "unknown," "cigarettes," or "faulty wiring." Certainly there are fires which, after the most thorough investigation, are unknown in origin. There is no doubt that cigarettes and faulty wiring are very real fire hazards and have contributed to enormous fire losses. But these categories are also convenient catch-alls for overworked and understaffed public authorities.

What to Look For

Obviously if the fire started in some place where there were eyewitnesses—more than one—whose accounts seem to support the discernible facts of the fire, then you probably don't need to probe further the first time a fire occurs in that area. If, on the other hand, the fire started in a location where there is no evident initiating cause, then the matter should be investigated.

You should also be alert to several suspicious circumstances that need examination:

- Two or more fires occurring almost simultaneously in different locations.
- Alien flammable substances in the vicinity of the office. Not necessarily exotic chemicals; they can be as commonplace as old rags, trash, or flammable packing materials. Ask yourself if they should reasonably be where you found them.
- Numerous wastebasket or trash bin fires.
- Windows, doors, desks, or files forced open at the fire site.
- Fire equipment, alarms, sensors, and extinguishers sabotaged or missing.
- An explosion occurring where neither equipment nor materials could contribute to such a blast.

- Evidence of deep charring or that the heat build-up was more rapid than the contents of the area should indicate.
- Evidence of missing inventory in the area.

Remember that most fires start as tiny flames. The majority are accidental, but you cannot afford to overlook the possibility that one was intentionally set. If there is a wastebasket fire, ask yourself what might have been destroyed if it had spread. You might discover the true explanation for the fire and ward off a dangerous situation before it gets out of hand.

Who Investigates?

The expert investigation of fires and their causes is a highly specialized field and requires the services of a trained and experienced investigator. Except in the case of infrequent wastebasket fires or other small fires without a repetitive pattern, a special investigator should be called in.

Large companies with a large asset risk employ one or more trained investigators to look into fires in their premises. This is not practical or necessary for many companies, but they may, however, find it worthwhile to research in advance the availability of arson investigators. Some major insurance companies and associations have investigators who are available to their insureds.

Training

A professional fire investigator should also be consulted to train your security people in the causes of fire and arson, as well as elementary fire investigation procedures.

Once such procedures are established, it should be normal practice to investigate and report any fire on company property. It would be wise to assist all tenants, if possible, in determining the cause of any fire they may have. This cooperative effort is simply a wise move to extend your lines of defense. Any fire in your building is a danger to you, and if an arsonist has selected a nearby tenant as a target, you can be as much the victim as the intended office.

Security and Professional Fire Investigation

In any situation where an investigator is called, security must seek to keep the fire scene undisturbed. This is easier said than done. Fire service people are taught and trained to promote good public relations by immediately cleaning up the premises as much as possible. Such action destroys valuable clues and hampers or eliminates the possibility of a thorough and accurate investigation. Everything at the fire scene is evidence. If anything must be moved, careful photographs should be taken before clearing begins, and the debris moved should be handled with care and secured in a safe place.

Security officers should also gather as much data as possible, so that they can assist the investigator, and keep a file for future reference. This information should include:

- Date, time, and location of fire.
- How the fire was discovered, by whom, and who turned in the alarm.
- Nature of the fire, and cause, if known.
- Description of area, including materials used or stored therein.
- Names, departments, addresses, and statements of witnesses.
- List of personnel who worked in or had access to fire site.
- Dates and occasions of previous fires in that area.
- Names of any employees having access who were under notice or warnings at the time.
- Estimate of loss.
- Details of insurance coverage.

Not necessarily incorporated into the report, but readily available for reference should be:

- A list of employees discharged for cause in the past year.
- Access control records.

Retain all material relevant to the fire under lock and key.

It is important to the community as a whole, and valuable to you as a company, to maintain open lines of communication with your local fire department. They can help you by giving timely warning of new developments that could concern you and, as you feed information back to them, they can sharpen their insights into the growing problem of arson.

1. The increase of fire. In 1992, there were over 3 million fires in the United States causing more than $4 billion in property damage and killing 12,000 people.
2. The consequences of industrial fires. There were 58,200 fires in industrial buildings, causing $750 million in property damage. Tragically, 43 percent of industries who suffer a serious fire never rebuild in the same community.
3. Basic fire behavior. For a fire to start and spread, three things must be present at the same time, in proper quantities:
   Oxygen, which is present in adequate quantities in the air we breathe.
   Fuel, that is, something that will burn. Fuel may be a solid, liquid, or gas.
   Heat, necessary to raise the fuel to the temperature above its ignition temperature. Sources of heat include welding torches, electrical equipment, and noonday sun.
   To prevent fire, you must remove or separate one or more of the three sides of the fire triangle.

4. How a fire starts.
   - *Initial or incipient stage*—The beginning phase starts with a small flame, low heat, and the release of flammable and poisonous gases. This phase may last for a split second, minutes, hours, or even days, depending on the fuel and oxygen available.
   - *Free-burning phase*—With fire involving ordinary solid fuels, after about 5 minutes the fire will enter the second and most destructive phase—the free-burning phase. Here large quantities of smoke, heat, and gases are released until the oxygen or fuel is used up. In tightly confined areas, the fire will lower its oxygen supply to a point where it cannot burn freely. However, heat and unburned gases will continue to build up.
   - *Smoldering phase*—The smoldering phase may well be the most dangerous, because a sudden supply of oxygen to the fire once again completes the fire triangle. Visible flame and extreme heat can flash suddenly or explosively and raise to temperatures easily exceeding 1000°F.

5. Fire Hazards.
   - *Fuel* hazards include such things as improperly handled or stored flammable liquids, accumulations of oily rags and rejected parts, especially near heat sources.
   - *Heat* hazards include overloaded or damaged electrical equipment; improper discarding of smoking materials in restricted areas; electrical, heating, cooking equipment, or soldering guns left on after working hours.
   - Some of the common hazard areas and dangers are laboratories; toilets; storage closets and lockers; shops and supply rooms; painting areas; crawl spaces—especially under buildings; trash bins and trash houses; boiler rooms; concession stands; cafeterias and snack bars; contractor work and contractor storage rooms; combustibles stored too close to heaters or boilers; worn or defective electrical wiring; rubbish not removed or in improper containers; open or leaking containers of flammable materials; flame- or heat-producing equipment left on after-hours; and equipment left running near combustible materials.

6. Fire protection equipment to know and check on patrol includes emergency exit doors; sprinklers; emergency telephones; sprinkler control valves; fire hose valves; fire hydrants; post indicator valves; exit signs (properly illuminated).

7. To verify that an extinguisher is operable:
   - check the pressure gauge to see if the extinguisher is full.
   - check the date with the inspection tag.
   - check to see if the wire or plastic seal is broken.

8. There are four classes of fire:
   Class A—Ordinary Combustibles. Class A fires are those that involve ordinary combustible solids such as wood, paper, cloth, plastic, and rubber. When they burn they leave an ash.

Class B—Flammable Liquids. Class B fires involve flammable liquids such as gasoline, paint, solvents, and greases.

Class C—Electrical Equipment. Class C fires occur in energized electrical equipment or wiring. Make sure you've got the right extinguisher or you may be in for the shock of your life.

Class D—Combustible Metals. Class D fires involve combustible metals such as magnesium and sodium. These fires require "dry powder" extinguishers. Most other extinguishing agents, especially water, will react violently and dangerously when applied to burning metal.

9. Types of fire extinguishers:

Pressured Water (H_2O). Pressurized water extinguishers are used on Class A fires. They usually contain 2-1/2 gallons of water under air pressure and will discharge a stream of water 30–40 feet for about one minute.

Carbon Dioxide (CO_2). Carbon dioxide extinguishers are used for Class B and Class C fires. They discharge a CO_2 gas stream 3–8 feet for 10–30 seconds. These extinguishers come in several sizes and smother the fire by excluding the oxygen. Place your hands only on the part of the horn that is designed for holding. It gets very cold elsewhere.

Dry Chemical. Dry chemical extinguishers contain special chemicals which can extinguish Class B and Class C fires, and in some cases, Class A, B, and C fires. Check the label to determine which type of dry chemical is in your extinguisher. These extinguishers discharge a stream of powder for 10–20 feet for about 15–30 seconds. It leaves a dust residue, so use it on delicate electrical equipment only as a last resort.

10. Proper operation of a fire extinguisher.

H_2O Extinguisher

- Locate the correct type of extinguisher
- Carry it to the fire scene in an upright position, usually by the handle.
- Next, remove or free the hose or nozzle from its holder.
- Holding onto the nozzle with one hand, pull the locking pin from the valve. Pull sharply away from the valve.
- Direct the stream onto the burning materials, not into the smoke and flame.
- Move the nozzle from side to side, starting at the bottom of the fire. Remember, solids hold heat; you may have to tear the fuel apart to fully extinguish the fire.

CO_2 Extinguisher

- When using a CO_2 extinguisher on a Class B or Class C fire, it will be necessary to be within 2–3 feet of the fire because of the limited range of the extinguisher.
- Crouching down may help you stay below the heat and get closer. Direct the CO_2 across the surface of the liquid at the point where the fuel and flame meet.
- Moving the nozzle from side to side, start at the edge of the fire nearest you and push it away to the far side. Continue the discharge until all flames are out. Never turn your back on a fire; it may reignite.

Dry Chemical
- Dry chemical extinguishers are used in the same manner as the carbon dioxide type, except you should stay back 5–6 feet from the fire.
- The impact of the chemical under pressure may blow flammable liquids out of their containers if you get too close. Continue to extinguish until the fire is completely out.
- While the procedure just described will work for most extinguishers, there are some dry chemical extinguishers that require a slightly different procedure. After releasing the hose and nozzle, a lever must be pushed down to open a cylinder of gas to pressurize the extinguisher. Next, open the valve on the nozzle and direct it as before.

APPROACH ANY FIRE UPWIND AND KEEP YOURSELF BETWEEN THE EXIT AND THE FIRE. Try to isolate the fire by closing windows and doors; shutting down air conditioners, fans and blowers; and turning off gas and electrical equipment in the immediate area.

11. Proper use of fire hoses. Hose streams should only be used on fires too large for extinguishers. Don't begin using them until evacuation and notification of the fire department have taken place. Operation of hose lines usually requires more than one person and some training by qualified personnel is desirable.

12. Fire emergency procedure. Every organization should have a fire evacuation procedure. If your organization is planning to adopt one, or is modifying an existing one, the following example may be helpful.

SAMPLE FIRE EMERGENCY PLAN STATEMENT

A fire emergency report should be directed to the security officer on duty in the control center or to the security director. He or she will be responsible for calling the fire department or emergency brigade over the public address system by announcing the evacuation procedure. Here is an example:

"ATTENTION—ATTENTION, PLEASE. THIS IS AN EMERGENCY. WE ARE EVACUATING THE BUILDING. PROCEED TO THE STAIRWAY EXIT. DO NOT USE THE ELEVATORS. WALK DOWN IN A SINGLE FILE. EXIT ON THE FIRST FLOOR AND ASSEMBLE IN THE PARKING LOT, NORTH OF THE BUILDING."

- Call the security officer on patrol and advise him or her to direct the fire department to the location of the fire emergency. If the location is in the main building, elevators may be brought to the first floor level by use of a special key.
- The fire department will be directed to arrive at the proper entrance.

When the emergency brigade is alerted over the public address system, the following action will be taken:
- The brigade members on the fire floor and those on the floor above and below will respond to the indicated location. On the way to the location, each member may pick up a fire extinguisher to assist in fighting the fire. Discuss your policy for this procedure.

- As soon as the security director or chief of the emergency brigade arrives on the scene, he or she will determine the need to evacuate.
- If evacuation is decided, the chief of the emergency brigade will call the security center, using an identifying code word, and instructing the security officer to direct the evacuation over the public address system.

"THIS IS THE FINAL ANNOUNCEMENT. ALL PEOPLE SHOULD BE IN THE EXIT STAIRWAYS. WILL THE EMERGENCY BRIGADE ADVISE CONTROL CENTER AS EACH FLOOR IS CLEARED."

- When the evacuation is announced over the public address system, the brigade members on each floor will ensure that people leave in an orderly manner by way of the *stairwells*.
- The brigade members on each floor will survey the area quickly to ensure that all people have left. As the floor is cleared, the last brigade member to leave will call the security center on an emergency phone and advise that the floor is cleared.

All employees should become familiar with the following fire emergency procedures:

Reporting Fire Emergencies. Anyone who discovers a fire must immediately report it to the security control center. Be sure to give all specific locations—floor numbers and side of building (north, south, east, west).

Emergency Evacuation (Employee Action). When you are alerted over the public address system to evacuate the building, you should do the following:

- Return valuable records and documents to the vault, if material you work with is kept in the vault, or
- Place all important documents in the drawers of your desk or file cabinets.
- Proceed quickly, DO NOT RUN, to the nearest stairway.

The building staff will take manual control of the elevators. There is a possibility that the elevators can malfunction during a fire, with the only way to exit the building by way of the stairs. In the event a particular type of emergency allows you the use of the elevators, you will be directed to them by the emergency brigade.

How Fires Develop—
The Four Stages of Fire Development

1. Incipient Stage—Invisible particles generated by thermal decomposition, no visible smoke, flame, or appreciable heat. Minimum hazard.
2. Smoldering Stage—Combustion products now visible as smoke. Flame or appreciable heat still not present. Moderate to major hazard.
3. Flame Stage—Actual fire now exists. Appreciable heat still not present, but follows almost instantaneously. Major hazard.
4. High Heat Stage—Uncontrolled heat and rapidly expanding fire can cause severe damage. Extreme hazard.

Sprinklers

One of the most effective means of reducing fire damage is the automatic sprinkler system. Although a sprinkler system can often extinguish a fire, its primary function is to retard the growth of the fire until the fire department arrives. A sprinkler system often remains dormant for many years, but must be fully operational when needed. Although sprinkler systems have an impressive record of performing as designed, failures have resulted in extremely large insurance losses. Many of these failures are caused because the system is not fully operational when fire strikes. There are two main weaknesses in any sprinkler system: 1) the flow of water to the system can either be shut off or not working properly, and 2) the fire department might not be promptly notified.

Supervisory service and waterflow service are the two types of central station service for sprinkler systems. Supervisory service makes sure that the sprinkler system is in operating order at all times. Sensors detect unsafe conditions such as closed valves, insufficient water pressure, freezing temperatures, and power failures at the fire pump. These supervisory sensors transmit a signal to the central station where an operator records the signal and notifies the responsible people to make quick repairs and restore protection.

Waterflow alarms protect against sprinkler leakage and the outbreak of fire. Water flowing through the sprinkler system initiates a fire alarm signal to the central station. The central station operator dispatches the fire department and notifies the subscriber.

Sprinkler contractors are skillful in installing sprinkler systems, but their interest in alarm systems is usually limited to providing an alarm outside of the building. The owner or the insurance company must take the responsibility of arranging for alarm systems to supervise critical points in the sprinkler system and provide a means of promptly notifying the fire department in case of fire.

Appendix I

Education and Building Safety

Educating employees and designated tenant representatives about fire prevention, protection, and evacuation should be a continuous program. Any structural changes or interior layout changes must be incorporated into the program as they occur. The following guide may be useful in establishing a fire-safety indoctrination program.

- Show all employees where primary and secondary fire exits are located and demonstrate, if necessary, how such exits may be opened. Explain the purpose of closing exit stairwells and the importance of keeping doors from the corridor closed at all times. If possible, employees should take a walk down these exits to familiarize themselves with the area.
- Explain procedures for reporting fires discovered by employees or tenant personnel. Always emphasize the importance of reporting *first*, before any effort to extinguish the fire is attempted.
- Touch doorknobs before opening doors. Opening a hot door can be deadly.
- Distribute a fire safety summary with all points and procedures reviewed.
- Explain the building emergency alarm or notification system.
- Explain that elevators are *never* to be used as a means of emergency exit.
- Explain the need to act quickly and emphasize the need to remain calm and avoid panic.
- Demonstrate available firefighting equipment or show a manufacturer's film on its proper use. Few employees know how to use extinguishers or corridor fire hoses.
- Explain what should be done if all escape routes are cut off by fire or smoke. In explaining such an extreme and rare emergency, point out that they may move quickly to a point farthest from the fire, closing doors between them and the smoke; enter a perimeter office with a solid door; and move readily flammable material out of that office if time permits.
- Since air pressure may expand and exert enormous pressure on the doors and walls, barricade the office door with heavy non-combustible furniture. (Assume that all upholstered furniture is combustible.)
- Open the top and bottom windows in the office. Smoke will exhaust through

the top while fresh air enters through the bottom. Break the window if necessary.

- Stay by the window and keep low where the air is cooler and cleaner.

BUILDING SAFETY

Much can be done to prevent office building fires—the first priority in fire protection planning.

- Reduce the fire load in each office and throughout the building.
- Use fire-resistant furniture. Remove any upholstered furniture and polyurethane cushions. Also use fire-resistant drapes and fire-retardant finishes.
- Keep combustibles from accumulating, particularly in refuse areas, chutes, and receiving areas.
- Reduce the amount of and control the handling and storage of highly flammable chemicals throughout the building.
- Identify less-obvious fire risks. Most wiring insulation materials burn when exposed to fire, causing a great deal of smoke. Wiring should be encased in metal conduits or ducts. The area between suspended ceilings and the concrete slabs above frequently contain fuel sources such as nonmetallic ducts and conduits; cable and wiring with insulated conductors; catwalks; and duct connectors and coverings. Such combustibles should be reduced or eliminated.

Preventing the Spread of Fire and Smoke

Where the floor is concrete, its integrity must be maintained. The over-all fire-resistant integrity of a concrete floor can be jeopardized by cutouts. Look for trouble spots such as:

- Vertical flues. Fire barriers equal to the fire-resistance of the floor should be installed where these exist.
- Wire connections between floors. These should be covered and the openings sealed with thermal insulation to prevent the transmission of smoke and heat between floors.
- Air conditioning ducts. These and other floor openings should be treated and sealed with fire-resistant materials and positive fire-stop seals.
- Fire and smoke venting systems should be incorporated in all new construction.
- Sprinkler systems should be installed in new construction as well as high-risk buildings and offices and those adjacent to such.
- Fire detection and alarm systems, both manual and automatic, should be installed throughout the building.

- Each office building and tenant should implement fire emergency plans and training programs to insure the safe evacuation of building occupants.

These are just some of the recommendations being made in cities that have high-rise office buildings. The ones mentioned here are the most important. While we hope such risks can and will be eliminated, fire protection planning cannot wait until they are. We must, in the meantime, be guided by the need for fire prevention and life safety, and always stay on the alert for new problems arising in our offices or the buildings they are located in. In reviewing building and office plans, you should ask yourself these questions:

- Are floor diagrams conspicuously posted?
- Are exit routes well lit, fairly straight, and free from obstructions?
- Are elevators posted to warn against their use in an emergency? Do these signs point out the direction of fire exits?
- Are all handicapped persons identified and their evacuation planned for?
- Is lighting adequate? Do corridors have emergency lighting during power failures?
- Who will notify personnel of decision to evacuate? Who will make the decision to evacuate? Who will operate the communication system? Who is assigned to provide information on the progress of the emergency, and by what means?

SUMMARY

With over a thousand office fires occurring each month in this country, building and office managers share a problem that needs careful thought. Fortunately, the majority of these fires are relatively small, at least in terms of the monetary damage suffered. But each has the potential of being a major disaster. You can never let down your guard in your constant fight with the ever-present threat of fire.

Appendix II

Fire Safety

FIRE SAFETY REQUIRES EVERYBODY'S COOPERATION AND PARTICIPATION

Fire prevention and fire safety. Subjects you've heard about since the first grade. Subjects you may think of as boring until you visualize yourself trapped in a fire, unable to escape. Death by fire is horrible, tragic. The injuries, too, can be awful, painful and disfiguring, their effects lifelong. Every year, two out of three deaths in residential fires occur between 8 p.m. and 8 a.m—while most people are sleeping. Most of the nearly 6,000 people killed by fire every year—and the almost 27,000 more who are injured—could be alive and well today because most fires can be prevented. We think that once you know some pertinent statistics, you'll agree that fire prevention and fire safety are worthy of close attention.

Your Home or Office

One way to keep a fire from spreading is to reduce the materials fueling it. Therefore, you should limit the number of flammable items used in decorating and keep your area neat and clean. Curtains, drapes, and other cloth hangings should be kept to a minimum and made of fire-retardant fabrics.

Your home may have limited electrical capacity: Do not overload the circuits. Refrigerators, stereo systems, and other UL-approved appliances should be plugged into wall outlets—never connected to light sockets.

Extension Cords

Overloaded electric cords and outlets ignite floor coverings and upholstered furniture and are the third leading cause of fires. Preventing these fires is simple: Use only Underwriters Laboratories– or National Electrical Code–approved extension cords in good condition and properly rated. Do not splice extension cords; never run them through doorways or partitions, or cover them with rugs.

Candles

Candles and other sources of open flame should be strictly forbidden. The only exception is candles attended by those observing religious holidays.

Smoking

Smoking is the leading cause of fire deaths. If you must smoke, please do so safely. Use deep ash trays with grooves or snuffers that hold cigarettes completely. Empty them regularly into a covered metal container. Be sure that all cigarettes are completely extinguished before disposing of them. And please don't smoke in bed or when you're sleepy.

Fire Safety Equipment

Since smoke detectors effectively alert you to a developing fire they should be inspected annually. Batteries in portable units should be replaced annually. Emergency exit doors and fire escapes are for your protection. They should be kept clear of obstructions. Corridor fire doors are used to control smoke. They must be kept closed at all times.

Any abuse of, or tampering with, fire alarms, smoke detectors, or extinguisher systems is strictly forbidden. It puts your life and the lives of others needlessly in danger. Penalties could include fines and serious disciplinary action. Pulling a false alarm or maliciously causing a smoke detector to initiate a general alarm is a violation of state laws and may be punishable by a fine or imprisonment.

Fireworks and Flammable Materials

Firecrackers, fireworks, gasoline, kerosene, other flammable fuels and their containers, motorcycles, mopeds, other fuel-powered items, and flammable and combustible materials should not be stored inside your home or office.

Fire Drills

Fire drills—practicing evacuation procedures—are an important component of fire safety. They are intended to teach behavior that can help you survive a fire emergency, alert you to alternate escape routes, and help you understand your responsibilities in the event of a fire. Consider holding fire drills periodically during the year. We strongly urge active participation. It could save your life.

Chapter 8

Bomb and Physical Security Planning[1]

INTRODUCTION

Bombing and the threat of being bombed are harsh realities in today's world. The public is becoming more aware of violent incidents perpetrated by vicious, nefarious segments of our society through the illegal use of explosives. Law enforcement agencies are charged with protecting life and property, but law enforcement alone is not enough. Every citizen must do his or her part to ensure a safe environment.

The information contained here is designed to help both the public and private sectors prepare for the potential threat of explosives-related violence. While the ideas set forth are applicable in most cases, they are intended only as a guide. The information provided is compiled from a wide range of sources, including actual reports from the Bureau of Alcohol, Tobacco and Firearms (ATF).

If there is one point that must be emphasized, it is the value of preparedness. Do not allow a bomb incident to catch you by surprise. By developing a bomb incident plan and considering possible bomb incidents in your physical security plan, you can reduce the potential for personal injury and property damage. By making this information available to you, we hope to help you better prepare for bomb threats and the illegal use of explosives.

BOMBS

Bombs can be constructed to look like almost anything and can be placed or delivered in any number of ways. The probability of finding a bomb that looks like the stereotypical bomb is almost nonexistent. The only common denominator among bombs is that they are designed to explode.

Most bombs are homemade and are limited in their design only by imagination of and resources available to the bomber. Remember, when searching for a bomb, suspect anything that looks unusual. Let a trained bomb technician determine what is or is not a bomb.

BOMB THREATS

Bomb threats are delivered in a variety of ways. The majority of threats are called in to the target. Occasionally these calls are made through a third party. Sometimes a threat is communicated in writing or by a recording.

There are two logical reasons for reporting a bomb threat. Sometimes, the caller has definite knowledge or believes that an explosive or incendiary bomb has been or will be placed and he or she wants to minimize personal injury or property damage. The caller may be the person who has placed the device or someone who has become aware of such information. The other type of caller wants to create an atmosphere of anxiety and panic that will, in turn, result in a disruption of the normal activities at the facility where the device is purportedly placed.

Whatever the reason for the call, there will certainly be a reaction to it. Through proper planning, the wide variety of potentially uncontrollable reactions can be greatly reduced.

WHY PREPARE?

Through proper preparation, you can reduce the accessibility of your business or building and can identify those areas that can be "hardened" against the potential bomber. This will limit the amount of time lost due to searching, if you determine a search is necessary. If a bomb incident occurs, proper planning will instill confidence in your leadership, reinforce the notion that those in charge do care, and reduce the potential for personal injury and property loss.

Proper planning can also reduce the threat of panic, the most contagious of all human emotions. Panic is sudden, excessive, unreasoning, infectious terror. Once a state of panic has been reached, the potential for injury and property damage is greatly increased. In the context of a bomb threat, panic is the ultimate attainment of the caller.

Be prepared! There is no excuse for not taking every step necessary to meet the threat.

HOW TO PREPARE

In preparing to cope with a bomb incident, it is necessary to develop two separate but interdependent plans—namely a physical security plan and a bomb incident plan.

Physical security provides for the protection of property, personnel, facilities, and material against unauthorized entry, trespass, damage, sabotage, or other illegal or criminal acts. The physical security plan deals with prevention and access control to the building. In most instances, some form of physical security may be already in existence, although not necessarily intended to prevent a bomb attack.

The bomb incident plan provides detailed procedures to be implemented when a bombing attack is executed or threatened. In planning for the bomb incident, a definite chain of command or line of authority must be established. Only by using an established organization and procedures can the bomb incident be handled with the least risk to all concerned. A clearly defined line of authority will install confidence and avoid panic.

Establishing a chain of command is easy if there is a simple office structure, one business, one building. However, if a complex situation exists, a multi-occupant building for example, a representative from each business should attend the planning conference. A leader should be appointed and a clear line of succession delineated. This chain of command should be printed and circulated to all concerned parties.

In planning, you should designate a command center to be located in the switchboard room or other focal point of telephone or radio communications. Management personnel assigned to operate the center should have the authority to decide whatever action should be taken during the threat. Only those with assigned duties should be permitted in the center. Make some provision for alternates in the event someone is absent when a threat is received. Obtain an updated blueprint or floor plan of your building and maintain it in the command center.

Contact the police department, fire department, or local government agencies to determine if any assistance is available to you for developing your physical security plan or bomb incident plan. If possible, have police and fire department representatives and members of your staff inspect the building for areas where explosives are likely to be concealed. (Make a checklist of these areas for inclusion in command center materials.) Determine whether there is a bomb disposal unit available, how to contact the unit, and under what conditions it is activated. In developing your bomb incident plan, you must also ascertain whether the bomb disposal unit, in addition to disarming and removing the explosives, will assist in searching the building in the event of a threat.

Training is essential to deal properly with a bomb threat. Instruct all personnel, especially those at the switchboard, in what to do if a bomb threat is received. Be absolutely certain that all personnel assigned to the command center are aware of their duties. The positive aspects of planning will be lost if the leadership is not apparent. It is also critical to organize and train an evacuation unit that will be responsive to the command center and has a clear understanding of the importance of its role.

We have suggested that the command center be located near the switchboard or focal point of communications. It is critical that lines of communication be established between the command center and the search or evacuation teams. The center must have the flexibility to keep up with the search team progress. In a large facility, if the teams go beyond the communications network, the command center must have the mobility to maintain contact with and track search or evacuation efforts.

SECURITY AGAINST BOMB INCIDENTS

In dealing with bomb incidents or potential bomb incidents, two interrelated plans must be developed—the bomb incident plan and the physical security plan. Until this point, we have primarily addressed the bomb incident plan. Now, before continuing with that plan, we will discuss security measures as they apply to defending against the bomb attack.

Most commercial structures and individual residences already have some security in place, planned or unplanned, realized or not. Locks on windows and doors, outside lights, and similar devices are all designed and installed to contribute toward the security of a facility and the protection of its occupants.

In considering measures to increase security of your building or office, it is highly recommended that you contact your local police department for guidance regarding a specific plan for your facility. There is no single security plan that works in all situations.

The exterior configuration of a building or facility is very important. Unfortunately, in most instances, the architect has given little or no consideration to security, particularly toward thwarting or discouraging a bomb attack. However, by the addition of fencing and lighting, and by controlling access, the vulnerability of a facility to a bomb attack can be reduced significantly.

Bombs being delivered by car or left in a car are a grave reality. Parking should be restricted, if possible, to 300 feet from your building or any building in a complex. If restricted parking is not feasible, properly identified employee vehicles should be parked closest to your facility and visitor vehicles parked at a distance.

Heavy shrubs and vines should be kept close to the ground to reduce their potential to conceal criminals or bombs. Window boxes and planters are perfect receptacles for a bomb. Unless there is an absolute requirement for such ornamentation, window boxes and planters are better removed. If they must remain, a security patrol should be employed to check them regularly.

A highly visible security patrol can be a significant deterrent. Even if this patrol is only one person, he or she is optimally utilized outside the building. If an interior guard is utilized, consider the installation of closed-circuit television cameras that cover exterior building perimeters.

Have an adequate burglar alarm system installed by a reputable company that can service and properly maintain the equipment. Post signs indicating that such a system is in place.

Entrance and exit doors with hinges and hinge pins on the inside to prevent removal should be installed. Solid wood or sheet metal–faced doors provide extra integrity that a hollow-core wooden door cannot provide. A steel door frame that properly fits the door is as important as the construction of the door.

The ideal security situation is a building with no windows. However, bars, grates, heavy mesh screens, or steel shutters over windows offer good protection from otherwise unwanted entry. It is important that the openings in the protective coverings are not too large. Otherwise, a bomb may be planted in the building while the bomber remains outside. Floor vents, transoms, and skylights should also be covered. Please note that fire safety considerations preclude the use of certain window coverings. Municipal ordinances should be researched and occupant safety considered before any of these renovations are undertaken.

Controls should be established for positively identifying personnel who are to authorized access critical areas and for denying access to unauthorized personnel. These controls should extend to the inspection of all packages and materials being taken into critical areas.

Security and maintenance personnel should be alert for people who act in a suspicious manner, as well as objects, items, or parcels which look out of place or suspicious. Surveillance should be established to include potential hiding places such as stairwells, rest rooms, and any vacant office space for dubious individuals or items.

Doors or accessways to such areas as boiler rooms, mail rooms, computer areas, switchboards, and elevator control rooms should remain locked when not in use.

Good housekeeping is also vital. Trash or dumpster areas should remain free of debris. A bomb or device can easily be concealed in the trash. Combustible materials should be properly disposed of, or protected if further use is anticipated.

Install detection devices at all entrances and closed-circuit television in those areas previously identified as likely places where a bomb may be placed. Coupled with the posting of signs indicating such measures are in place, these are good deterrents.

It is necessary for businesses to maintain good public relations with their clients. Corporate responsibility, however, also involves the safety and protection of the public. The threatened use of explosives means that in the interest of safety and security, some inconvenience may have to be imposed on visitors to public buildings. The public is becoming more accustomed to routine security checks and will readily accept these minor inconveniences.

Perhaps entrances and exits can be modified with minimal expenditure to channel all visitors through a reception area. Individuals entering the building could be required to sign a register indicating the name and room number of the person they wish to visit. A system for signing out when the individual departs could be integrated into this procedure.

Such a procedure may result in complaints from the public. If the reception desk clerk explains to visitors that these procedures were implemented with their best interests and safety in mind, the complaints would be reduced. The placement of a sign at the reception desk informing visitors of the need for safety is another option.

RESPONDING TO BOMB THREATS

Instruct all personnel, especially those at the switchboard, in what to do if a bomb threat call is received. It is always preferable that more than one person listen in on the call. To do this, a covert signaling system should be implemented, perhaps by using a coded buzzer signal to a second reception point.

A calm response to the bomb threat caller could result in obtaining additional information. This is especially true if the caller wishes to avoid injuries or deaths. If told that the building is occupied or cannot be evacuated in time, the bomber may be wiling to give more specific information on the bomb's location, components, or method of initiation.

The bomb threat caller is the best source of information about the bomb. When a bomb threat is called in:

- Keep the caller on the line as long as possible. Ask the person to repeat the message. Record every word spoken by the caller.
- If the caller does not indicate the location of the bomb or the time of possible detonation, ask for this information.
- Inform the caller that the building is occupied and the detonation of a bomb could result in death or serious injury to many innocent people.
- Pay particular attention to background noises, such as motors, music, and any other noise which may give a clue as to the location of the caller.
- Listen closely to the voice (male or female?), voice quality (calm or excited?), accents, and speech impediments. Immediately after the caller hangs up, report the threat to the person designated by management to receive such information.
- Also report the information immediately to the police department, fire department, ATF, FBI, and other appropriate agencies. The sequence of notification should be established in your bomb incident plan.
- Remain available; law enforcement personnel will want to interview you.

When a written threat is received, save all materials, including any envelope or container. Once the message is recognized as a bomb threat, further handling should be avoided. Every possible effort should be made to retain evidence such as fingerprints, handwriting or typewriting, paper, and postal marks. These will prove essential in tracing the threat and identifying the writer. While written messages are usually associated with generalized threats and extortion attempts, a written warning of a specific device may occasionally be received. It should never be ignored.

DECISION TIME

The most serious of all decisions to be made by management in the event of a bomb threat is whether to evacuate the building. In many cases, this decision may have already been made during the development of the bomb incident plan. Management may provide a carte blanche policy that, in the event of a bomb threat, total evacuation will be effective immediately. This decision circumvents the calculated risk and demonstrates a deep concern for the safety of personnel in the building. However, such a decision can result in costly loss of time.

Essentially, there are three alternatives when faced with a bomb threat:

1. Ignore the threat.
2. Evacuate immediately.
3. Search and evacuate if warranted.

Ignoring the threat completely can result in some problems. While a statistical argument can be made that very few bomb threats are real, it cannot be overlooked that sometimes bombs have been located in connection with threats. If employees learn that bomb threats have been received and ignored, it could result in morale problems and have a long-term adverse effect on your business. Also, there is the possibility that if the bomb threat callers feel that they are being ignored, they may go beyond the threat and actually plant a bomb.

Evacuating immediately on every bomb threat is an alternative that on face value appears to be the preferred approach. However, the negative factors inherent in this approach must be considered. The obvious result of immediate evacuation is the disruptive effect on your business. If the bomb threat callers know that your policy is to evacuate each time a call is made, they can continually call and bring your business to a standstill. An employee, knowing that the policy is to evacuate immediately, may make a threat in order to get out of work. A student may use a bomb threat to avoid a class or miss a test. Also, a bomber wishing to cause personal injuries could place a bomb near an evacuation exit and then call in the threat.

Initiating a search after a threat is received and evacuating a building after a suspicious package or device is found is the third, and perhaps the most desired, approach. It is certainly not as disruptive as an immediate evacuation and will satisfy the requirement to do something when a threat is received. If a device is found, the evacuation can be accomplished expeditiously while simultaneously avoiding the potential danger areas of the bomb.

Evacuation

An evacuation unit consisting of management personnel should be organized and trained in conjunction with the development of the bomb incident plan, as well as with the cooperation of all tenants of a building.

The unit should be trained in how to evacuate the building during a bomb threat. Evacuation priorities should be considered, such as areas above and below the bomb site in order to remove those persons from danger as quickly as possible. Training in this type of evacuation is usually available from police, fire, or other safety departments within the community.

You may also train the evacuation unit in search techniques, or you may prefer a separate search unit. Volunteer personnel should be solicited for this function. Assignment of search wardens and team leaders can be made. To completely search the building, personnel must be thoroughly familiar with all hallways, rest rooms, false ceiling areas, and every location where an explosive or incendiary device may be concealed. When police officers or firefighters arrive at the building, the contents and the floor plan will be unfamiliar to them if they have not previously surveyed the facility. Therefore, it is extremely important that the evacuation or search unit be thoroughly trained and familiar with the floor plan of the building and immediate outside areas. When a room or particular area is searched, it should be marked or sealed with a piece of tape and reported to the supervisor of that area.

The evacuation or search unit should be trained only in evacuation and search techniques. If a device is located, it should not be disturbed. Its location should be well marked, however, and a route back to the device noted.

Search Teams

It is advisable to use more than one individual to search any area or room, no matter how small. Searches can be conducted by supervisory personnel, area occupants, or trained explosive search teams. There are advantages and disadvantages to each method of staffing the search teams.

Using supervisory personnel to search is a rapid approach and causes little disturbance. There will be little loss of employee working time, but a morale problem may develop if it is discovered that a bomb threat was received and workers weren't told. Using supervisors to search will usually not be as effective because of their unfamiliarity with many areas and their desire to get on with business.

Using area occupants to search their own areas is the best method for a rapid search. Furthermore, area personnel are familiar with what does or does not belong in their area. Using occupants to search will result in a shorter loss of worktime than if all were evacuated prior to search by trained teams. Using the occupants to search can have a positive effect on morale, given a good training program to develop confidence. Of course, this would require the training of an entire work force, and ideally the performance of several practical training drills. One drawback of this search method is the increased danger to unevacuated workers.

The search conducted by a trained team is the best for safety, morale and thoroughness, though it does take the most time. Using a trained team will result in a significant loss of production time. It is a slow operation that requires comprehensive training and practice.

The decision as to who should conduct searches ultimately lies with management, and should be considered and incorporated into the bomb incident plan.

Search Technique

The following room search technique is based on the use of a two-person search team. There are many minor variations possible in searching a room. The following discussion, however, contains only the basic techniques.

When a two-person search team enters a room, they should first move to various parts of the room and stand quietly with their eyes closed to listen for a clockwork device. A clockwork mechanism can be quickly detected without use of special equipment. Even if no clockwork mechanism is detected, the team is now aware of the background noise level within the room itself.

Background noise or transferred sound is always disturbed during a building search. If a ticking sound is heard but cannot be located, one might become unnerved. The ticking sound may come from an unbalanced air-conditioner fan several floors away or from a dripping sink down the hall. Sound will transfer through air-conditioning ducts, along water pipes, and through walls. One of the most difficult types of buildings to search is one that has a steam or hot water heating system. These buildings constantly thump, crack, chatter, and tick due to the movement of the steam or hot water and the expansion and contraction of the pipes. Background noise may also include traffic outside, rain, and wind.

The individual in charge of the room search team should look around the room and determine how the room is to be divided for searching and to what height the first sweep should extend. You should divide the room into two equal parts. The division is based on the number and type of objects in the room, not its size. An imaginary line is then drawn between two objects in the room; for example, the edge of the window on the north wall to the floor lamp on the south wall.

First Room-Search Sweep

Look at the furniture or objects in the room and determine the average height of the majority of items resting on the floor. In an average room, this height usually includes table or desk tops and chair backs. The first searching height usually covers the items in the room up to hip height.

After the room has been divided and a searching height has been selected, both individuals go to one end of the room division line and start from a back-to-back position. This is the starting point, and the same point will be used on each successive sweep. Each person now starts searching way around the room, working toward the other person, checking all items resting on the floor around the wall area of the room. When the two individuals meet, they will have completed a "wall sweep." They should then work together and check all items in the middle of the room up to the selected height, including the floor under the rugs. This first searching sweep should also include those items which may be mounted on or in the walls, such as air-conditioning ducts, baseboard heaters, and built-in cupboards if these fixtures are below hip height.

The first search sweep usually takes the most time and effort. During all the sweeps, use an electronic or medical stethoscope on walls, furniture items, and floors.

Second Room-Search Sweep

The team leader again looks at the furniture or objects in the room and determines the height of the second sweep. This height is usually from the desk tops to the chin or top of the head. The two persons return to the starting point and repeat the searching technique at the second selected search height. This sweep usually covers pictures hanging on the walls, built-in bookcases, and tall table lamps.

Third Room-Search Sweep

When the second sweep is completed, the person in charge again determines the next searching height, usually from the chin or the top of the head up to the ceiling. The third sweep usually covers high mounted air-conditioning ducts and hanging light fixtures.

Fourth Room-Search Sweep

If the room has a false or suspended ceiling, the fourth sweep involves this area. Check flush or ceiling-mounted light fixtures, air-conditioning or ventilation ducts, sound or speaker systems, electrical wiring, and structural frames.

Post a conspicuous sign or marker in the area indicating "Search Completed." Place a piece of colored Scotch tape across the door and door jamb approximately 2 feet above floor level if the use of signs is not practical.

The same basic technique can be expanded and applied to search any enclosed area. Encourage the use of common sense or logic in searching. If a guest speaker at a convention has been threatened, common sense would indicate searching the speakers platform and microphones first, but always return to the search technique. Do not rely on random or spot checking of only logical target areas. The bomber may not be a logical person.

In summary, the following steps should be taken in order to search a room:

1. Divide the area and select a search height.
2. Start from the bottom and work up.
3. Start back-to-back and work toward each other.
4. Go around the walls and proceed toward the center of the room.

WHEN A SUSPICIOUS OBJECT IS LOCATED

It is imperative that personnel involved in a search be instructed that their only mission is to search for and report suspicious objects. Under no circumstances should anyone move, jar, or touch a suspicious object or anything attached to it. The removal or disarming of a bomb must be left to explosives disposal professionals. When a suspicious object is discovered, the following procedures are recommended:

1. Report the location and an accurate description of the object to the appropriate supervisor. Relay this information immediately to the command cen-

ter, which will notify the police and fire departments, and rescue squad. These officers should be met and escorted to the scene.

2. If absolutely necessary, place sandbags or mattresses (never metal shields) *around* the suspicious object. Do not attempt to cover the object.
3. Identify the danger area, and block it off with a clearance zone of at least 300 feet, including the floors above and below.
4. Make sure that all doors and windows are opened to minimize primary damage from a blast and secondary damage from fragmentation.
5. Evacuate the building.
6. Do not permit reentry into the building until the device has been removed or disarmed, and the building declared safe.

HANDLING THE NEWS MEDIA

It is of paramount importance that all inquiries from the news media be directed to one appointed spokesperson. All other persons should be instructed not to discuss the situation with outsiders, especially the news media. The purpose of this provision is to furnish the news media with accurate information and ensure that additional bomb threats are not precipitated by irresponsible statements from uninformed sources.

SUMMARY

This data serves only as a guide and is not intended to be anything more. The ultimate determination of how to handle a bomb threat must be made by the individual responsible for the threatened facility.

Develop a bomb incident plan. Draw upon any expertise that is available to you from police departments, government agencies, and security specialists. Don't leave anything to chance. Be prepared!

Bomb Incident Plan

1. Designate a chain of command.
2. Establish a command center.
3. Decide what primary and alternate communications will be used.
4. Establish clearly how and by whom a bomb threat will be evaluated.
5. Decide what procedures will be followed when a bomb threat is received or device discovered.
6. Determine to what extent the available bomb squad will assist and at what point the squad will respond.
7. Provide an evacuation plan with enough flexibility to avoid a suspected danger area.
8. Designate search teams and areas to be searched.

9. Establish techniques to be utilized during the search.
10. Establish a procedure to report and track progress of the search and a method to lead qualified bomb technicians to a suspicious package.
11. Have a contingency plan available if a bomb should go off.
12. Establish a simple-to-follow procedure for the person receiving the bomb threat.
13. Review your physical security plan in conjunction with the development of your bomb incident plan.

Command Center

1. Designate primary and alternate locations.
2. Assign personnel and designate the decision-making authority.
3. Establish a method for tracking search teams.
4. Maintain a list of likely target areas.
5. Maintain a blueprint of floor diagrams.
6. Establish primary and secondary methods of communication. (Caution—the use of two-way radios during a search can cause premature detonation of an electric blasting cap.)
7. Formulate a plan for establishing a command center if a threat is received after normal working hours.
8. Maintain a roster of all pertinent telephone numbers.

ENDNOTE

1. Prepared by Stephen E. Higgins, Director, Bureau of Alcohol, Tobacco, and Firearms, ATF P 7550.2 (Washington, D.C.: U.S. Government Printing Office, 1987).

Appendix I

Suspect Package Alert

The following items are some things to watch for if a letter or package bomb is suspected. (If the addressee is expecting a package or letter, the contents should be verified.)

- The addressee is unfamiliar with name and address of sender
- The package or letter has no return address
- Improper or incorrect title, address, or spelling of addressee
- Title, but no name
- Wrong title with name
- Handwritten or poorly typed address
- Misspellings of common words
- Return address and postmark are not from same area
- Stamps (sometimes excessive postage or unusual stamps) versus metered mail
- Special handling instructions on package (i.e., special delivery, open by addressee only, foreign mail, and air mail)
- Restrictive markings such as confidential, personal, etc.
- Overwrapped, excessive securing material such as masking tape, string or paper wrappings
- Oddly shaped or unevenly weighted packages
- Lumpy or rigid envelopes (stiffer or heavier than normal)
- Lopsided or uneven envelopes
- Oily stains or discolorations
- Strange odors
- Protruding wires or tinfoil
- Visual distractions (drawings, unusual statements, and hand drawn postage)

Please be aware that this is only a general checklist. The best protection is personal contact with the sender of the package or letter.

Prepared by Department of the Treasury, Bureau of Alcohol, Tobacco and Firearms

Appendix II

Bomb Threat Checklist

The following are some general questions to ask a bomb threat caller to help keep him or her on the line and to ascertain as much information as possible about the bomb allegedly in the building.

1. WHEN IS THE BOMB GOING TO EXPLODE? _____
2. WHERE IS THE BOMB RIGHT NOW? _____
3. WHAT DOES THE BOMB LOOK LIKE? _____
4. WHAT KIND OF BOMB IS IT? _____
5. WHAT WILL CAUSE THE BOMB TO EXPLODE? _____
6. DID YOU PLACE THE BOMB? _____
7. WHY? _____
8. WHAT IS YOUR ADDRESS? _____
9. WHAT IS YOUR NAME? _____

EXACT WORDING OF BOMB THREAT: _____
SEX OF CALLER: _____
RACE: _____
AGE: _____
LENGTH OF CALL: _____
TELEPHONE NUMBER WHERE CALL WAS RECEIVED: _____
TIME CALL WAS RECEIVED: _____
DATE CALL WAS RECEIVED: _____

CALLER'S VOICE:
Calm___ Angry___ Excited___ Slow___ Rapid___ Nasal___ Stutter___ Lisp___ Raspy___ Deep___
Soft___ Loud___ Laughter___ Crying___ Normal___ Distinct___ Ragged___ Cracking voice___
Slurred___ Clearing throat___ Disguised___ Familiar___ Whispered___ Deep breathing___ Accent___

IF THE VOICE IS FAMILIAR, WHAT DID IT SOUND LIKE?

_____
_____
_____
_____

BACKGROUND SOUNDS:
Street noises___ Kitchen sounds___ PA system___ House noises___ Motor___ Factory machinery___
Animal noises___ Static___ Long distance___ Office machinery___ Voices___ Clear___ Music___
Local___ Booth___ Other _____

BOMB THREAT LANGUAGE:

Well spoken (education level)___ Message read by threat maker___ Incoherent___ Taped___ Foul___ Irrational___

REMARKS:

CALL REPORTED IMMEDIATELY TO: _____

YOUR NAME: _____

YOUR POSITION: _____

YOUR TELEPHONE NUMBER: _____

DATE CHECKLIST COMPLETED: _____

Prepared by Department of the Treasury, Bureau of Alcohol, Tobacco and Firearms

Chapter 9

The Lines
of Defense

In the preceding chapters, we have demonstrated that certain opportunistic and criminal forces are always in motion, alert to any vulnerabilities in the workplace. Robbers, burglars, rapists, muggers, arsonists, bombers, mobs, and industrial spies are pressing at the perimeter—while embezzlers and employee thieves are attacking from within.

For each potential danger, we have tried to present appropriate countermeasures, but as we have already pointed out, uncoordinated "solutions" developed on a problem-by-problem basis simply aren't effective. Neither is the philosophy of addressing problems after-the-fact, which at best only results in a massive effort to react against a loss that has already occurred.

As company policy, reaction is too risky; there just aren't that many businesses that can survive several or, in many cases, even one major loss. Management must be defense-minded and security-conscious on an overall basis, planning not just against losses already incurred, but against potential losses which present methods could allow. Proactive asset protection is called for.

What should the size and scope of your defenses against crime be? In the last analysis, only you can answer that. Each building and office's exposure to crime is unique. Although there are many problems common to all, when we get down to the nitty-gritty *you* must determine the formula for the defense of your office, building, or tenants. And it's not a simple formula to arrive at.

For the large and small business office alike, an evaluation will have to be made in terms of the vulnerabilities or potential risks, including diminished employee productivity and morale. Obviously, the very small office does not face the dangers larger offices are heir to, but it may still be a tempting target for external or internal attack. Small businesses should be obliged to set up a disciplined security routine and follow it faithfully, since in most instances one person will be both security administrator and sole member of the security force, in addition to all his other duties.

THE ROLE OF OFFICE SECURITY

In setting up your defenses, remember that, unlike a military installation, a business office is essentially a public place. Since it is either selling products or services to the public, its offices must be open to potential clients.

The office must be secure, but it can't be a fortress. The security system must include only as many controls and as much equipment as necessary to prevent loss without reducing productivity by over-control. While your security system must protect against external assault, the methods used can't unduly restrict customers, vendors, and others necessary to the profitable operations of your business.

The balance is a delicate one. While you must have some protection against even subtle and sophisticated attack, you have to avoid the strangling red tape that could suffocate your operations—a loss equal to or exceeding any loss you are trying to prevent. It requires careful judgment, but then we never said it was easy—few worthwhile things are.

THE ROLE OF EMPLOYEE COOPERATION

An effective security system requires a lot of hard, thoughtful work, and the co-operation and concern of all your employees. With their support, your system can be an effective, virtually impregnable defense.

Employee support should consist of willing cooperation in all anti-loss theft-prevention systems and an awareness of the need for security. This awareness and security-consciousness can maximize all security efforts. At the same time, it is important not to give the appearance that you encourage tattling; in developing a security awareness attitude in the office, you should not create an atmosphere of suspicion.

Cooperative employees will report unlocked or tampered-with doors, suspicious visitors, minor thefts, and many other incidents that keep a security operation effective but wouldn't be reported by an indifferent or uninformed staff. They will make the extra effort to keep personal and company property under lock and key. They also will be more careful and concerned about fire hazards, perimeter integrity, and unauthorized visitors, thereby reducing fire and general security hazards.

In short, an informed staff is invaluable in the war against office crime and loss. Any office or building that enlists the aid of its personnel and creates an atmosphere of intelligent awareness of potential dangers has taken a major step toward asset and loss control, providing a safe and secure workplace for its employees.

THE ROLE OF INSURANCE

Since no loss prevention system can be absolutely invulnerable, insurance is vital to protect against losses that may occur in spite of the best and most vigorously administered loss prevention program. But insurance can't pay for the loss of productivity in an office shocked by crimes of violence. It can't pay for the drop in morale (let alone the monetary losses) due to repeated theft. It can't replace customers lost due to business interruption and the destruction of valuable records. And it rarely can begin to pay for the man-hours required to piece together data lost by computer damage. The possibilities of irreparable loss are almost endless, and yet there is still a significant number of managers who feel that their security problems are under control because they "have insurance."

Let's not forget those incredible number of offices that have neither insurance nor an overall security program. There will always be a long-shot player—but *no* security program and *no* insurance? That's really pressing your luck and exposing the business to incredible liabilities.

If you, like Candide's tutor, Dr. Pangloss, believe that "everything's for the best, in this best of all possible worlds," then maybe you should risk those astronomical odds. But if you are living in today's world you will want to set up reasonable defenses against the enemies who lurk outside and within your office. They are there. Maybe they haven't gotten to you yet—but they will. Just be sure you're as ready for them as they are for you.

THE FUTURE

The paperless office concept with electronic mail, electronic files, modems, video text, and instant worldwide communications is a direct result of the microcomputer—a technology that provides for simple word processing to complicated financial forecasting and database management. All of this information can be available to all levels of employees and eases business operations, but it also makes it possible for them to access proprietary information.

The door is now open to increased white-collar crime opportunities. Challenges in the future for safeguarding this data call for responsible security people and concerned businesspeople to not only provide the usual levels of physical security but to adjust their philosophy of proprietary protection to decentralize security to all levels within the company—something of particular need to larger businesses.

Every employee will have to be aware of information security. Security awareness programs will by necessity be influenced and driven by risk analysis. The more networking between microcomputers and mainframes, the greater the risks. It will be necessary to emphasize the impact on the business of information theft should a loss or compromise take place. The next step would be to categorize the risks and apply the degree of security controls necessary to minimize or reduce these specific risks. Employee screening, administrative and technical safeguards, and physical security—all of these have been and will be addressed further in this book.

Chapter 10

Developing the
Security Function

How the security function is to be administered, whether by a manager having other responsibilities, or by a security professional heading a security department, will depend upon the needs and goals of the office or office building where security is needed.

The final program is rarely the result of a single planning decision; even where management intends from the first to establish a formal security operation, the eventual organization will vary with experience and circumstances.

In some cases, creating a specific security staff has occurred much more by accident than by planning. Each reaction to a crime took the company or building management further toward a security program. While some companies and high-rise building management evaluated their problems and organized their security departments, most office security departments developed gradually, in some cases, with the installation of better locks, then improved lighting, alarms, and so on. Eventually the hardware was supported by manpower—or manpower was supported by hardware—and a security operation evolved.

Although the gradual or reactive approach may eventually develop into an effective security operation, it can present very real dangers. Until a complete security effort is in effect, you are still exposed to all unrecognized risks. You may feel secure because you are guarding against minor risks while you have little or no protection against major risks. Experience has shown that management is well advised to plan, organize, and completely develop a security program, rather than just let it evolve as problems occur.

Once the need for an all-around security program is recognized, management needs to begin with an understanding of the nature of a private security force and how it relates to the operation of the company as a whole.

THE ROLE OF PRIVATE SECURITY

Private security has been defined as "the business of protecting business," but the following definition might be more helpful: Office security is a staff function, an integrated service department whose main purpose is to protect and defend company personnel and assets.

This definition, however, is still incomplete. It does not incorporate the factor of employee cooperation. Employee participation is both a security essential and an index of the security department's success judged by the degree of involvement and cooperation demonstrated by company employees. Without cooperation throughout the office, security cannot succeed. Nor does it give the feeling that the security group is providing a service for its customers.

SECURITY IS NOT LAW ENFORCEMENT

Private security forces and public law enforcement departments are two quite different entities. While the public tends to confuse the two, their scope, objectives, and methods of operation are necessarily different. Usually operational only within the confines of a building or office, private security is charged with the responsibility of asset protection and crime prevention, and creating and supervising systems to protect employees and property. Security forces rarely apprehend criminals. On the other hand, security departments can and do investigate speculatively, unlike law enforcement, which investigates only identified crimes, and then only to the extent necessary for prosecution. As previously noted, insurance recovery depends upon extensive proof. For the purpose of criminal prosecution, only proof of one theft is needed. Police cannot investigate inventory shortages or the "mysterious disappearance" of stock or equipment. Security can and does fill these needs.

Law enforcement acts on the premise that detecting, prosecuting and confining criminals frees society from these undesirable elements and in the long run, will prevent crime and protect persons and property. Private security is interested in direct, before-loss protection of persons and property, and generally has little interest in prosecution. The direct protection of private property by police—beyond alarm response and the passing of an occasional patrol car—is beyond the capacity of hard-pressed law enforcement, and no improvement in this situation can reasonably be expected. On the other hand, the well-planned presence of private security, backed by well-considered and supervised systems, prevents crime, protects property and personnel, and insures an atmosphere in which business can profitably be conducted.

In addition, private security enjoys a somewhat greater legal latitude. In the eyes of the law, any representative of security, from a guard to the director of security, is simply another employee, a "private citizen." Court decisions have continuously affirmed this over the years. The admissibility of voluntary admissions are legal requirements only applicable to sworn law enforcement. And police officers are held to be law enforcement officers at all times—even when moonlighting as security personnel. Only when deputized or acting at the request of law enforcement are private security personnel held to be subject to the laws governing law enforcement personnel.

As a private citizen a security officer may not coerce, intimidate, or make any material promise in return for an admission. As an agent of the company, his interrogations must not accidentally constitute an arrest within the widely construed meaning of the law, and his searches of employee property on company premises must be accomplished within local or state law. The right of any suspect being questioned by a private citizen is to refuse to answer and to leave. If the suspect is detained, or believes that he cannot leave, a citizen's arrest has occurred.

THE IMPORTANCE OF NOTHING

In security the best news management can get is that "nothing happened." Unfortunately, the problem of evaluating such good news is difficult. Money has been spent and energy expended to result in "nothing." All too often management may forget the origin of the security function and say, "See, we don't need security after all."

Actually, the security function tends to be established only after a sizeable loss or a significant series of losses contributing, of course, to the patchwork development of security operations. That some security is needed in every office is beyond question. How extensive this function should be is determined by an evaluation of the crime rate in the area, the history of loss or mysterious disappearance, the potential for loss, and the known or suspected risk to assets and personnel.

In the security field, half a loaf is worse than no loaf at all. When management knows there is no security, it tends to conduct itself accordingly. Where a fractional security function has been established, even though management knows it has merely hired doorknob shakers to make limited rounds of inspection, the delusion gradually develops that the company now has genuine protection and the warm glow of security embraces even those risks management knows do not have any protection.

For this reason, many contemporary offices and building managers are moving toward establishing the whole security function at one time or to the rapid upgrading of existing, limited security functions.

THE SECURITY PROFESSIONAL

Today's security director is not only seasoned, but remains capable of growth, with the ability to adapt to changing circumstances as the business being protected grows. In the past, security directors have almost invariably been drawn from the ranks of retired law enforcement—police, FBI, and military—and this is still true to a large degree. While many of these people have been highly successful in adapting to their new field, perhaps an equal number have not. Those who were not successful tended to be rigid in their attitudes. They brought with them the mission and attitudes of police officers and tried to apply the adversary techniques familiar to them to their new circumstances.

The security man and woman must be cooperative, innovative, and flexible, seeking out the best solutions for assignments without depending upon tradition—and in office security, there is very little tradition. As in other security fields, this inevitably leads to reinventing the wheel, developing by trial and error systems that have already been tested in practice. It is unfortunate, but understandable, that many office security personnel feel isolated and alone.

Each security administrator or executive must be involved with all the security problems at the office, and at the same time develop and maintain outside security contacts with as many security directors in the community as possible. Regular informal communications and cooperation with local police and fire department officials are included, as well as professional and trade associations, trade publications, and state and federal bulletins. In short, outside contacts and information are vital to a competent security operation. They afford the security director the opportunity to continually update approaches to the job and remain apprised of new dangers or criminal techniques that might endanger the company. The ability to work cooperatively and constructively with these outside contacts is as essential as the need to develop and maintain such contacts. Even the part-time security administrator of the smaller office needs these contacts and cooperation.

SECURITY ATTITUDES

Within the office, the security professional must be able to communicate. Even though the job necessarily precludes the image of being everybody's pal, everything the security staff should be must be apparent in the conduct of the administrator. The individual must be friendly without being intimate, conscientious, able to lead and act independently, a person of obvious integrity and ability. Given this kind of example, these qualities will be mimicked in the security staff; without it, the best security team will disintegrate. With these qualities the security mission can gain the cooperation of all office personnel.

THE FORMAL AND INFORMAL ORGANIZATIONS

It is important for the security manager to be aware of, and sensitive to, relationships within the organization. Too many office administrators prefer to maintain the fiction that the office operates on the basis of the formal organization, within the strict confines of company policy as outlined by management in announcements, memoranda, and handbooks. Competent security managers, like effective office managers, know better. They know that there is a formal organization and an informal organization that, although not often in opposition to the organizational charts, is created by the alliances and antipathies inevitable in any society. Both know that it is the informal structure that creates the day-to-day operational process, as well as the office grapevine—the route of unofficial communication and an important index of company morale. Given a sensitive appreciation of the informal organization, as well as solid knowledge of the formal leadership, the security manager is in an excellent position to keep abreast of the real state of the office, and to spot problems as they develop.

Only time on the job will fully tie your new security manager into your informal organization but, if the security director is to be really effective,the new job indoctrination should include a briefing on this shadow organization.

ROLE OF MANAGEMENT PHILOSOPHY

Many managers find it difficult to verbalize their general philosophy and approach consistent with the job to be done and company policy or attitudes. They may want a free-and-easy, open atmosphere while still recognizing that too much openness can be an invitation to criminal attack. Other managers may prefer a strict, by-the-numbers operation, and yet recognize that rigid policies can result in low morale and high employee turnover. In many ways it is up to security to strike the proper balance between what is said and what is meant, and to proceed on an approach appropriate to the climate of the particular office. The security approach always should be in harmony with the overall atmosphere, for in such harmony—or the lack of it—lies the difference between a positive and negative security contribution.

YOUR SECURITY PROFESSIONAL

As we can see, the security function has passed far beyond the lone watchman isolated from the work of the company. Your security professional expects to be, and should be, a part of the management team. He must be able to speak to employee groups on safety issues and the response to fire and bomb threats; to develop and implement contingency programs for emergency response; to know the capabilities and limitations of security equipment and staffing; to construct and supervise an appropriate training program for his security people; to develop procedures for the protection of confidential information, to set up a review program to regularly reevaluate all security systems in the office; and to educate management in security's role in loss prevention. And these are only a sampling of the areas the security professional should be able to direct with confidence.

Clearly we are describing the kind of professional necessary to handle office security. Further, we recognize that there is no single yardstick for office security programs or for the responsible security officer; growth is inherent in the responsibilities of the position and much must still be learned on the job.

Security is largely a self-taught field, though some colleges do offer degrees in security. Not only does the most relevant training come through experience, no real substitute for experience has been found. The rare security executive who feels he has nothing to learn is understandably regarded with extreme skepticism by his peers, as he should by management.

SECURITY IN THE TABLE OF ORGANIZATION

Because of its vital importance, the contemporary security function should be the concern of company management at the highest level. Experience has amply demonstrated that if security is to be effective it must have—and must be *seen* to have—the support of top management. Without this support, security cannot possibly command the respect and cooperation necessary to the success of its protective goals and objectives.

While the visible support of top and middle management is a *sine qua non* of competent security, opinion differs as to the level of management at which security should report. Many advocates support the notion of having security report directly to the president or the highest ranking financial executive in order to avoid the common experience of having adverse information blocked or diluted in transmission. On the other hand, carried to extreme such an arrangement could burden an already-overworked top officer with excessive detail. Whoever the responsible executive may be, it is important that she be genuinely involved and familiar with company risks in order to evaluate whether the security operation is controlling and reducing those risks. In many offices, this role simply cannot be squeezed into top management's portfolio but it should be as near to the top as possible.

The solution, it would seem, would be to tailor the decision for the particular situation. Where the top executive *can* be involved, and where the risk of loss is recognized as great, the responsibility for security supervision may be placed there; where the risk is believed to be less and top executives are already fully occupied, the responsibility should logically be placed on the highest-ranking executive available whose other assignments are most compatible with evaluation of security administration. In situations where there is a particularly high risk, or where there has been a high incidence of loss, it might be wise to delegate other responsibilities away from the top in order to make room for security supervision at the highest level. In any event, security's access to top management must *never* be wholly blocked.

SECURITY ADMINISTRATION

In small offices, the direct administration of the security operation, as well as its supervision, is often assigned to executives or administrators having other primary responsibilities, such as treasurer, controller, head of administration, or office manager.

In larger offices and in large buildings where there is a security staff requiring supervision and security administration is clearly a full-time position, the operational responsibility is assigned to a security administrator. Titles for this position range from executive security officer and director of security down through security manager, security supervisor, and chief of security, depending upon the structure of the particular office and company organization, and the degree and kind of responsibility delegated.

Whatever the title, the top security administrator, in terms of available company information, should:

- be aware of, and have access to, the operations of every department.
- understand and have access to company statistics.
- be aware of company planning prior to implementation, particularly building plans and alterations, and office relocations.
- understand and have access to computer operations.
- be involved in, and knowledgeable about, personnel department operations, and have access to personnel records.
- be knowledgeable about, and have access to operations such as purchasing, equipment and equipment replacement, petty cash handling, mail room operations, and the various company accounting procedures.
- be involved in management discussions and policy decisions in all areas which may affect, even marginally, office security and safety.

While access to some of these areas may seem unusually liberal to the executive unfamiliar with the function of security, professionals in the security field can illustrate from examples the need for every one of them.

Obviously, the development of an effective, operations-integrated security function is almost as great a challenge as security's assignment of loss prevention. Without the necessary access, information, authority, and contingency planning, however, the goal of security will never be truly fulfilled.

Chapter 11

Trade Secrets and Industrial Spies

If your company has a captive market all to itself, you're not actually concerned with this chapter. Pass on—unless you think you may have a competitor or two tomorrow. In that case, read on. Because as long as you have competition—or possible competitors—someone will be watching you.

The discussion of the need for well-defined areas of confidentiality assumes that you are in a business whose success, or survival, depends on developing and keeping a reasonable share of the potential market in the face of pressures created by others—a definition that fits virtually every business in the free world.

Every competitive situation starts with the gathering of information, from two little boys circling each other in a school yard, each trying to decide if the other one is tougher and stronger, to the high-powered sports organizations that gather, screen, and evaluate the films of opposing football teams to give their own team a competitive edge. Most information-gathering is legal and ethical—part of the business of business. But some of it—and from all indications a growing part of it—is straight cloak-and-dagger.

Every business must reduce the vulnerability of its confidential information to discovery by either legal or illegal means. Think right now of the planning advantage you would have if you had before you a schedule of the new product plans of your closest competitor. Of if you had the minutes of the last meeting of their executive committee. Or reliable advance information on their new advertising campaigns. Curiously enough, a high percentage of this information is available—too late to be of benefit to others. You certainly don't care if the competitors get hold of your new pricing structure, or your new packaging plans, or the fact that you're test marketing in Chillicothe, Ohio—after it's well-launched. After all, you can't keep them from eventually knowing. But what you need and must maintain is "lead time"—your jump on the market.

THE INTELLIGENCE OPERATION

It is vital to remember that every competitive business in the country—however ethical—must know what the competition is doing. As in chess, the winner will be the player who is able to successfully balance the needs of her attack *and* her defense. Many players are famous for a slashing, bold attack; but unless they also present a reasonable defense, they will surely lose. So it is with business, and information is an essential of both attack and defense. Some businesses have large departments that do little but gather, evaluate, and digest information pertinent to their company's markets and competition. The information is constantly updated and produced in volumes on virtually any topic. Actually, there is more information available from non-secret sources than anyone would usually need to generally predict or plot an action, reaction or plan, be it their own or someone else's.

There are reports on labor, statistics, business, agriculture, electronics, and government, to name a few. There are reports to guide you to reports. There are guides to lead you to guides. There are special industry publications. There are marketing organizations who will do research for you. There is the Library of Congress and your local public library, if you can't get to Washington. And, of course, you must not overlook the obvious:

- major metropolitan newspapers.
- magazines—especially general business magazines or trade journals in your specific field.
- government publications—largely from the Department of Commerce. (A list of subjects and titles that would probably circle the earth.)
- Annual reports—required for publicly held companies.
- in-house publications.
- business letters and bulletins.
- business and professional association publications.

It has been said that during World War II foreign agents were able to plot the production of our war materials by simply reading published reference material. Our own OSS in that same period did most of its work by carefully digging through tons of data on everything from weather to observed movement of coal cars. The cloak-and-dagger operatives dropped behind enemy lines were glamorized; but the heart of the operation was research of mountains of data, *almost all of which was readily available.* This mundane method of intelligence-gathering has grown with the years; in security circles a famous trade magazine is still known as *Aviation* Week.

THE SHORTEST DISTANCE BETWEEN TWO POINTS

It is a common error to believe that complicated and roundabout means must be used to achieve an end. This is perhaps best typified by the advertising agency producer who was anxious to persuade a certain star to appear in a series of commercials. The producer and his assistant spent three days in the most devious machinations, trying to get in touch with the actor to discuss the project. They set up a luncheon date with someone who knew his agent's sister-in-law; they called the cousin of the director of his last show. Nothing. Finally, when things looked their bleakest and the sponsor was adopting an ominous tone, their secretary suggested, "Why don't you try the phone book?" Amused by her naivete, they did. There he was, listed in the book just like common folk. They called him up and made the deal. You must not overlook the obvious.

WHAT'S THE PROBLEM?

All of the methods of gathering business information are not, however, as harmless as those we have discussed. While data gathered from published sources, rumor, industry gossip, common vendors, loose talk, and legally observable activity represent the bulk of amassed competitive intelligence, the business community today is also faced with the very real problem of the professional, or quasi-professional, espionage agent.

The industrial spy is a difficult and elusive adversary. In the absence of any figures establishing the extent of this activity, it is difficult to objectively define the nature and scope of the problem. The wide diversity of viewpoints on the subject further complicates the matter.

- Security organizations, when interviewed, state that they never engage in wiretapping, bugging, or illegal methods of industrial espionage. On the other hand, several have been caught in the act.
- Business executives interviewed feel the problem is minimal, nonexistent, or confined to a few businesses.
- Small private operators would prefer that you believe the worst, especially if they're in the "debugging" business. On the other hand, qualified professionals have found bugs in phones, walls, office audio systems, and electrical outlets, just to name a few.
- Any electronically minded teenager, radio engineer, or telephone serviceman can "bug" an office, phone, or home by adapting readily available equipment.

It seems impossible to sketch in the true parameters of the problem of electronic espionage.

Bugging

The use of electronic surveillance equipment by private investigators and others, including government, became a matter of increasing concern to lawmakers, culminating in the passage of the Omnibus Crime Control and Safe Streets Act. One of the sections of this act established federal penalties for the interstate use, possession, sale, advertisement, or transportation of eavesdropping equipment; such equipment is no longer advertised. Many states have also established their own strong penalties against the manufacture, sale, possession, and use of eavesdropping equipment. For example, federal law permits recording by, or with the permission of, a party to a conversation, while certain state laws forbid recording without permission from *all* parties to the conversation. (See Appendix I for states that permit consensual recording.) It is difficult to evaluate the deterrent effect of such legislation because there are no reliable records—former or present—on the number of illegal listening devices found.

Many persons or firms who have been bugged are reluctant to reveal the fact, particularly since the culprit is usually unknown and unidentifiable. Though it is difficult to estimate with accuracy, it is safe to assume that many violations do occur and that most of these are either undetected or unreported. Virtually all go unpunished.

Availability of Equipment

When consideration is broadened to include highly sophisticated equipment in the hands of government agencies, it must be said that the equipment available today makes virtually total surveillance possible. These devices can pierce the privacy of the home, office, or moving vehicle. They can, of course, monitor all normal lines of communication. No regular line of communication is secure. Conversations can be heard in public places, despite noisy surroundings.

The kind of surveillance being used for illicit, unethical, and illegal penetration of rival business communications is not so sophisticated and it doesn't need to be. Effective hardware for simple eavesdropping is inexpensive to create and easily installed. The required components are readily available to the general public, even though sophisticated equipment is not. Through the use of simple scanners, television sets, and various communications receivers, conversations over cellular phones and faxes are easily overheard or monitored. The Privacy Act is well known to the at large "scanner" people out across America. They are well aware, however, that it is impossible to effectively enforce the privacy laws and continue to amuse themselves by listening to cellular phones.

The do-it-yourself bugging devices are far cheaper, more available, and more effective than anti-bugging equipment. Effective electronic countermeasure equipment is expensive, requires expert operators, and is not generally available to private security agencies, let alone the public.

Definitions

Wire communication means any communication made in whole or in part with the aid of wire, cable, or other like connection between the point of origin and the point of reception furnished or operated by a common carrier providing or operating communications facilities.

Oral communication means any oral communication uttered by a person exhibiting an expectation that the communication is not subject to interception under circumstances justifying the expectation.

Intercept means the aural acquisition of the contents of any wire or oral communication through the use of an intercepting device.

Intercepting device means any electronic, mechanical, or other device or apparatus which can be used to intercept a wire or oral communication other than any telephone or telegraph instrument, equipment, or facility, or any component thereof, furnished to the subscriber or user by a communications common carrier in the ordinary course of its business and being used by the subscriber or user in the ordinary course of its business; or, being used by a communications common carrier in the ordinary course of its business, or by an investigative or law enforcement officer in the ordinary course of his duties.

Contents, when used with respect to any wire or oral communications, includes any information concerning the identity of the parties to the communication or the existence, substance, purport, or meaning of that communication.

Cellular Phones

Cellular phone transmitters operate at high frequencies (800 and 900 MHz). You should be aware of the fact that conversations on a cellular phone or your home portable phone (40 and 50 MHz) are on open airways, which means that individuals with a radio scanner can listen to your calls. Be advised that someone may be listening to your conversations.

The cellular phone, unfortunately, is used by the criminal element for illegitimate purposes. They know they can't be taped or tapped into. Cellular services are designed to jump between various radio frequencies in order to travel between "cells."

Cellular phones can be secured inside your car by means of a 6- by 6-inch personal pad cable or with a secure-it disc that costs about $14.

We strongly suggest that you carefully and frequently check your phone bills before payment. AT&T is currently designing a cellular telephone that scrambles over-the-air signals; the snoopers who intercept the calls will hear chirping sounds.

Fax Machines

Receiving obscene fax messages from unknown parties is handled no differently than receiving obscene phone calls: contact the telephone company's business office, place a trap on the line, and follow their established procedures.

You can't control junk mail over your fax machine. However, you can notify the sender that you no longer wish to receive their material. After all, you are paying for the cost of the paper and the line. When you know you are receiving a junk fax, pick up the receiver to interrupt the transmission and cancel material being sent.

Some fax machines now are capable of broadcasting from memory, sending out the same document to 125 people. Newsletter subscriptions are being sent over fax machines. Vendors automatically advise customers that it's time for service on their products by way of this device.

Fax machines can be secured to furniture in a number of ways, such as the use of a furniture mounting device that costs about $60, or an anchor pad unit that costs about $150.

The fax machine has become such a common tool in today's office that most companies own or lease their own machine. Rapid communication, routine correspondence, and less money spent on overnight delivery all and more make the fax machine a very necessary tool.

WHERE DO YOU STAND?

Naturally, if you are in a highly volatile business that depends to a great degree on new products regularly introduced, or unusual hard-hitting merchandising gimmicks, you already know the danger of leaking information. But if you feel that espionage is someone else's problem and not yours, perhaps you need to ask yourself a question or two.

Most managers feel they have so little information of interest to a spy that they can't have an espionage problem. If you fall into this group, try this test: Ask yourself what information *you* would like about your competitors. What value would drawings, plans, market research, future product information, trade secrets, and fiscal matters of your closest competitor have for you? It is a rare company official that can honestly say, "None."

But most firms do have secrets—or information that should be secret. So your first defensive step is to identify those secrets, the confidential material that might be actively sought by less-than-scrupulous competitors. Who would pay to get your computer payroll printout? A competitor seeking to raid you of your key engineering personnel. Who would go through your trash? Anyone seeking bid carbons, computer information, materiel sources, or discarded drafts of key proposals.

IDENTIFYING YOUR SECRETS

To establish what information in your company should *remain* in your company, you must identify key information throughout the company, as well as how valuable each type of information would be to others. This applies to all aspects of your business—whether it's machines, processes, systems, or procedures and pricing, planning, new products or financial information.

As you identify this information, ask yourself how available the same information may be from other sources. There is more than one case where a company has gone to considerable lengths to protect information that has been the subject of a press release or a professional paper, and is actually available in publications or, at the least, is in non-restricted distribution.

If you find areas that you consider valuable to you, potentially valuable to others, and not otherwise available—you should then break down the areas into component parts:

- Plans—physical layout or activities, new product planning, research problems and successes.
- Prices—unit, bulk, favored-customer discounts, profit margin, and marketing breakdown.
- Performance—up- and downtime of equipment, the capability of a machine, system, method, or special process.
- Problems—limitations of equipment, capitalization, cost overruns, systems, production difficulties, transportation, acceptance, and sales.
- Personnel—Who knows what? What do they know? What key executive is discontented and why? How are the company's pay scales determined?

Obviously many segments of the total information picture, such as announced prices, will be known outside the company, but the more these elements remain confidential, the safer you are.

Remember that, even without any effort at espionage, a good analyst can develop an astonishingly accurate picture by putting together scraps of information. The fewer scraps you give him, directly or through industry gossip, the more difficult his job becomes, and the more likely he is to guess wrong.

IDENTIFY CURRENT PROBLEMS

The moment you identify a secret, you can see a potential problem. But ask yourself, what has been happening before? If you have never before exercised any control over company secrets, you may have experienced some of the following:

- Competitors constantly ahead of you or on the market at the same time you introduce a new product or price.
- You are losing more than your share of big bids (particularly by very narrow margins) and barely picking up small or medium ones.
- Marketing programs seem to go sour from the start.
- Your business negotiations and decisions seem to be anticipated.
- Competition is hiring away your key executives, often just when they are most needed.
- The mail room knows your secrets before your secretary—and your secretary likes to talk.
- Your proposals and presentations seem to appear in part in competitors' proposals.

PLUG LEAKS

The average office is not capable of dealing with a determined professional spy, but in most cases, simple precautions can prevent most problems.

If something is secret, handle it that way. An overall company policy should be formulated. Such a policy should emphasize the basic security practices that prevent careless loss of information, rather than the sophisticated countermeasures necessary to thwart the professional spy. Where you feel that professionals may be at work, you must resort to more elaborate policies and measures.

A basic security policy should define areas, actual work, statistics, and documents that should be classified as secret or, more commonly, "company confidential." Decisions should be based on business and industry conditions that exist under normal circumstances. For example, in the chemical industry many things may be secret—the name of a project, work areas, papers, formulas, and plans. On the other hand, the management of a retail food store chain may only need to keep secret store grosses, the location of the next store, or the prices in next week's ad. (The latter information actually was once the subject of espionage—corporate spies photographed the prices from drawing boards in an art department.) In any event, once confidential information is identified, employees should follow company procedure in handling it.

DOCUMENTS

Any document classified secret or "company confidential" should be marked as such. Inexpensive rubber stamps, and stamp pads in a conspicuous color, can be purchased from local stationers for this purpose.

Storage of Proprietary Information

Documents considered secret are about as safe from examination in an ordinary filing cabinet with a lock as they would be in a desk drawer. Special filing cabinets or vaults are needed which resist undetected entry.

Numbering and Logging

Classified documents should be numbered ("Copy 4 of 7") and only allowed out of central files on a sign-out basis. Each item taken from the file should be described in an appropriate log and signed for by an authorized recipient. When documents are returned, the clerk should sign the log to indicate the return of the copy, and by whom it was returned. Obviously this does not protect you against photocopying, but it narrows responsibility to trusted persons.

Distribution

Access to, and distribution of, confidential and critical information should be strictly limited on a "need to know" basis. Some persons will need to see some confidential material, but others won't. For this reason you will want to limit the number of copies generated and indicate distribution on the document, requiring an accountability from each recipient. A method frequently used to update and/or reduce a confidential distribution list is to insert a sheet stating, "unless the person or department who originated the confidential document is notified to the contrary and in writing—the particular report/file/computer run will cease to be delivered with this document."

Public Communications

All press releases should be examined for the possible accidental inclusion of confidential information. If the release (or annual report or prospectus) relates to a subject area in which there is confidential information, the text should be cleared by a designated executive knowledgeable about that area.

Employees must be cautioned against discussing confidential subjects and information with nonemployees, including their families, and even with fellow employees who do not have a "need to know." You cannot stress this precaution too much, getting an employee to talk to a person they trust has been successfully used in espionage time and time again. (Note: When the use of public telephones or cellular phones is unavoidable, the use of scramblers must be a serious consideration.)

EMPLOYMENT PRACTICES

Companies frequently categorize levels of employees for whom more detailed background investigations need to be performed prior to an employment offer. In some industries the choice is not the company's, but necessary for compliance with federal regulations (such as the Securities and Exchange Commission for stock brokerage positions). At the very least, all employees who would have access to or exposure to company confidential material or critical business data should have a background investigation within the limits of applicable laws. Depending upon the level of risk determined by a proprietary information vulnerability study, enforceable agreements should be obtained. Such confidentiality contracts and pledges as nondisclosure and noncompetition clauses, ethics, and other industry specific documents should be agreed upon, signed, and witnessed. Without the proper legal considerations it would be difficult, if not impossible, to pursue any breach of confidentiality in the courts.

Sensitive Work Product

Certain levels of proprietary information should not be allowed to be taken home for study or additional work. Risk is also great if documents taken on business travel are taken out for work and study purposes on planes. How often have we witnessed travelers curious about a fellow passenger's correspondence and reports. The removal of highly sensitive papers should be on a need-only basis and then with proper instruction as to transporting and handling.

Meetings

Business meetings and conferences concerned with highly sensitive information should be held in company space. When this is not possible, meetings should be conducted in a controllable facility. Advance announcements should be on a need-to-know basis and with as little lead time as possible. Certainly, any electronic sweeps of the facility to determine if surreptitious recording devices are present should be made in advance and the specific room(s) kept secure. When important meetings must be held on company property, all related offices and conference rooms should be screened just as you would for any off-campus activity. It is possible to provide an acoustically and electronically protected facility or room that is safe, secure, and defensible.

In cases of top-secret meetings, it is often wise to meet in the company conference room and from there to go to another, unannounced location. This eliminates the chance of prebugging. At such meetings, briefcases should be banned, and telephones removed from the room, since either can be rigged to act as an eavesdropping device. If the matters to be discussed are of a particularly sensitive nature, and you have reason to suppose that the room may have been bugged despite all your precautions, you can provide some protection by playing a radio or record player at normal volume. Unfortunately, eavesdropping professionals can filter out all sounds above or below voice frequencies.

Paper Shredders

Paper shredders must be located in a convenient place for all employees to use and near areas where classified documents are originated or retained. Confidential documents and tab runs should always be shredded, pulped, or burned —never discarded in wastebaskets. (See Appendix II.)

Shredding is more important today than it ever has been. Should sales reports, bid proposals, research and development plans, or merger and buyout strategies fall into the hands of the unauthorized, the damage caused to your business could be incalculable. A wide variety of shredders are available in the marketplace. Caution should be exercised in the selection of shredder size, type, and supplier.

Access Control

In all company security programs, access control is of prime importance. Strict control must be maintained over traffic into classified areas or where classified material may be exposed on desks. Authorizations for entry into such areas should be pruned to the smallest practical number, and the list regularly reevaluated and revised. Badges must be worn and with distinctive colors. You must make it clear that it is the responsibility of employees to challenge unauthorized or unknown persons in their area, even if they, too, are employees.

General Vigilance

Office security should act as a constant watchdog for all classified systems to insure the integrity of proprietary information. In these, as in all security systems, constant vigilance is required. It is vital that the systems themselves be supervised and regularly evaluated for continued effectiveness. No system will continue to operate on its initial momentum alone.

In this respect, classified papers should be checked for accurate stamping, paper shredders must be used as prescribed, and wastebaskets checked. Classified files must be properly secured. Classified materials, wherever held, should be audited periodically and any misuse reported. Management should be kept constantly updated on violations, violators, and potential leaks of classified information.

If you employ these basic techniques, the amateur spy, the random information peddlar, and the disgruntled employee should no longer have you at a disadvantage; you will have neutralized much of their effectiveness.

PROFESSIONALS

There is every reason to believe business spying is on the increase, the use of professionals is limited to exceptional companies and exceptional circumstances. Use of professional techniques to spy on a competitor leaves a company open to lawsuits, loss of public confidence, adverse publicity, and a host of other unpleasantness—as those linked to the Watergate caper can testify.

Normally, the average business only needs to protect itself from carelessness by hiring and promoting loyal, competent personnel, by denying unauthorized access to sensitive material, and by training employees. These measures require thought and a careful study of your operation, but they certainly are not difficult to achieve. Be on guard for any breakdown in your system. It has become common knowledge and even admitted to by numerous foreign governments—many of them our long-time allies—that they spy and conduct covert operations to obtain industrial secrets. Obviously they employ professionals to accomplish this and when possible recruit employees to provide the type of information we have been discussing. Governments often need only to subscribe to trade magazines or obtain public information through government forms required to be filed by corporations. Think of how often employees are called upon to provide scientific or technical presentations at seminars, conferences, and workshops. Many publish data that is critical or valuable to the companies' specific interests.

EMPLOYEE EDUCATION AND SECURITY AWARENESS

Few measures you take to protect your classified information will be as effective as the concern of your employees. If interested people have been educated to understand and appreciate company policies regarding secrets, your problem is virtually solved. Trade shows and the meetings of professional associations are notorious (and legal) sources of information from unguarded conversations. Establish an audit trail on company secrets—disclosure of which in many cases can mean disaster to any company.

Appendix I

State Laws that Permit Consensual Recording

**STATE LAWS THAT PERMIT CONSENSUAL
RECORDING OF ORAL COMMUNICATIONS
WITH THE PERMISSION OF A PARTICIPANT
(AS OF APRIL 1993)**

Alabama—Criminal Code Sec. 13A-11-31
Arizona—Criminal Code Sec. 13-3001 to 3017
Arkansas—Smithey vs. State 590 SW2d 676
Colorado—Revised Statutes 18-9-303, 18-9-305 (4.7b)
Connecticut—Chap. 959(a), Sec. 53a-187 through 189
District of Columbia—DC Code Sec. 23-542 *et seq.*
Georgia—All parties must consent - Sec. 16-11-60 to 16-11-67[*]
Hawaii—Title 38 Sec. 803-42(7)(B)(3)
Idaho—Sec. 18-6701 through 6718
Indiana—Federal Law
Iowa—Sec. 727.8
Kansas—Article 40, Sec. 21-4001-4002
Kentucky—Penal Code Sec. 526.010-.080
Louisiana—Rev. Statutes 15:1303
Maine—Title 15-Sec. 709-712
Minnesota—Chap. 626A
Mississippi—Sec. 41-29-531
Missouri—Sec. 542.402
Nebraska—Article 7, Sec. 86-701-712
Nevada—(Telephone prohibited) one party consent NR. 200.650 must have Atty.
   Gen. opinion
New Jersey—Sec. 2A-156A 1 through 26
New Mexico—Article 12, Sec. 30-12-1-11
New York—Penal Law - Sec. 250.00 *et seq.*
   Criminal Law - Article 700
   N.Y. Civil Practice Law & Rules - 4506

North Carolina—Cri. Law Article 30A, Sec. 14.227 1 and 2
North Dakota—Sec. 12.1-15-02-04
Ohio—Baldwin's Ohio Revised Code Sec. 2933.52
Oklahoma—Title 21 - Sec. 1202
Oregon—Sec. 133.721 through 739
    Sec. 165.535 through 540
    Sec. 133.992(2)
Rhode Island—Sec. 11-35-21 through 23
South Carolina—Sec. 17-29-10 through 17-29-50
South Dakota—Sec. 23A-35A-21
Tennessee—Use Federal Law
Texas—Article 18.20
U.S. Virgin Islands—Use Federal Law
Utah—Michie's Utah Code Annotated 77-23a-4
    Sec. 76-9-401, Sec. 76-5-403
Vermont—Use Federal Law
Virginia—Sec. 19.2.61 through 2-70
West Virginia—Sec. 62-1D-1 through 62-1D-16
Wisconsin—Sec. 968.31
Wyoming—Michie's Wyoming Statutes Sec. 7-3-602(B)(iv)

---

*Supreme Court supports one party consent

Appendix II

Paper Shredding
and Recycling

Documents in the wrong hands are a threat to your company!

The U.S. Supreme Court decreed that any discarded documents may be considered public information unless conscientiously disposed. Protect sensitive papers—shred them first.

Information on paper to be recycled has an even greater chance of improper disclosure than paper that is thrown away. Waste paper is usually collected and removed daily. While paper to be recycled waits for days or weeks to be collected and processed. While waiting, sensitive information on this paper is accessible for accidental or intentional viewing!

Shred it first. Then store it and recycle it. (Yes! Shredded paper can be recycled.) Shredding cuts paper fibers which makes it less desirable to recyclers. But, when unshredded paper is mixed with shredded paper, the results are fine. Shredding also increases the bulk of the material so it takes up more space, and this is inconvenient for some recyclers.

The key question is: "What is the value of the information on the paper?" If it is not of value, then it should not be shredded, but if it is important, shred it first!

Shredded Paper as Packing Material

A great second use for waste paper is for packing material—usually after being shredded by a strip cut shredder. Using shredded paper as packing:

- Reduces or eliminates the expense of packing material purchases.
- Reduces disposal service volume and expense.
- Uses biodegradable paper in place of plastics.
- Reduces the space needed to store packing material.
- Provides better protection from shipping damage for many items.

Types of Material to Be Shredded

Company confidential/high security documents that have been duplicated (by microfilming or photocopying) may be used by your competition to your disadvantage):

- financial reports
- customer lists
- marketing plans
- blueprints
- sales reports
- future plans
- and many other documents

Old or Inaccurate Data

An old or obsolete report may not be of use to you or your company, but it would be considered "golden" by a competitor, supplier, or even a customer. An erroneous report can foul your planning if it is confused with accurate data. Be sure to shred old spreadsheets, correspondence, product studies, and telephone call reports.

Government Classified Documents

Those dealing with classified documents such as blueprints, reports, plans, and contracts are generally instructed regarding the correct handling and destruction of classified information—often requiring special methods of shredding.

Obsolete Forms

They may be obsolete within your company, but they look fine to the outside world. Blank checks, credit memos, purchase orders, and other negotiable documents and forms can be forged and cashed.

Personal and Personnel Information

Government Privacy Act regulations and sound company policies dictate that information about personnel be handled or destroyed properly, including resumes, referrals, credit reports, job applications, tax forms, and insurance forms. Civil or criminal punishments for improper disclosures are a real threat.

Tips for Selecting the Right Shredder

- Do a complete audit of the types and volumes of paper to be shredded. (Almost everyone underestimates the volume of material that should be shredded.)
- Do you need a wide throat for printout?
- Will there be periodic file cleanings when higher volumes need to be handled?
- Will paper volume increase in the future?
- Check with other departments that do not have a shredder.

If this will be the only shredder in your company or the only one on your floor, every department and everyone will use it.

- Do a company-wide needs analysis and have multiple departments fund the purchase of the right shredder for everyone's needs.
- Be careful about comparing capacity specifications. Determine the capacity for yourself. Many shredders are made outside the United States and their sheet capacity ratings are for a lighter paper. Check the specifications for common U.S. paper weights.
- Ask for a demonstration. See if the unit is easy to use and can handle the types and volumes of paper you need to shred. Have the people who will use the unit try it. Check the shredder's capacity!

Materials for Shredding

Personnel documents
Payroll data
Computer printouts
Correspondence
Blueprints
Old files
Customer lists
Business plans
Confidential report overruns
Obsolete reports
Production schedules
Engineering notes
Bids and quotations
Labor negotiation data
Profit and loss reports
Meeting minutes
"Bad" copies
Obsolete forms such as checks and
    purchase orders
Marketing plans
Design ideas and concepts

Patent application material
Vendor files and quotes
Unneeded extra copies
Old employment applications
Resumes
Salary information
Status reports—periodic and year-
    to-date
Price list data
Assembly data/bills of material
Paper documents after microfilming
Old purchase orders
Engineering documentation
Meeting notes
Drafts and interim copies
Advertising schedules
Expired documents in personnel
    files
Government classified materials
... and much more!

Reprinted by permission of Cummins–Allison Corporation.

Chapter 12

Computer Security

There are very few businesses of any meaningful proportion that do not use what has been called the marvel of the twentieth century—the computer. The use of computers in most businesses is considered essential. At the same time the computer has become a focal point for people and groups who see it as a means to commit fraud, steal information, or disrupt competitors to name but a few possibilities.

In spite of the risk potential and business's ever-increasing reliance on the computer, many firms continue either to ignore these risks or to rely heavily on the complexity of the computer to keep outside individuals ignorant of the means to compromise it. But computer programming now is taught to junior high school students; there is not much "mystery" about the computer anymore.

Dependence upon the ignorance of the general public for protection is a sign of a total lack of understanding on the part of management of computer operations and computer science. Unless they have had some meaningful indoctrination in computer operations they may feel, as many laymen do, that the computer is mysterious, mystical, and infallible.

Some of this inadequacy in computer security is understandable. In the years following World War II, businesses and institutions of every type jumped into the computer age. Many of them tried to convert huge chunks of their accounting operations into data processing overnight. Technicians and programmers frequently worked around the clock. Establishing security controls in a chaotic period such as this would have been impossible, and the attempt discounted as absurd and unnecessary. The point was to get the program running—not to get it running in a manner which would satisfy some vague (and as yet unknown) security requirement. The day has now passed when computer programs need be run on a crash basis; unfortunately, many companies continue in that manner, leaving themselves wide open to catastrophic loss.

The evidence is overwhelming that this attitude is simply no longer rational. An effective security program is essential to any computer operation and it must have the vigorous support of an informed management. It may be difficult for a security director to explain to the company's president that they have an exposed and vulnerable machine that could wipe out the company, but he has to get that message across somehow.

And the more the leadership understands, the more they will come to see the grave consequences of data damage or loss, whether by accident or by malicious intent. Realizing that the threat is a constant one, they will agree that a comprehensive physical and financial security program is necessary to safeguard the computer system.

PHYSICAL SECURITY

Physical security of computer installations has become a matter of increasing concern. Not too many years ago a computer was considered to have great public relations value, and the computer facility was displayed in a street-level fishbowl for inspection by interested spectators. This is no longer the case; today most companies no longer publicize their computers and rarely, if ever, acknowledge their precise location. Computer rooms are no longer on many company tours. Where computers were once on display, today they are, while not exactly concealed, secured against unauthorized traffic and generally located well away from visitor traffic.

Some items that must be considered in determining the location of computer areas are:

- *Power source.* Record of dependability and availability of backup power; quality of maintenance and reputation for speedy, efficient response to failures.
- *Fire department.* Speed of response, training received. (Each city has a "fire rating" based in part on the effectiveness of the fire force. Check with your insurer.)
- *Labor force.* Remote locations can make it either difficult or easy to get and keep competent personnel. Locations in high crime areas might have an adverse effect on personnel retention, as well as increasing insurance premiums for the installation.
- *Access.* A remote or rural site is easier to isolate and defend, but may present personnel problems. Fire and police service, too, may not equal big-city standards.
- *Natural phenomena.* Your choice of site should take into account the possibility of flood, earthquake, heavy snow, frequent electrical storms and the effects each could have on your operation.
- *Maintenance.* How long will it take manufacturer maintenance personnel to arrive at your location?
- *Space required.* Your machine configuration and the amount of peripheral equipment required for your operation may take more space than your headquarters building can provide.

ELECTRIC POWER

Any fluctuation in line voltage can cause data transfer inaccuracies; this problem should be anticipated and compensated for. While some computer operations are not greatly hampered by electric line fluctuations or momentary outages, the damage to other operations may be catastrophic. Where this is true, or might be true, the recommended practice is to isolate the computer from the primary power source by uninterruptible power source or surge strips, which in turn supply the computer through alternators. The computer is then effectively buffered from the usual line voltage power problems. Standby diesel or gasoline generators are adequate for alarms, lights, and safety equipment. Air conditioning should have a separate power supply (and multiple manual power cutoffs) for fire protection.

FIRE

Fire protection is a team effort involving those charged with planning and installing the system and the safety and security personnel who are responsible for monitoring and testing the system. Should a fire occur, the company fire brigade, local fire department, security staff, and employees are all involved.

The building owner bears the ultimate responsibility for the proper installation and continued effectiveness of the fire system. A building that "meets code" is seldom truly adequate. Fire protection begins in the planning stage. The services of an architect are essential in fire design for new construction, and are sometimes required for a fire system retrofit. Consulting engineers must ensure that all systems work in harmony and are mutually supportive. The system design team also includes the building owner, key operational chiefs, and the insurance underwriter.

The wise owner will have the underwriter check with the Insurance Services Office (ISO) for design and construction guidelines. The ISO establishes building rating criteria for underwriters' use in setting premiums on specific buildings. Construction materials, number and size of exit points, and occupancy factors are only three of the many criteria considered in establishing insurance credits for the owner.

In planning for fire protection, the design team must prepare for all possibilities. The fire system layout should consider all protective requirements for the business's personnel and property. The fire system hardware must include the equipment necessary to cope with potential problems. Building and fire system expansion are also key elements in long-range planning for a fire protection system. Lastly, a review of facility fire protection requirements, continual testing, and system maintenance and updating needs to continue after installation.[1]

FIRE CAUSES

Stated succinctly, the major causes of fire are:

1. Fire in adjacent occupancies.
2. Accumulated combustibles, usually waste paper.
3. Electrical fires.

Electrical fires are not a common cause of fire in computer centers. The largest losses have occurred due to fires originating outside the center and burning through. In most cases the center had good fire protection, but little thought or effort was expended to protect the remainder of the building. It is, an expert said, as if they thought they would be able to climb through a charred building to an untouched computer center.

Accumulated waste paper ignited by cigarettes or matches is the second most common cause of computer center fires; hence the importance of having extinguishers—and personnel trained to use them—available to put out paper fires before they get out of hand.

A fire in a computer facility is worsened by damaging side effects. In many cases, the fire itself—that is, heat and flames—may be minimal, but damage from smoke, dust or fumes may be enormous. While this can be true anywhere, it is especially true in computer areas.

ALARMS

Although the human nose can detect a fire faster than many artificial sensors, we should hardly depend on it, particularly when we realize that magnetic tape begins to deteriorate at 150º. A sophisticated fire detection system is necessary to protect any computer installation.

There is no doubt that the best time to install a fire warning and extinguishing system is during initial construction of the computer center. At that time the cost of installing detectors throughout the facility is relatively small. Doing it later may be more costly, but it must be done. Detectors should be placed on ceilings, under raised floors (if any), in suspended ceilings, within air ducts, in cable conduits, and within the equipment itself.

The fire sensors most acceptable for the critical risks faced by the computer facility are ionization detectors, which sense the charged ions that are the precursors of fire, preceding smoke or flame.

Equally important is to check the fire detection system periodically to be sure it is fully operational.

FIRE EXTINGUISHING SYSTEMS

Directly related to a fire detection and alarm system is a method of controlling and extinguishing fires. The detection system we have discussed can directly trigger an extinguishing system, or sound the alarm, or both.

The extinguishing system of choice for computer installations today is one using an inert, non-lethal gas called Halon. (It should be noted that Halon 1301 is an ozone-depleting chemical. The U.S. government has issued a ban on its use effective December 31, 1995. Further, the Montreal Protocol will be calling for a worldwide phaseout by 1994.) Carbon dioxide systems have been used with success, but such a system requires immediate evacuation of personnel for life safety. Dry chemicals also are effective but leave a residue on the equipment and in the air which must be very carefully cleaned and filtered out before the machines can be used again.

By 1994 the Ansul Fire Protection Corporation of Marinette, Wisconsin, will offer for commercial use a substitute for Halon 1301. It is called INEGEN (R). INEGEN is a mixture of three inert gases: approximately 52 percent nitrogen, 40 percent argon and 8 percent carbon dioxide.

Sprinkler systems—indeed, water from any source—can be more disastrous than the fire itself. Water can short-out electrical circuits, damage delicate components, and wreak havoc with tapes. Equally firm opinions favoring sprinklers, however, are held by the Factory Mutual Group of insurance companies. To this apparent stalemate, IBM has said, "If your insurer requires sprinklers, install them. Just make very sure they never go off."

Portable Extinguishers

CO_2 extinguishers should be placed throughout the facility, including the tape library—usually a fire vault. Hand extinguishers cannot replace a total extinguishing system, but are invaluable in bringing small fires under quick control, avoiding the expensive discharge of the main fire-extinguishing system.

Fire-Resistant Equipment

In the event of a fire, specially insulated file and tape cabinets protect records and programs from a severe fire. The quantity of tape and records needed, however, has led to the practice of operating the tape library from a fire-resistant records vault. If a tape "safe" or cabinet is used it should carry a three-hour UL rating for fire-resistance, as should the door of the records vault. Always remember, however, that many tapes are necessarily exposed in the operations area at any given time.

It is important, too, that you determine the fire resistance of materials in the computer area. A $6.7 million loss was recently sustained when an overheated light fixture ignited a supposedly fire-resistant ceiling, wiping out a tape library and a computer room.

Off-Premises Protection

Whatever countermeasures are taken to protect the computer center and its operation, nothing is invulnerable. The investment in data, and the company's dependence upon its ready availability, is such that extraordinary measures must be adopted to protect the data.

Off-site storage is an effective safeguard for programs, payroll information, and data that are vital to a company's operation. This is done by off-site storing of duplicate tapes updated according to various schedules. Some of the data stored may only require revision once a month, whereas others should be up-dated more frequently. How these duplicate tapes are created is a matter be-tween your pocketbook and your data manager. Whether they shall be the product of simultaneous operation, or copied through the use of journal tapes, only your needs can determine. Suffice it to say that off-site storage of duplicate data could be the best investment you ever made. Learn from the example of a company that stored its backup list of equipment inventories and, after a disas-trous fire, had a precise list of hardware that existed nowhere except among the liabilities of their insurers. In no other manner could they have proved their loss so quickly.

BACKUP COMPUTER OPERATIONS FACILITY

It is customary to set up a computer of the same model with similar peripherals in order to form a mutual assistance pact in the event of disastrous loss. Con-trary to popular belief, however, a virtually identical hardware system may not be compatible with yours. In locating potential backup facilities, actual tests must be made periodically to positively prove that your company's critical pro-gram can still be run at the backup installation. This could mean contracting with more than one other data center, but in any event, it is a reciprocal arrangement whereby either will support the other in the event of computer loss. Periodic tests are necessary to verify that the other installations are still compatible and their schedule capable of providing time to you should it be-come necessary. Equipment and program changes by either you or your backup installation could alter emergency support arrangements. For these reasons, technical communication between parties should be maintained. A mutual aid pact is not only an economical security arrangement, but in all probability it is the only feasible contingency for both parties against disaster.

MAGNETS

Before we leave this discussion of physical computer security, let's touch on the damage potential of a magnet.

Almost everyone has read stories of how someone with a dime-store magnet in his pocket wiped out the data of a major corporation just by passing through the tape library or by putting a magnetic flashlight near a tape drive. Some of these stories have been dignified by publication in respectable newspapers. In a way, it's a shame the stories aren't true, because there's no question but that they add to the ever-growing mythic atmosphere surrounding the computer. The facts, though less amusing, are more comforting for computer personnel.

Tests have shown that a distance of about 12 centimeters (5 inches) between tape and a magnet is enough to prevent erasure. Other tests have shown that al-most half of that distance is still safe. In fact, during one test, it was not until a pocket magnet was moved over the entire surface of one side of a tape reel that marginal erasure occurred. This is not to suggest that you can afford to be careless with magnets. You can't. If someone were able to smuggle in a fairly sizable electromagnet and assemble it within the protected area, even your problems would have problems. The point is that care must be taken to avoid not only undue exposure to magnets, but also the hysteria which has been generated in some quarters regarding magnets and computers.

Above all, become well-acquainted with your data processing manager and your computer manufacturer's representatives—they know ways to damage computers and data loss so simple and effective that they're too dangerous to publish here.

COMPUTER ESPIONAGE

Much has been written about the cloak-and-dagger aura that surrounds the complex operation of a computer. We regularly watch television programs that deal with incredible data thefts accomplished with ease by instruments too sophisticated to detect. By and large, this is another amusing fantasy of the entertainment world. Industrial espionage exists, certainly, and it requires strong countermeasures to prevent, but it rarely takes the form that we see on TV and in the movies.

Electromagnetic or acoustical eavesdropping are both possible but they are difficult to bring off successfully. A central processing unit cannot be monitored in this manner, but a typewriter terminal, remote terminal printout, or display could be. There is usually so much interference from these terminals, however, that any data interception is difficult. Most industrial spies know that a well-placed bribe is far more effective than the clandestine installation of eavesdropping equipment. Monitoring devices are glamorous, but they are usually unneeded; the information sought is probably being thrown out in the trash as an unneeded copy.

When an industrial spy does resort to hardware, he is more apt to use the old-fashioned bug in some form of data communication lines. The information that is transmitted over lines from machine to remote terminals, for example, is in a digital form and, although it may sound like nothing at all to the untrained ear, it is recognizable to anyone with computer expertise. Since this data can be retrieved by wiretapping and other forms of monitoring (and then printed out on any compatible terminal), more and more companies are scrambling or encoding sensitive data, as well as the transmission of such information. These techniques are one more way in which access to information is denied to unauthorized people, whether internal or external. Computers have a natural talent both for encrypting and, it must be said, for decoding the less sophisticated ciphers. Whoever is zeroing in on your computer knows computers. For any code to be effective, you should change it frequently, as well as take expert cryptographic advice in setting up your information encoding system.

Above all, don't overlook the obvious. Many companies get so interested in the "007" aspects of counterespionage that they forget the little things that are even more likely to do them in, like all those printouts and printer ribbons in the trash barrels.

There are ways that spies can get at the data in your computer, ways that range from monitoring your computer traffic and buying your computer center trash, to bribing an employee. There is even data theft from one computer to another. But it is important that you keep the problem in perspective; you cannot afford to be casual about the possibility of such theft, and yet you cannot panic yourself into supposing that you are surrounded by electronic superspies.

Only you can really determine whether your database in any given area is worth stealing. Some part of it probably is. It's valuable to you, or you wouldn't have it in a computer, but you must determine its worth in terms of time, trouble, expense, and risk. And only after this determination, and an effective determination of the degree of value, can you decide how far you should go in setting up protective counterespionage measures.

American high-technology companies have cause for concern. Their inventions and trade secrets are threatened from both within and outside the United States. A sting operation engineered by the FBI is said to have nabbed more than a dozen Japanese businessmen. The seriousness of the problem has spurred the chairman of a U.S. Senate subcommittee to write:

> We believe it is important for us to receive from officials in the private sector who have responsibility for the security of sensitive information some specific examples of the types of problems American industry faces in this area as well as other input concerning the scope of the problem and possible solutions.

The severity of this problem convinced California legislators to pass tough legislation that is directed specifically at high-technology thieves. Under the California law, any person who is convicted of "knowingly buying, selling, receiving, disposing or concealing" stolen semiconductor devices or computer equipment is guilty of a felony. The statute carries a term of up to three years imprisonment. It also covers the forgery or unauthorized removal of a company logo from a microelectronic product.

The California law, however, is an exception; both at the local and federal levels, prosecutors have to deal with antiquated laws. Even if conviction results, imprisonment is also the exception; funds and training for government investigators in this area have been slow in coming.

DATA ACCESS CONTROL

Any computer system must have routine safeguards, mainly procedural, which are primarily designed to protect it from misuse, carelessness, or ignorance. Such safeguards limit computer access to those people who are familiar with its operation and know what they are doing. These rules and procedures, if strictly administered, will go most of the way toward providing the security you need, even though security is not their first objective.

In most applications it is also important to take additional steps to prevent unauthorized users from obtaining services from the installation, and to keep authorized users from getting to data which they are not permitted to have.

In today's technology, some system of authorization and user identification is necessary to protect computer programs and files. A few years ago sensitive business information could be protected at the computer itself. Physical access to the facility could be limited, and authorized persons could be supervised in such a way to review all machine access. Today companies are operating on so-called management information systems where consoles, transmitting, and receiving devices of various kinds are remotely located, some of them thousands of miles away. Some of these remote stations include visual displays that could be viewed by strangers. It is evident that a tight security system must be established over these remote points or their access in order to control the flow of proprietary data.

There are three ways to identify a user who wishes to access the system from a remote terminal or telephone: by a password, by a key or card, or by a physical characteristic which is, in theory, unreproducible.

Password

The most common system is the use of a password or identifying phrase. Upon a remote signal to the computer, the users are asked to declare their name and the system password. The software could then identify the individual and verify access authority.

The problem with such a system is that passwords are readily picked up by unauthorized persons. They are also frequently written down to avoid forgetting and they tend to become generally known. Variations on the fixed password system are used to overcome its difficulties. The one-time password system can be based on a series of passwords. The series is sent by registered mail to authorized users. Other systems use algebraic variations of an assigned random number often involving the date. Another type of system employs an extended check and cross-check over a series of questions.

The problem with a password system is that it can get totally out of hand. While it is relatively simple by this means to restrict the system to a handful of specially cleared employees, its wide application drastically restricts the potential of the technology at hand, hampering a sizable number of employees who should have some machine access. Over-involved identification procedures waste time and the more complex they become, the more time will be uselessly expended in simply accessing the system. At some point we begin to encounter the point of diminishing returns.

Finally, there is no way to know if a password system has been compromised until the damage is done and that fact verified.

Cards and Keys

Personal computers (PC's) and other equipment may be fitted and programmed for card access. Such a system speeds up the process for approved access. In the event a card becomes lost or stolen it can deprogram them and, when the appropriate hardware is installed, withhold suspect cards. Other new technological identification hardware such as voice and fingerprint verification may also be considered and integrated into the access control program.

Terminal/PC Security

Any data access control system should limit the accessibility of remote terminals and PC's. Here we return to solid ground from the more rarified atmosphere of the mainframe computer. We can secure the rooms that house remote terminals and PC's as well as the terminals themselves. Keys or combinations to release these facilities are distributed as necessary.

In addition to the physical security of a remote terminal and PC, data security at the terminals must also be considered. Any access system must consider the location as well as the user. Certain data might be denied to certain locations. As an example, the personnel manager would be permitted to retrieve payroll information but not from a location outside the personnel department. If she were in some other part of the building and sought payroll information from an unauthorized terminal, the information should be automatically denied to her by programmed controls. System controls must monitor each access request by a user to ensure that such data is authorized for release to that person and place. Unfortunately, many systems have no means of identifying the remote terminals in use except by the code supplied by the end user.

MULTI-LEVEL ACCESS

In order to get the greatest use possible out of the computer operation, it is usually necessary to specify differing levels in various programs that personnel are permitted to access. It is possible, even probable, that only a limited number of people would be permitted full access to an entire program. Even fewer should be able to reach the computer's basic instructions. On the other hand, there may be many people whose work would be considerably more productive if they had access to use (not change) a part of such programs. A rigid and inefficient system that simply denies them access is not in the company's best interest. The more rational approach is to encourage access up to some cut-off point. This is a "permissions" system that takes over after an authorized user has logged on. The names of valid system users can be explicitly programmed to have certain specific rights to a file, such as read-only, write-only, append-only, or execute-only. In this way a file can be put to its maximum use by allowing differing and restricted use simultaneously to users at various levels of authorization.

CARELESSNESS—THE GREAT ENEMY

The computer is invaluable to a company because, among other things, it stores an incredible amount of information that is almost instantly available for retrieval. If the integrity of that charge is compromised in any way (and it happens all too often) the information in the computer can get out of control, and in many cases, is permanently lost.

This breakdown of information control is usually the result of inadequately trained personnel. Ignorance is probably by far the greatest security problem in computer centers. It is responsible for more serious problems and constitutes a greater potential hazard than all the criminal activities to which companies might be subjected.

STORAGE

Careless storage of tapes can be a very serious problem. Excess heat or humidity begins to destroy the tapes by flaking off the metal oxides. Tapes too tightly wound print through from one layer to the next. Tapes that are roughly handled lose data. The lesson here is obvious. The data on these tapes is the very reason your company is involved with a computer operation; the tapes containing the data must be handled only with the greatest respect and care by competent personnel.

CRIME BY COMPUTER

The crimes that have been committed by imaginative souls playing games with computers catch the public's attention in part because it's a new method of criminality. Embezzlement and theft were committed long before the introduction of computers, but the mystique of the computer, the apparent ease of the theft, and the dollar value usually involved capture the imagination, for example:

- A brokerage firm executive over a period of years transferred $50,000 into his personal account via computer.
- "Computer-assisted crimes account for more than $100 million in annual losses. In one such caper, a computer consultant took his unsuspecting employer for more than $10 million. Although computers are quickly replacing guns as instruments of crime, to date the government and many states have yet to enact laws to address the problem."[2]
- A bright young man determined through discarded computer printouts how a warehouse was ordering parts and with the use of a Touch-tone phone stole over a million dollars in parts.
- Even our own Internal Revenue Service has been bilked by its own employees, as well as outsiders. In a dozen cases, 900 claims for returns well over $2 million were paid out by computer-generated checks.

There is no end to these stories. And we can only wonder who, how, and how many have never been caught.

It is not easy to combat computer embezzlement. Audits are complex and necessarily incomplete and control over authorized users is limited. Certain steps can be taken, however. As in all accounting functions, duties and responsibilities should be separated. Programmers should not have direct access to the computer, as their superior knowledge of program construction constitutes a severe temptation. Software programming safeguards must be built in to allow the computer to recognize very specific responsibilities and authorities in various operations.

In some companies outside computer security specialists who operate independently from computer line management may be desirable. Many large auditing firms have developed a formidable expertise in auditing for (and against) embezzlement. In either case, the outside experts should be responsible to top management for audit and verification of all security procedures.

COMPUTER-PROGRAMMING PERSONNEL

In the last analysis, no system of safeguards can prevent internal theft by computer unless you are able to recognize those people who are in a position to do the company harm and take steps to protect company assets from them. In order to protect against them, you must first understand them.

Let us state categorically that you cannot protect your company against these people by guards or access systems or validations of any kind; they are your computer personnel and related servicepersons. They set up your systems and they can destroy them and your entire company in the process. You must understand them as people and as professionals in order to set up defenses.

Let us quickly interject that these people are probably the least likely, as a group, to align themselves as "the enemy." As a group, they are not inclined to criminality, but if you fail to recognize who they are and what they do for your company, they could be nudged into an attitude of indifference, or even of active hostility. When either of these attitudes develop, you've got trouble in your computer.

In addition, allowances must be made for the fact that programmers are mathematicians, mathematicians play games, and computers are great games. It has been said that MIT's computer must be the most secure in the world because it has long been the dream of virtually every student there to outwit its controls. Benign, vigilant control, and generous access to smaller, non-critical computers are the safety valves that protect against computer games-playing.

SCREENING

We will assume that you have screened your personnel very carefully before hiring them. We will assume that you have followed the procedures proper to filling any sensitive position. You've double-checked previous employers personally if possible. You've satisfied yourself that the background and training of each employee is up to the standards set for each position. You've properly indoctrinated each employee in the peculiarities of your operation.

During this period you've kept the new employee busy, but your indoctrination program doesn't push him into operation too rapidly. You now have a computer operation staffed with high-grade professionals who meet your specifications and who, having had ample opportunity to see what they can expect and what is expected of them, find the company meets their specifications.

Once your computer operation is adequately staffed, you must take a look at each position and evaluate the harm that each could do. There are three basic functional positions in a computer department: maintenance-repair (usually on the hardware supplier's payroll); network administrator; and system programmers. There are sweepers, librarians, messengers, as well as middle management people, but although all of these people can represent very real security problems, they usually do not have the unique one-to-one intimacy with the computer.

The maintenance engineer must from time to time "dump" the system to correct problems that appear. A "system dump" is trade jargon for an image of a computer memory at a given moment. It's not the entire database or all of its information, but it is a copy of everything the computer is working on at that moment. It's purely a matter of chance how much information is revealed, but the possibility of exposing confidential data always exists. In addition this technician flips switches to check circuits and is generally into most of what the machine is doing. Techniques have been developed to keep engineering personnel away from program material under specific circumstances, but in the long run these measures are meaningless. Many malfunctions can occur on a computer and, in accordance with Murphy's Law, they frequently do. The technician will eventually be in every part of the machine, which means virtually unlimited access.

The network administrators run the machine. They work around the clock and on weekends. They are usually alone at 3 a.m., which means they can do anything they want to. Naturally the operator logs all the operations—but there's no one on hand to certify the log's accuracy. There's almost no action that cannot be reasonably explained.

The last and most dangerously able to cause harm is the systems programmer. If her authorized access if virtually unlimited, she is in a position to alter the system. This ability is potentially the most damaging of all, since she knows how to change any program in the system and then change it back again—undetected. She also can erase any information in the system and easily cover it as a routine operation.

You cannot eliminate these opportunities for crime. All three of the employees we have mentioned must, in order to function, be in a position where they can do you harm. They could, in fact, put you out of business. There are no ultimate controls that can both prevent catastrophes and still allow the computer center to function. A totally theft- and espionage-proof computer would be an unusable machine.

Your best security measure is an enlightened relationship with your computer people, and top-notch security-conscious leadership. If your computer personnel feel they are properly appreciated, they will be your strongest allies. If they feel unappreciated or taken for granted, they can be dangerous enemies.

INSURANCE

Insurance is your final security defense against disaster. Even though we have provided a security program for our computer facility, we cannot completely eliminate the elements of risk in a computer system. As a result, we must provide the final shelter of financial insurance.

In purchasing electronic data processing insurance you should consider an "all risks" policy. Besides insurance against embezzlement, including catastrophic losses, you will need a policy that includes coverage for all:

- equipment losses
- data losses
- reconstruction of data files
- costs of back-up operations
- loss of income

Obviously much professional advice will be necessary in choosing the proper coverage. The costs of insurance may well be influenced by the effectiveness of your computer security program. There is profit in protection, and it is frequently evidenced in reduced insurance premiums.

ENDNOTES

1. Lawrence J. Fennelly, *Handbook of Loss Prevention and Crime Prevention, Second Edition,* (Stoneham, Mass.: Butterworth-Heinemann, 1989), p. 69.
2. August Bequai, *New York Times,* May 9, 1984.

Appendix I

Ten Steps Toward Increased Computing and Data Security

The increased availability of personal computing technology has dramatically changed the way people work. Powerful, easy-to-use hardware and software tools have enabled workers to provide for their own information requirements without the need for constant interaction with large data centers and information systems professionals. The use of personal computers, however, carries with it added responsibilities to ensure continued, uninterrupted operation. This section attempts to outline ten prudent steps which can be taken to increase computing and data security.

The first responsibility in maintaining a secure, uninterrupted computing environment is to provide for physical security. Computer hardware is stolen and malfunctions, and there are several steps that can be taken to avoid these losses and interruptions:

1. If at all possible, keep equipment in an area that can be locked when unattended and lock the door when not in use.
2. If equipment must be kept in an open area, install devices which either secure the equipment to a desk or table, or sound an alarm if it is removed.
3. Record and maintain a list of all serial numbers. In the event of theft, serial numbers are essential to facilitate the return of recovered stolen goods. Without identification, recovered equipment often cannot be returned.
4. It is sometimes advisable to engrave equipment with an identifying mark to aid in recovery.
5. Insure all equipment against loss or damage.
6. Develop a maintenance strategy for all hardware components. Either buy a maintenance contract or maintain spare parts and/or computers to allow swapping in the event of failure. Such a strategy ensures availability and avoids unplanned expenses.

Computer hardware is the most obvious thing to protect and certainly is important, but it is also the most easily replaceable component of a computing system. The second, but more critical area of responsibility to ensure uninterrupted operation is data security. Data security can be defined as the prevention of accidental or intentional disclosure, modification, or destruction of computerized data. While we often think of security as the prevention of intentional misuse, it is the accidental causes (most often overlooked) that cause the most problems. Hardware malfunctions and inadvertent keystrokes cause more loss of information than all the criminals in the world could ever hope to. Again, there are prudent measures which can be taken to ensure continued operations.

7. All data files should be backed up daily. This single procedure will provide more data security than any other possible measure. As mentioned earlier, hardware can be readily replaced, but the data which is maintained on the computer cannot unless it is backed up. A single hard disk contains hundreds of million characters of data, and one hardware malfunction can render it all useless. Every personal computer system has software available in its operating system to provide daily backups either totally, or on an incremental basis.

8. Maintain copies of your data backups, program backups, and forms in an *offsite* location. If a catastrophe such as a fire or flood were to happen, backups kept in the same area would also be destroyed. In addition, special custom-made forms often require a long lead time to replace. If offsite, archived copies are available, operations can easily be restored using other computer hardware.

9. Limit use of your personal computer to authorized persons. User authentication can only be carried out by limiting access to the computer. Often, adequate physical security is all that is necessary. Turn off and/or lock the computer when it is not in use. If the PC is in a public area, use passwords to limit access. And use separate directories or libraries for individuals if multiple people share a PC. In this way multiple users cannot inadvertently disrupt another's work.

10. Finally, exercise software testing controls and verify results. "GIGO," or "Garbage In, Garbage Out" is an old expression often used to describe computer programs. Today unfortunately the term has come to stand for "Garbage In, Gospel Out" as people become more dependent on personal computers. Results should never be trusted or relied upon simply because they were produced by a computer without verifying the accuracy of programs with test data.

Reprinted by permission of Dennis M. Devlin.

Appendix II

Computer Viruses

This is the most insidious of all computer diseases. In addition to anything else it may do (like planting logic bombs to bring down the system at a crucial time), it copies itself into any other program with which it comes in contact. These "infected" programs, in turn, copy themselves into any other program with which they come in contact. A virus planted as a test in the University of Southern California computer system infected all of the system's programs in 21 seconds. For best (or worst) results, the virus should be planted initially in a highly privileged and frequently used program like an editor or linker.

Because computers are interconnected to form vast networks, the impact of a virus can be devastating. Assuming that an intelligent and determined foreign adversary elected to invoke the logic bomb strategy with a computer virus, who can say for sure that the United States' most critical defense computers are not already contaminated?

Poisoned E-mail

The idea is to reprogram the victim's terminal to hurt him in some way by sending a message via electronic mail (E-mail). You have to know what kind of terminal your victim is using and how it is configured. Both terminal type and configuration tend to be somewhat standard within organizations.

This attack works against terminals that have one or more (usually twelve) function (F) keys programmable by sequences of escape characters (that is, strings of characters starting with ASCII 27 or ESC). Most modern terminals and personal computers possess this feature.

Knowing the victim's configuration means you have to know which keys he or she has programmed and what they have been programmed to do. For example, users often use the F1 to display their current directory. Other tasks assigned to function keys are listing files and displaying the time. For this attack to be effective, the victim must habitually use these keys; most terminal users do.

You attack your victim by sending an E-mail message with an escape sequence embedded in it. Depending on the system, such a sequence begins ESC; or ESC[. Then a string of commands follows that will make the key do what the victim expects it to do but will also make it do something you want it to do. If the victim uses F1 to list the current directory, it may have been programmed with the following string:

ESC[1 lc P<CR> (where, *<CR>* means "carriage return").

Such a command string conforms to the syntax:

<control characters> <key designation> <command string> <termination>.

The command string "lc" means "list current directory"; P means to program a function key.

The control characters alert the terminal that an equipment function is to be performed; the number dictates which key; the command string tells what is to be done (the characters are stored in a buffer dedicated to the selected key); and the termination ends the process. When a signal such as this is sent to a terminal, nothing is displayed on the screen while the terminal is being programmed.

Let us say we want to compromise our victim's files. We must be sure that the function key does what the victim expects it to do; the key then copies the victim's files into a place where we can grab them and then the key wipes out any trace of the transaction.

The command string would be:

lc <CR>
*cp -c * / usr / acct / smartin&.*
<control sequence to clear the two previous lines from the screen and to position the cursor at the start of the line two lines above the current position—in other words, to wipe out the evidence>

The poisoned E-mail sets the victim up. The trigger is pulled the next time he or she pushes the F1 key to inspect the directory. The effect of this command sequence will be to cause all the victim's files (* stands for "all") to be copied to the perpetrator's disk area.

This program runs as a background process so it does not interfere with whatever the victim is doing. The last string of control characters clears the lines containing the offending instructions and also a line containing a process number reported by the operating system (an auditing provision intended to let the user know what is happening). The cursor is placed immediately after the command string expected by the user.

Reprinted with permission from John M. Carroll, Computer Security, Second Edition, (Stoneham, Mass., Butterworth-Heinemann, 1987), pp. 241-44.

Appendix III

Hacking

The large number of personal computers in the hands of the public has led to the prevalence of hacking—electronic trespass into computer systems remotely accessible by telephone lines. Hackers are typically young, male computer enthusiasts ranging in age from 8–39, with the average age 14–15. They make a game out of defeating access-control systems and are often loosely organized into clubs or circles. They exchange experiences and information through hacker boards—free, privately operated electronic bulletin board services (BBS) accessible by home computers with modems.

Hackers sometimes do damage: wiping out on-line files; changing passwords so legitimate users are denied access; stealing credit card numbers and using them to obtain goods and services; and crashing systems. They constitute a vast computer underground, even conducting "tele-trials" of people who have offended them. One reporter critical of hackers was tried, convicted, and sentenced to "electronic death." The hackers allegedly arranged to have his telephone, gas, and electricity turned off, flooded him with unordered mail order merchandise, and fraudulently obtained his credit report and posted it on bulletin boards.

Hackers also often obtain long-distance telephone service free by using techniques such as "boxing" (using hardware devices or computer programs to generate the musical tones the telephone company uses to open access to long-distance trunks); stealing telephone credit card numbers; using telephone company lingo to deceive operators into thinking they are company employees making official calls; or fraudulently obtaining access codes to long-distance services.

The first thing the hacker has to know is a computer's telephone number. Most system managers wisely avoid publishing these numbers. Hackers sometimes call on public lines, however, and deceive secretaries by claiming to be legitimate users who have forgotten the number. The hacker may enter the premises with a big envelope and claim to be a private courier and then read the number off a telephone. Or he can don khaki coveralls, enter a telephone closet or vault, clip a linesman's test handset across any pair (or all pairs, if time permits) of terminals bearing red tags, dial the local ANI (automatic number identification) number, and listen while a computer-generated voice tells him the number.

If deception or penetration doesn't work, the hacker may obtain an autodialer and program his personal computer to record the number dialed if answered by a 1,000 or 2,000 Hz tone. Hackers do not have to dial all 10,000 numbers in a telephone exchange; computer numbers are rarely more than +200 numbers removed from a company's published number.

Telephone Protection Devices

Devices are available that may foil the hacker who scans a telephone exchange to get computer telephone numbers. But no device will help if employees are disloyal and give out the numbers, let themselves be deceived, or let unauthorized persons roam around the premises.

The silent answer/callback modem is a protective device. When somebody dials into a computer, it does not answer with a high-pitched tone. Instead an intelligent modem answers with a synthetic voice and requests the user's access code (usually four-digit number), and a microprocessor checks it against a prestored list. If it is valid, the modem hangs up and calls the user back on the officially listed number (also prestored). Then the usual log-in procedure begins.

Some hackers have defeated the callback technique by call forwarding—every telephone exchange has a test and service number. Those familiar with the procedure can deceive the operator (or computer) who answers into honoring a request to forward all calls to a given number to a different number. Provided the hacker has the user's access code, he or she will be called back on a phone under his or her control.

The callback ritual can be awkward for sales representatives or executives reporting in. The best way to accommodate them is to have a time schedule where they will be allowed to log in without a callback.

Employees who call in from cars may be vulnerable to interception by persons who monitor VHF mobile radio-telephone frequencies (for example, 153 MHz) with scanners. The same is true for executives who call in from yachts, except that marine radio-telephone frequencies are in the 2–3 MHz band.

Protection by Password

The second line of defense is the password. The hacker's usual way of breaching this defense is to steal or guess the password. Many passwords are easily guessed. One way to discourage password guessing is to impose a quota system. Each would-be user gets two or three tries, and if she can't get the password right, the system logs her off.

Quota systems, however, penalize users who are forgetful or just poor typists, but they don't bother hackers who are probably stealing long-distance service from the telephone company anyway and are not upset at being logged off. Some hackers use telephones with an automatic redialing feature and let their personal computers try guess after guess, call after call, until they get the password right.

Some quota systems seal a user's account if the log-on quota is exceeded on the premise that such action will save files from harm. Hackers have worked around this precaution by systematically going through the whole computer system (that is, making three unsuccessful log-ins on every account) and forcing the closure of every account, thereby bringing down the system.

The best kind of quota system writes a warning message on the security officer's console so the officer can take action. This procedure works well if the offenders are on-site but not much good if they are a continent away. Provisions for automatic telephone number identification can help in tracing some hackers, but some foil that ploy by traversing complex access routes through several gateways or by using a "cheesebox"—an unauthorized call-forwarding device favored by those who want to make untraceable calls.

Among the passwords that are the easier to guess are master passwords or service passwords that often grant their users special privileges within a system. A system must, when delivered, have a master password programmed into it that enables its owner to get in for the first time, after which the owner is expected to change the password. When a large number of users must be admitted to a system at one time, a default password is used; this too must be changed once users get in. Often it is not, or the user is slow in using the default password, in which case somebody else gets in first, changes the password, and has fun with the account while the owner is locked out. Default passwords are widely used in schools and colleges at the start of a semester. Other easily guessed passwords are used by computer servicepersons.

When allowed to choose their own passwords, users often pick ones that are easy to remember. Initials (the most common ones are JB and JM), backwards initials, personal names, street names, automobile license numbers, or the last four digits of the user's telephone or social security number are some examples. A hacker can get some of these passwords by consulting a telephone book, city directory, or by scanning license plates in the company parking lot.

Two Bell Laboratories engineers wrote a password-breaking program that automatically tries all usual sets of initials backward and forward, 400 first names, and 100 street names. They were said to have discovered 85 percent of the passwords on the computer the first time they tried it. Many password-breaking programs are available on hacker boards.

It helps in guessing passwords to know about formats. The National Bureau of Standards recommends a minimum of four numbers. Many computer systems are limited to six characters and users tend to select letter sequences that are pronounceable. Some systems allow up to 10 characters and company protocols sometimes insist that they be alphabetic (upper and lower case) and numeric and use at least one punctuation mark. Passwords also should be required to be changed from time to time.

There are several strategies for improving password security. One is to make them longer—ten or twelve characters instead of six or eight. The second is to increase the possible number of symbols from twenty-six upper-case alphabetic characters to as many as ninety alphanumeric and special characters. The third is to use one-time passwords. Distribute a list of 500 or so, and use the top one on the list for each session. This method defeats interception of passwords by wiretaps. The fourth way is to encrypt passwords and compare the encrypted form.

Password encryption can be strengthened by adding (concatenating) the password with a number that is a numeric transformation of the current date (like adding 50 to the day of the month). This procedure can be carried out automatically at each end of the line before the password is encrypted. The encrypted versions are compared for authentication. Another improvement in password selection is a two-stage password. The user must give a project/programmer number (in a format like 9999/9999 or 9999,9999) or a user name plus a user identification number and then authenticate that with a password. There are even three-stage passwords where the user must give a four-digit access code to an intelligent modem before beginning the log-on procedure on the computer.

Project/programmer numbers and user names and IDs are often used for intracompany billing, and hackers have recovered them by rummaging through company trash, although most system managers protect passwords by making them nonprinting (also known as *echo-suppression*) or covering them with a strikeover mask.

Hackers have been known to retrieve passwords by personal reconnaissance: entering company premises ostensively to take lunch orders and looking for passwords written on or under desk blotters, taped on or under retractable desk arms or drawers, or taped to visual display screens. Some hackers are skillful enough to discover a password by watching the user's fingers on the keyboard, a practice called *shoulder surfing*.

Deciding whether to let users choose passwords or to assign them has always been troublesome. If the user chooses them, a hacker who can learn something about the user can often guess the password; if the password is assigned, the user may write the word somewhere for fear of forgetting. One answer may be use of the pass phrase. The user selects a phrase, sometimes as long as the user likes (up to at least 128 characters), and the log-in routine hashes and mashes it to produce a one-way encryption that is stored internally.

Wiretapping and Piggybacking

A truly determined hacker still has two ways to steal passwords if all else fails: wiretapping or piggybacking. To wiretap he needs to access either the line into the computer or out of the home or office of a legitimate user. The terminals are located in junction boxes in the basements or hallways of office or apartment buildings, in terminal boxes on poles, or in front lawns in suburban areas. An ordinary audiocassette recorder can copy the usual 300-baud tone signals on a voice-grade telephone line. It can be played back through an acoustical modem and the result printed. Although the echo of the password is suppressed, its actual transmission from user to computer is not.

Reprinted with permission from John M. Carroll, Computer Security, Second Edition, *(Stoneham, Mass., Butterworth-Heinemann, 1987), pp. 293–99.*

Chapter 13

The Thief
You Pay

PART I: THE "INVISIBLE MAN"

It's closing time. Office personnel have put away their papers, locked up their desks, and left for the day. A few industrious folks are clearing up reports or finishing that last column of figures, but they'll be gone soon. Then office security will lock up the office for the night.

Alarms will be turned on, windows and doors checked, and the night security force will begin its regular routine. All doors to the building will be secured. If after-hours employees are working, the main entrance will be opened for them and relocked by a security officer after they have signed his after-hours book. Only one elevator is operating. It's the end of a good day. No incidents have been reported, and the night is even more uneventful. Security has only routine reports to submit. And yet $1,000 was stolen from this office today.

At 9:00 the next morning, the thief returns to steal again. He waves good morning in the lobby. He chats with acquaintances on his way up in the elevator. He nods to the receptionist and moves purposefully to an interior office where he begins his day's work. Who is this bold bandit? He is an employee of yours. He is a thief you pay.

CAN YOU RECOGNIZE HIM?

Unfortunately there is no dependable way that the potentially dishonest employee can be recognized even if honesty and psychological testing were administered as a pre-employment screening tool. The causes that trigger dishonesty generally come after the thief you pay has been hired. Your employment practices can, of course, eliminate applicants with a high-risk potential; tests can often tell you if they are honest *when they are hired*. But you must accept the fact that *anyone*—male or female, new employee or veteran, accountant or clerk, salesman or engineer, janitor, secretary, or high-ranking executive—can be a thief.

It is generally accepted by bonding companies and professional security people that potential workers divide into three groups insofar as security is concerned. The first group, about 25 percent, will be consistently honest no matter what opportunity to steal is given to them. Another 25 percent are outright thieves; in any environment, they will be actually looking for ways to steal. The honesty of the remaining 50 percent is up to you. This group could be on either side, depending on the circumstances. If the opportunities for theft are there, then the temptation is there and given sufficient temptation—particularly the example of others—this 50 percent will steal also.

Obviously these percentages are at best an approximation of a difficult-to-define situation, but it should give you food for thought. Because it means that, barring effective hiring precautions, you start with 25 percent of your employees just biding their time until they can steal you blind, and another 50 percent who could easily go the same way! In other words, you are faced with the possibility of having 75 percent of the employees of your company ripping you off, unless you institute a thoughtful and vigorous program to protect the assets and the profits of your company.

WHY DO THEY STEAL?

Since we have no fail-safe method of recognizing the potentially dishonest employee at first sight, perhaps we can develop a technique for advance warning. If we know why trusted persons steal, perhaps we can watch for specific patterns that will indicate the potential is there, and that the time may have come for them to make their play.

There is no simple answer to the question of why otherwise honest people begin stealing from their employers, for there seems to be no single motivating factor that triggers that attitude.

Some employees may begin to steal because of a sudden temporary financial emergency. Usually they think of their theft as borrowing and tell themselves they will replace the money they've taken. Theft of goods is usually excused by such thoughts as "I need it more than they do," "They owe it to me," and "Everybody else does." Curiously enough, a significant number of first-time thefts by nonprofessionals are for others: to help with a friend's hospital bill or to give a hand to a relative who's in trouble.

Some employees steal simply because they feel like living the good life for a while or that they must make an impression on someone. Some steal because they think—or, rather, tell themselves—they "have it coming to them." Some steal to avoid losing status when they're hit by financial problems. And, in a great many cases, they begin to steal for no other reason than that they can't resist the daily opportunities that a lax or naive management lays before them: "They'll never miss it."

Nevertheless, despite the seemingly unrelated causes of employee theft, it is possible to generalize some principal factors. First in importance is a pattern of financial irresponsibility. This does not necessarily mean a person with expensive tastes, or even one having a need to show off by spending. This is simply someone who has never been able to come to grips with her own economic realities. She is always in financial hot water, a person often looks to a few of your company assets to bail her out. A credit check usually identifies her for you.

Second is the "swinger"—the high roller with the fancy car and fancier lifestyle. He may spend a lot of time at the track or casino and make a few trips to Las Vegas or Atlantic City every year. In between junkets his bookie sees a lot of him. He's a "natural" for theft.

The third category is the employee caught in a genuine crisis—often an extended illness, either her own or someone in the family. Or it could be a devastating judgment against her in some liability action. She is a victim of circumstances and needs help—fast. You may find that your assets provided that help, without your knowing it.

Obviously employees falling into one or more of these categories should be handled with care and their opportunities to steal watched. You should also watch for any of the following danger signs:

- close and regular association with someone from a vendor company
- gambling (beyond the office pool on the World Series)
- borrowing from co-workers
- bouncing personal checks
- heavy pressure from creditors, including telephone threats, visits to the office, and garnishment of wages
- misuse of personal checks, such as obtaining cash with undated or postdated checks
- excessive drinking or other forms of substance abuse
- obvious spending in excess of known income
- refusing to relinquish custody of records during the day or to assign them to others
- consistently passing up vacations and, more rarely, refusing promotion

It is safe to say that employees will steal from the place that is most familiar to them—the workplace. It is where the thief you pay feels most confident and assured that he can get away with a theft.

WHAT IS STOLEN?

The temptation exists to say that anything that isn't nailed down could be—and probably has been—stolen. Unfortunately, even if it is nailed down, it's still fair game for the determined or desperate thief.

It is common for employees to conduct their "sideline" job on the spot—no overhead for them! Buying and selling to or through contacts made in the course of legitimate business and delivering by company truck, as well as using company telephones, postage meters, files, and even computers, is amazingly common.

One company executive we know made an unexpected visit to his office on a weekend and discovered his computer room in full operation. It seems a computer operator who had been with the company for twelve years had gone into business for himself and had set up a thriving data processing service bureau using company equipment.

We know from experience that anything may be stolen. The following list of attractive items for theft is made up of most of the things your office likely contains:

Cash

Stolen through padded expense accounts, by kickbacks, or from cash storage accessed through unauthorized keys, combinations, or carelessness. Cash is also attacked indirectly, through counterfeit or stolen forms (blank checks, vouchers, invoices, etc.), or through collusion with vendors or customers—paying for goods not received, failing to show short counts, overloading, providing information to hijackers, approving altered invoices.

Equipment

Cellular phones, faxes, PC's, postage meters, tools, software, typewriters, calculators, dictating machines, projectors, and tape recorders all have a ready market. One enterprising executive we heard about sold his company's manufacturing equipment.

Furniture

Desks, chairs, tables, lamps, file cabinets, clocks, rugs, lighting fixtures, stereo speakers, and paintings.

Supplies

In addition to petty attrition, supplies may be stolen in gross lots—pens, pencils, pads, paper clips, etc.

Proprietary Information

Computer programs, mailing lists, accounts, customer lists, bid estimates, research data, preferential discount schedules, sales plans, advertising, promotional, and merchandising programs.

Time

The theft of this precious asset goes on in every business environment every day. We all admit that time is money and productivity is certainly reduced with its theft either by hourly or salaried wage earners. Good security can enhance productivity by placing control within management's hands so time thieves are more readily identified.

Misuse of Assets

Even the misuse of the smallest item can cause a critical erosion of profits. Very few employees—and not many employers—consider a pen here, a pad of paper there, as theft. But in an office with 100 employees it certainly represents a considerable cost over the course of a year.

In addition to the theft of company property, let us not overlook personal property theft in the office, a regular occurrence in many places. We have discussed the "hit-and-run" thieves from the outside who prey on purses left on desktops and wallets in jackets hung on office doors or coat racks, but it is a sad fact that a significant number of these thefts of personal property may be by fellow workers.

Unfortunately, personal property is difficult to protect and security cannot be directly committed to safeguarding such items. Essentially, anyone who keeps personal property in the office is risking its loss. Until the crime rate in the office declines, each employee can best protect personal property by bringing as little as possible to the office. Wallets and purses can be placed in locked drawers (petty thieves usually are not familiar with these simple locks), kept on the person, or put out of sight in occupied or locked offices.

Employees should be made aware of this risk to their personal property. It is equally important that they recognize the plain fact that, while security will institute every possible safeguard, security's responsibility is for their safety and that of the company's property and operations. Security cannot assume responsibility for personal property brought to the office, things about which they do not know and whose handling they cannot control.

COLLUSION—THE CONCERTED EFFORT

While the dishonest employee working alone can do enormous damage to an employer over a period of time, he is an even more formidable problem when working in collusion with others. His confederates may be coworkers, or they may be vendors or customers, messengers, truck drivers, or servicepersons, all on different payrolls. The most costly combination is a group of your employees working with a group of outsiders.

Security people agree that employee theft involving more than one person is far more serious than the "lone-wolf" operation. Detection is more difficult because, with two or more working on the caper, there are better opportunities for cover-up. Key members of the ring will be those employees whose job it is to enforce and oversee security procedures. The combination is so effective in many cases that the only way the ring can be exposed is by placing an undercover man in the company within or near the suspected group.

"INNER OFFICE": SPECIAL DANGER

In terms of dollars and financial damage, the main office is the Achilles' heel of most business operations. This is the sensitive nerve center of the entire function. This is where approvals and authorizations originate. This is where receipts and invoices are handled. The thief in the office, working alone or with confederates, indeed has the fate of the company in his hands.

And his hands are none too gentle. When we consider that an estimated 33 percent of business failures are the result of employee dishonesty, we shouldn't have to sell the need for internal business security. (Note: The fact that one third of our nation's business failures is a result of employee theft and dishonesty has been a steady rate for the past 20 years, according to the U.S. Department of Commerce.)

HOW THEY DO IT

In reviewing theft in the office, we find that its forms are limited only by the ingenuity of your staff. Remember that you've gone to a lot of trouble to train your staff in the systems they help operate. And the better they know the system, the better they know how to use or evade it. Look over these examples to see how many could apply to your operation:

- Receiving clerks and truck drivers getting together to falsify counts. Uncounted items are resold, or (in a "long count") a cash kickback is made.
- Payroll and personnel employees creating false "hires" or retaining resigned employees on the payroll, thus producing authentic checks made out to nonexistent employees.[1] (These false checks are frequently cashed by confederates to protect the perpetrators.)
- Computer programmers and operators working in collusion, or programmers working under insufficient supervision and having direct access to the computer. Increasing business dependence upon computerization makes many companies extremely vulnerable to this type of virtually undetectable attack.
- Maintenance personnel and outside servicemen who cooperate to steal office machines for resale.
- Purchasing agents or accounting personnel working in conjunction with vendors to produce false accounts payable records. Payments are split. The accounts payable clerk or supervisor falsifies shipment receipts and issues vouchers on the vendor's invoice for goods not shipped. Vendor-purchasing agent collusion may also involve approving purchase of merchandise at an inflated price. (Vendor kicks back extra profit to purchasing agent.)

---

1. One classic case was uncovered only because the company cashier cashed paychecks for nonexistent employees through an employee who was an ardent union member. The company learned of the "shadow" employees because their union contract called for all new hires to join the union. "Where are our new members?" was the union's demand.

- Mailroom and supply clerks combine to pack and mail merchandise to themselves for resale or personal use.
- Mailroom supervisor and accounting clerk produce false figures that exceed amount of money placed in company postage meter while the excess cash goes into their pockets.
- Stockroom clerk and janitor (or janitor alone or in combination with trash pickup personnel) remove office equipment and supplies in trash.
- Issuing checks in payment of bills from fictitious suppliers and depositing them by means of false endorsements to accounts set up for that purpose. Another version is to set up a new company bank account—without telling the company.
- Raising the amounts of checks after voucher approval.
- Taking incoming cash and not crediting customer accounts.
- Forging checks and destroying the cancelled checks when they have cleared the bank, then concealing the transactions by altering bank statements and forcing footings in the cash books.
- Padding payrolls as to overtime and rates. Employees "kick back" to the authorizing supervisor. One firm discovered it was paying $40,000 per month for unworked overtime.
- Paying creditors' invoices twice and appropriating the second check.
- Pocketing unclaimed wages.
- "Lapping"—pocketing small amounts from incoming payments and applying later payments on other accounts to cover shortages.
- Appropriating checks made payable to cash or the bank which they were intended for payment of notes and creditors, or presigned blank checks.

These are only a few of the methods of internal crime committed regularly in offices around the world. But the known cases represent only a tiny percentage of the probable crimes; it is estimated that for every thief who is caught there are thousands who get away with it for years until they have accumulated enough to retire in comfort—at your expense.

PART II: INTERNAL SECURITY

Internal theft is clearly an enormous problem. The yearly cost to American business staggers the imagination—and the figure continues to climb. Certainly, the estimates of billions lost in white collar crime represent actual loss; however, the overall impact of business interruption makes it significantly worse.

We all are aware of the dramatic increase in crime generally across the country in the past decade. As shocking as those figures are, bear in mind that inside, or employee, thieves outsteal the external criminals (like automobile thieves, burglars, and armed robbers) by about five to one—and only a minuscule percentage of them are caught and prosecuted. The next time you find yourself shaking your head over the crime rate—which almost entirely represents external crime—remember the rest of the facts, the internal criminal you are more likely to be the victim of.

Fortunately you *can* do something about internal theft. You can reduce losses by dishonest employees to relatively unimportant amounts—if you set up a continuing program of prevention, education, and control.

The first essential step is to accept the possibility that some of your employees *might*, under the proper circumstances, steal from you. You must not join that astonishingly large group of employers who are blind to the possibility of dishonesty among their employees.

Security professionals report case after case where an employer was willing to believe that workers of competitive firms stole from *their* employers, but refused to believe that any of "his people" would steal from him. Management, they report, is always aghast to find how actively some of the most-trusted employees have been lining their pockets at company expense.

You need not believe all the figures cited here in order to establish effective defensive programs. What is important is to recognize the potential of internal theft, the crippling losses you could suffer—and may be already suffering—at the hands of one or two dishonest employees.

With that threat in mind you will be better able to establish a program of countermeasures to secure your operation against the thief on your payroll.

LOSSES CAN BE CUT

The first step in instituting countermeasures against internal theft is to adjust your attitude. It is outrageous—and immoral—to accept employee dishonesty as part of the "cost of doing business." Although it is probably true that there will always be petty pilferage and loss due to dishonest employees—no system of internal control can absolutely prevent every kind of theft. A continuing effort is essential if such a system is to be as effective as possible. No percentage of loss to embezzlement or pilferage is acceptable; theft is contagious, and today's petty theft is tomorrow's theft ring. Whenever and wherever theft begins, sincere efforts must constantly be made to reduce it.

Every business necessarily makes an effort to reduce costs and enlarge profits. In highly competitive fields this effort is truly a matter of corporate life or death. If a company in such a competitive situation finds its overhead is higher than industry standards, it must cut these costs to an acceptable level simply to stay in business. It's good business sense, whatever the competition, to regularly examine and reduce costs wherever possible. Certainly, internal theft is a totally absurd area to budget for in your operating costs.

As we have noted, there are two elements that exist in the crime of embezzlement—desire and opportunity. If management permits the opportunities for theft to present themselves regularly, the day will inevitably arrive when a need or the desire for more money combines with the opportunity, a temptation too strong to resist.

Management has a very real moral obligation to protect the integrity of its employees by taking every possible step to avoid presenting those opportunities for theft that will tempt otherwise honest people to take advantage of the trust placed in them. This is not to suggest that employers must bear the responsibility for thefts by their employees, but it is their obligation to remove the opportunities, and hence the temptation, and to make such theft "unthinkable" by all but the most determined employee-thief.

BEGIN AT THE TOP

A plan for internal security, like any plan involving policy, must begin at the top.

At the management level, more than at any other point or in any other area of the office, enthusiasm and total commitment are an absolute necessity. Even if a large percentage of your staff probably is never in a position of handling cash, merchandise, or papers that they could use to divert assets to themselves, they are still a part—an important part—of the climate of honesty in your office. Management's vital involvement must be continuous and clearly supported from the highest level. Without this support, security cannot be effective.

It may be necessary to overcome objections to the institution of internal security procedures; we all know there are people who instinctively resist anything new. These people must be sold by the tact and firmness that you would use in instituting any other new procedure. However, once you have proved that security measures are both necessary and beneficial, you will find that most employees are glad to cooperate.

INITIATING A PLAN FOR INTERNAL SECURITY

Screen Applicants

Certainly the key to any system of internal security is the basic honesty of the employees. If all the employees are honest, the system will be foolproof. If a high percentage of them are thieves, the system may be tested to the breaking point.

The best place to screen out bad risks is in the human resources office, *before* they're put on the payroll. A careful, selective employment policy may take more time and cost a few more dollars, but it will pay for itself many times over. The savings in reduced turnover, employee training, and greater efficiency can repay the costs—let alone the savings realized in the reduction of internal losses.

It is important that you use an application form that, among other things, asks for a chronological listing of all previous employers. This provides a reference source; but it can also show a gap where the applicant didn't wish to list a previous employer, such as the county jail. Dates of employment are facts previous employers usually have no objection to verifying—or contradicting. It is imperative therefore that you verify each applicant's previous employment data. Frequently, when completing an application, dates will be stretched out to cover periods where unacceptable time was served, either for a bad work experience or actual jail time. Certain types of self-employment, such as child care in the home, are difficult to confirm. Simply asking for a client list, however, can discourage the wrong type of applicant. You will find simple requests such as these will cause a percentage of your applicants to remove themselves for consideration. There are other methods to accomplish the above, such as asking for a signed waiver that authorizes you to obtain confirmation information about the application data before an interview starts. Also, it is advisable to mention in any newspaper ads that all applicants will be subject to a background check prior to employment.

Check References Properly

You will, of course, ask for business and personal references—these must be checked. In checking these references, however, remember that the applicant has selected them. She obviously hasn't selected someone who will give her a bad report. It is important that you check another contact at each previous employer by telephone, if not in person.

Why check by telephone? Because people tend to be considerably more candid on the telephone than in a letter. In addition, you have an opportunity to hear the inflections with which they respond. If a former employer says, "Oh, yes, Smith was a good worker," the manner in which he says it has real significance. There are enough different inflections in such a line to keep an actor, much less a former employer, busy for quite a while. But a form asking the same questions comes back with only a "yes" or a "no." It can't give you any shadings; you get no additional insight into Smith as a potential employee. Another vital question for previous employers is, "Would you rehire her?"

Applicants for supervisory jobs, including those promoted to these positions, should of course be checked more thoroughly than is possible simply by following up an application.

Consider Professional Backgrounding

Professional backgrounding involves extra expense, but is paid for many times over each time it turns up the fact that an apparently acceptable candidate has an unacceptable past that was conveniently not mentioned. This backgrounding involves a discreet investigation into the past and present of a potential employee, and can uncover serious problems that you should know about—in character, work habits, and past performance—but could never effectively uncover by your own efforts.

It is conservatively estimated that 93 percent of all employees known to have stolen from their employers are not prosecuted; they are mostly fired without charges being brought. These workers are, in fact, unknown as thieves except by a few persons where they formerly worked. They are not known even to the police. Someone from this select group could be applying for employment in your firm now. Another sobering thought is that one out of every 49 American adults is on probation, parole, or in jail.

A professional investigator could do background checks for you—granted, at some expense. But when you think of the potential losses just one dishonest employee can cause, you know the value of this information if the position under consideration is sensitive in any way. Personnel and security experts alike agree that less than 20 percent of the work force is responsible for 80 percent of personnel problems of all kinds. Any measures than can cull out that 20 percent save time, money, morale, and administrative headaches. And backgrounding is legal, discreet, and confidential.

It can be very useful to announce on the original employment application that employees must be bonded if hired. This announcement will instantly dampen the enthusiasm of the professional thief; he knows bonding entails fingerprinting and giving permission for access to criminal records. Knowing he will almost surely be exposed by a bonding investigation, he will withdraw his application and move on to a company with less stringent requirements.

Interviews

Every applicant who presents him- or herself for an employment interview comes equipped with their complete history known only to themselves. Preemployment background checks can and often do overlook an important detail. Revealing reactions to specific questions during an interview are of crucial importance. Most human resource interviewers concentrate on job skills and abilities called for in the specific job description, but this is simply not enough. The experienced and skillful security practitioner working in conjunction with the interviewer decreases your odds of hiring an applicant with something to hide.

Examination of Public Records

Law enforcement agencies and the various courts provide final disposition of cases. A closer look at the records where possible, or simply obtaining additional details in connection with the investigation relative to the case, presents a completely different set of facts. An example of this is a conviction for simple assault which may or may not have been plea bargained due to insufficient evidence to support sexual assault. Another frequent conviction is reckless driving; it often starts out as a driving under the influence, but for one reason or another ends as a misdemeanor.

When you discover information such as the examples cited above, you must be careful in how you handle it because it is illegal in most areas to deny employment due to an arrest that did not lead to a conviction for the crime charged. It is legal of course to reject an applicant for a criminal conviction. At the very least you certainly could look longer and harder at all the material prior to making a decision.

Investigate Before Promotion

It can also be important to investigate any employee being considered for promotion or transfer to a more responsible or sensitive position. Remember that without opportunity there is no temptation. Employees suddenly thrust into a new situation, where they are regularly tempted to steal and have the opportunity to do so, are placed in a wrenching position—especially if their personal circumstances place them under financial pressure.

The model citizen ten years ago may be having an extramarital affair today that is squeezing him for his last penny. The young man with a modest interest in stocks and bonds when he was originally hired may now be the wolf of Wall Street under heavy pressure in a declining market. By determining the real situation, you are in a position to help the employee work his way out of his family or financial problems before he moves on to new responsibilities and temptations. This kind of interest on your part in employees' personal problems not only builds company morale, but also reduces losses from theft.

Polygraph Examinations for Certain Jobs

In some cases where the position under consideration is highly sensitive, it could be valuable to screen prospective employees or candidates for promotion by the use of a polygraph test, if this is legal in your state. While this procedure is a matter of some controversy, veteran security professionals generally agree that the lie detector can, in the hands of competent and ethical professionals, play a constructive role. A polygraph test can quickly establish the validity of the truthful applicant's statements of background. This can be particularly valuable where the applicant has claimed experience or training in areas difficult, time-consuming, or expensive to check out. The polygraph obtains information that cannot be gathered from any other source, such as the application, background investigation, psychiatric testing, or psychiatric examination.

It is of course important for you to check the legal status of the polygraph in your state before you consider its use. Several states forbid its use as a requirement for employment, but permit it to be used on a voluntary basis. Many firms do, however, use the polygraph for hiring practices, as well as investigations, and those that do report its use as helpful.

You must make your own decision as to whether polygraph use is indicated. Only you can make the final decision, but you might be well advised to contact some polygraph examiners who are members of the American Polygraph Association and learn more about your state laws and the methods used by ethical examiners, before the need arises.

It is important to acknowledge that polygraph examinations generally are between 70 to 90 percent accurate and the success rate frequently depends upon the skills and experience of the operator. Approximately 12 states have passed laws prohibiting employers from giving lie detector tests for preemployment, whether voluntary or not. There are precedents too numerous to mention from state and local laws to interpretations by the National Labor Relations Board and the Equal Employment Opportunity Commission concerning the use or misuse of polygraphs. It is safe to say that in order for a company to avoid any charge of defamation of character, violation of the law or public policy, or circumvention of the equal employment practices, a clear understanding of all existing laws and precedence must be understood.

Chapter 14

Drugs in the Workplace

CONTROLLED SUBSTANCES

Overview of Controlled Substance

Security officers must be familiar with classes of drugs, their reactions within the body, and their slang names. Officers need this information to recognize the behavior associated with drug abuse, and they may find it important in a variety of control and investigatory activities.

Controlled substances can be broken down into five major classes: depressants, stimulants, narcotics, marijuana, and anabolic steroids. In addition, hallucinogens such as LSD, glue, and hydrocarbons require security scrutiny.

- Depressants (barbiturates) will produce behavior resembling alcohol intoxication: stumbling and staggering as in a drunken state; falling asleep, difficulty concentrating; dilated pupils.
- Stimulants (amphetamines) will produce excessive activity: irritable, argumentative, or nervous behavior; excitable talkativeness; increased blood pressure and pulse; long periods without food or sleep.
- Narcotics (opiates and their derivatives) will produce constricted and fixed pupils; itchiness; flushed skin, muscular twitching, sniffles, watering eyes and cough; appetite loss; lethargy or drowsiness.
- Marijuana will produce dilated and bloodshot pupils; distortions and hallucinations; rapid, loud speech with frequent laughter; distorted depth and time perception.
- Anabolic steroids will produce increased muscle mass; increased secondary male sex characteristics in both males and females (deepened voice, increased hair growth, and acne).

Of the many slang and street terms, the following are fairly common. A general knowledge of these terms may be useful when questioning a suspect, dealing with abnormal or aggressive behavior, or overhearing a conversation.

- Amphetamines: bennies, roses, cartwheels, dexies, oranges
- Barbiturates: barbs, good balls, yellow jackets, blue birds, reds, red devils, tuies, rainbow

- Chloralhydrate: Mickey Finn, Mickey Peter
- Cocaine: coke, snow, just, flake, snowbirds, happy dust, C
- Codeine: schoolboy
- Heroin: H, smack, joy powder, horse, harry, junk, sugar
- LSD: acid, cubes, the Big D, sugar
- Marijuana: pot, Mary Jane, weed, hashish, grass, rope, hay, tea, Acapulco gold, stinkweed, sweet lunch
- Mescaline: peyote, buttons, plants
- Morphine: M, mud, Miss Emma, unkie, morph[1]
- Crack, which is also known as rock cocaine, is the result of changing the structure of cocaine hydrochloride from a salt to a free base. By heating the salt form in the presence of alkali the cocaine is changed into a form that can be smoked. Smoking allows the cocaine to go directly to the lungs and the bloodstream as opposed to being inhaled through the nose, as with ordinary cocaine.

SUBSTANCE ABUSE[2]

Substance abuse refers to abuse of any substance that can cause personal harm or harm to others. This problem is pervasive. Millions of people abuse substances. Students, housewives, retirees, and employees are among the many different kinds of people who abuse substances to varying degrees.

Abuse by employees in particular adds a business dimension to the adverse effects, besides personal harm and harm to others. Let's look at associated characteristics and examples of the employee who:

1. Abuses prescription or nonprescription drugs from retail stores
2. Obtains and uses illegal drugs
3. Sells and uses illegal drugs
4. Drinks alcohol or smokes marijuana before work, during breaks, and during lunch
5. Sniffs glue or industrial or cleaning fluids to get high
6. Abuses any type of substance in order to withstand a monotonous, assembly-line type job
7. Steals products or sensitive information to support a drug habit
8. Operates dangerous machinery while in an intoxicated state, and then causes an accident
9. Slows production or makes a mistake due to substance abuse
10. Is absent because of the ill effects of alcohol or other drugs.

If the employee abuses substances after hours, there is almost certain to be a spillover effect of this lifestyle into the workplace. An employee may take tranquilizers to calm down during the day, and then consume barbiturates to sleep at night. To make it through the workday the same person may abuse amphetamines. This is often called "downer-upper" addiction. Many employees consume illegal and legal drugs before arriving at work and while on the premises. Drinking alcoholic beverages prior to work, and then out of a coffee thermos during work, is common.

Excessive absenteeism and poor job performance are expensive side effects of substance abuse. Both cost businesses billions of dollars each year. Outsiders also are known to exploit drug-dependent employees through the promise of money, drugs, or the threat of blackmail in order to obtain their assistance to commit a crime.

No occupation is immune to substance abuse. Those afflicted are from the ranks of blue-collar workers, white-collar workers, supervisors, managers, and professionals.

CAUSES

One might ask why anyone would want to abuse substances. This is a difficult question to answer. Several explanations can be offered, but causes vary. A person may want to escape a boring existence, overbearing problems, or to bolster self-confidence. Peer group pressure is another cause. Curiosity and emotional immaturity are other variables. A search for personal or religious insight can be the reason. Or a truck driver or student, for example, may abuse stimulants in order to work longer hours and achieve certain goals.

COUNTERMEASURES

Unenlightened management ordinarily ignores substance abuse in the workplace. As with so many areas of loss prevention, when an unfortunate event occurs (such as a drug-related crime, production decline, or accident due to substance abuse) these managers panic and then react emotionally. Experienced people may be fired unnecessarily, arrests made, and litigation threatened. In contrast, with the first sign of abuse, action should be taken as soon as possible to reduce the problem and possibly salvage the employee. Preemptive action can be cost-effective and prevent additional losses because the employee is still experienced and training dollars have been invested.

If management suspects substance abuse or the use of illegal drugs in the workplace, an undercover investigation will detect the magnitude of abuse. In certain states urine surveillance is lawful; an employer can request that an employee undergo urinalysis as a condition of further employment. Because drug use has frequently been shown to have a high relationship to employee theft, some firms require urinalysis for all job applicants.

Loss prevention practitioners should be aware of substance abuse problems, characteristics, and remedies. Cost-effective decisions have to be made regarding the salvageability of an employee versus the costs to the business resulting from crimes, accidents, and other losses.

One commonly used strategy to impede substance abuse is education and prevention. This approach is the hallmark of many government-sponsored programs. If people are knowledgeable about substances and their side effects, their own personality, as well as the methods to deal with life stresses, then abuse can be reduced. Numerous kinds of educational media are available—posters, advertisements, educational kits, and games. Counseling is another important component and such programs are often found in schools. But businesses can also establish contracts with local government drug abuse agencies, or private concerns that specialize in this area, to salvage employees.

Alcoholism

Alcohol is the most abused drug in America. An alcoholic is defined as someone who cannot function on a daily basis without consuming an alcoholic beverage. Although alcohol is stressed here, we must not forget that many other substances are detrimental to people and the workplace. For example, a heroin addict or a chronic marijuana smoker are also liabilities. Heroin addicts are rare in the workplace since they cannot afford to work; to support their habit they must commit crimes that net them more money than wages from working would. Most managers have yet to recognize the seriousness of chronic marijuana use. But as more marijuana abusers advance to increasingly responsible positions, management views will very likely change.

The National Academy of Sciences has reported that the medical, social, and industrial costs of problem drinking may run as high as $60 billion a year—including at least $19.6 billion in lost productivity. After a five-year study, General Motors found that employees with alcohol-related problems drained 70 percent of the benefit dollars from the company's sickness and accident policies.

Alcoholism is usually considered the fourth most serious disease in the United States, behind heart disease, cancer, and mental illness. Estimates of the number of alcoholics in the United States range between nine and fifteen million. These figures do not include the millions who are on the fringe of alcoholism. It is often a hidden disease whereby alcoholics hide the problem from family, friends, physicians, and themselves. Some major symptoms of alcoholism are heartburn, nausea, insomnia, tremors, high blood pressure, morning cough, and liver enlargement. The alcoholic often blames factors other than alcohol for these conditions.

TYPES OF SUBSTANCES

Four terms can help the reader understand the impact on users of various substances.

Psychological dependence: Users depend so much on the feeling of well-being from a substance that they feel compelled toward continued use. People can become psychologically dependent on a host of substances, including alcohol, marijuana, nicotine, and caffeine. Restlessness and irritability may result from deprivation of the desired substance.

Addiction: In addition to psychological dependence, certain substances lead to physiological addiction—when the body has become so accustomed to a substance that the drugged state feels "normal" to the body. Extreme physical discomfort results if the substance is not in the body.

Tolerance: After repeated use of certain drugs, the body becomes so accustomed to the drug that increased dosages are needed to reach the "high" of earlier doses.

Withdrawal: The person goes through physical and psychological upset as the body becomes used to the absence of the drug. Addicts ordinarily consume drugs simply to avoid pain, and possible death, from the effects of drug withdrawal. Symptoms vary from person to person and from substance to substance. An addict's life often revolves around obtaining the substance, by whatever means, to avoid withdrawal symptoms.

Narcotics

These drugs include opium, its derivatives, and their synthetic equivalents, including heroin, morphine, codeine, and methadone. Such drugs are used to relieve pain and induce sleep. The method of consumption is injection, oral, or inhalation. Both psychological and physiological dependence is typical, besides a potential for tolerance. Heroin has been touted as the most serious illegally abused drug in the United States. The situation was particularly bad during the 1960s and 1970s when hundreds of thousands of heroin addicts committed assorted crimes to obtain money to pay for their habit. Since then, many heroin addicts have turned to methadone, which can be obtained at medically approved clinics, thereby preventing crime and black market dealings. But there are still many street addicts who prefer heroin and are prone toward criminality. When heroin is "mainlined" (injected), a "rush" is experienced. There is an intense period of sensation and then a feeling of well-being. The feeling of pleasure eventually deteriorates to a struggle to avoid withdrawal. Symptoms are constricted pupils, lethargic behavior, scars where needles are injected, and poor appearance due to personal neglect. The paraphernalia of the heroin addict consists of a hypodermic syringe, pin, or eye dropper, a spoon, and matches to heat the heroin. A belt is tied around an arm or leg to cause a vein to swell.

Depressants

These substances fall into several categories. Barbiturates: phenobarbital and secobarbital (Seconal); tranquilizers: Valium and Librium; nonbarbiturate hypnotics: methaqualone (Quaalude); and miscellaneous drugs: alcohol and chloroform. A depressant affects the central nervous system. Barbiturates are ordinarily prescribed for insomnia, while tranquilizers calm feelings of anxiety. Other depressants are used prior to surgery. Abuse of these drugs can lead to psychological and physiological dependence—withdrawal is painful and can be fatal, although depressants have a tolerance potential. These drugs are taken orally or injected and addicts may have to commit crimes to support their habit. Symptoms are similar to that of an alcoholic: drowsiness, slurred speech, disorientation, constricted pupils, irritability, and slow reflexes.

Stimulants

There are several types of stimulants, including the more common ones: caffeine, amphetamines, and cocaine. These drugs affect the central nervous system and generally cause increased alertness soon after consumption, but restlessness and irritability are characteristic of long-term usage. There is a tolerance potential, plus a susceptibility to psychological dependence. Physiological dependence is nil.

Caffeine is found in coffee, tea, cola drinks, and No-Doz. Increased alertness may be followed by insomnia, gastric irritation, and restlessness.

Amphetamines are widely used stimulants that are swallowed or injected. They are prescribed for narcolepsy (chronic sleepiness). Illegal amphetamines typically originate from legitimate sources. Abuse is characterized by anxiety, talkativeness, irritability, and dilated pupils.

Cocaine is referred to as a glamour drug. It is expensive and the high is short-lived. The history of cocaine is interesting: It used to be an ingredient in Coca-Cola and Sigmund Freud experimented with it. The user inhales cocaine into the nose or injects it. Symptoms of abuse are similar to those of amphetamines, with the addition of damage to nasal membranes and the potential for hallucinations and hostile behavior.

Hallucinogens

These substances can produce a trance, fright, and irrational behavior. The most popular hallucinogen is marijuana; LSD is another.

Marijuana and its derivative, hashish, are widely used; millions of people smoke marijuana occasionally to relax. Because of widespread cultivation of the plant to produce rope prior to the Civil War, marijuana grows wild in almost every state. Because its use it widespread, many states have decriminalized it. Its effects depend on the individual and the potency. There is no physiological dependence but psychological dependence is possible; research on tolerance is inconclusive. As with alcohol, nicotine, and other dangerous substances, marijuana abuse can be detrimental to an employee's health.

LSD was popularized in the 1960s by the youth counterculture because its effects were touted as a consciousness-expanding experience. The effects vary greatly but there is no physiological dependence. Bizarre hallucinations, that can be either beautiful or terrifying, are a consequence of using LSD.

Inhalants

By inhaling volatile chemicals, intoxication can result, either from one's own volition or by accident due to poor ventilation. The awareness of both causative factors should be understood by all employees.

Three types of inhalant chemicals are volatile solvents, aerosol propellants, and anesthetics. Volatile solvents include a variety of glues or cement, cleaning fluid, paint thinner, and paint remover. Aerosol propellants are used in a variety of consumer products, but because of pollution problems, usage has diminished. Anesthetics such as nitrous oxide (laughing gas) and ether are found in medical facilities for surgical purposes.

Those who seek a high gather the substance or gas in a plastic bag and place it over their mouth and nose before breathing. Direct breathing from the container holding the substance is another method. Physiological dependence is nil, but tolerance and psychological dependence may result. The effects are numerous and varied: intoxication, a chemical odor on the person, drowsiness, stupor, and hallucinations.

ENDNOTES

1. Russell L. Colling, CPP, *Hospital Security, Third Edition*, (Stoneham, Mass.: Butterworth-Heinemann, 1992), pp. 470–71.
2. Philip P. Purpura, CPP, *Security and Loss Prevention*, (Stoneham, Mass.: Butterworth-Heinemann, 1984) pp. 443–49.

Appendix I

Testing Hair for Illicit Drug Use

Use of Hair Testing

Use of hair as a test medium avoids the limitations of infrequent urine testing. Hair testing is relatively well-established and uses a number of the same technologies as urine-based tests, including enzyme, radioisotope, and fluorescent immunoassays. The methodologies are identical; the distinction is in the medium.

Hair has several advantages over urine in testing for drug abuse:

- Hair greatly expands the time window for the detection of an illicit drug. Urinalysis of a single specimen generally can detect the presence of drugs for a period of several days to a week or two, depending on the drug. Hair analysis can detect drug use for several months or more, depending on the length of the hair.
- Brief periods of abstinence from drugs will not significantly alter the outcome of hair analysis.
- Hair is relatively inert, easy to handle, and requires no special storage facilities or conditions. Compared with urine samples, it presents fewer risks of disease transmission.
- Having some hair snipped from the head is less invasive and embarrassing for most people than supplying a monitored urine specimen.
- Collecting comparable samples for repeat testing is easier with hair than with urine.
- Contaminating or altering a sample to distort or manipulate test results is much more difficult with hair than with urine. Preliminary research shows that even treating hair with a variety of strong compounds will not completely eliminate traces of illicit drugs.

Conclusions

Radioimmunoassay of a single hair specimen (RIAH) detects more drug exposure than is self-reported or detected by a single urine test. The degree of this underreporting appears to vary to some extent with the type of drug. These research findings are most relevant for cocaine: It was detected in a relatively large number of subjects, and three disparate types of data—self-report, urinalysis, and RIAH—were available. Although more work must be done in establishing standard protocols and procedures for using RIAH as a routine screening device, sufficient information is available to support the utility of hair testing for detecting drugs of abuse.

Hair testing appears to have a number of advantages, besides its less invasive method of collection—the extended time window for results, the stability of the medium, and the difficulty of tampering with the medium to evade positive test results. Some practical difficulties may occur, however, in collecting specimens from individuals with short or no hair.

RIAH's applicability in the monitoring of offender drug use may very likely permit a better determination of drug exposure over longer timeframes than is currently available using urine screening methods conducted less than twice a week. In fact, hair-based testing could be conducted with less frequency than urinalysis to achieve a comparable level of confidence.

Finally, hair testing appears to hold promise as a useful tool in drug epidemiology. Yet, a substantial amount of field testing is still required before it attains the degree of acceptance now accorded urinalysis testing. Nevertheless, the outcome of this project indicates that such testing ought to continue.

Prepared by Tom Mieczkowski, Harvey J. Landress, Richard Newel, and Shirley D. Coletti, National Institutes of Health, January 1993.

Chapter 15

Building Factors

Since there are so many factors that can be discussed in office security, the following variables are addressed to methodologically examine and define an existing crime problem.

When scrutinizing the environment in which an office building exists or will be constructed, it is important to get accurate information regarding the area outside of, as well as inside, the complex boundaries. Is the location in a downtown area? Is the location primarily residential? If so, are the residents mainly in homes or apartments? Are there subdivisions with well-secured perimeters and access control? Is the area considered to be a low- or high-crime area? Why and by whom? A low-crime rating, location-wise, does not mean that your building is coincidentally secured. It could mean that other crimes are or will be displaced to your location. Violence is always foreseeable. When planning your security, there is no set radius formula that demarcates a safe zone from a violent zone. If this is so, then the key question to consider is "How can adequate security be determined and by whom?"

Business can retain security experts, contract guard services, or hire their own corporate security force. An interdisciplinary approach, based on our experience, has always generated a more precise definition of the crime problem. It is always wise to contact the crime prevention unit of local law enforcement for a number of reasons. First, the crime prevention unit is usually a repository of crime information. Information from patrol officers can be invaluable and incidents officially reported to police are quantitative. However, qualitative information concerning patrol officer perceptions of your location may not support officially reported quantitative data. The crime prevention unit can assist in painting a clear picture of crime through security surveys and follow-up recommendations.

Local associations can also assist in crime definition and choice of potential prevention resources. Real estate associations, nationally, are creating programs for realtors to understand violence, drugs, gangs, and cults, to name several crime problems. The Chamber of Commerce invites various security and police professionals to address its membership. Crime stoppers and crime watch groups may be able to assist in evaluating the building and surrounding areas.

Another source of assistance is local neighborhood newspapers that often publish news not found in larger newspapers with broader appeal. An example of this are associations formed specifically to address the crime problems of concerned citizens, professional groups, church groups, and women's resource centers.

Continuing education programs at community colleges, vocational schools, four-year colleges, and universities regularly conduct seminars and short courses on crime. Costs, if any, are nominal and can include college credit and/or continuing education credit for mandatory retraining stipulated for numerous professional licenses.

Building owners and managers should specify who is responsible for security. Unfortunately, this may be an afterthought, even with many occupants in the building. A number of questions need consideration:

1. Which businesses stay late after dark?
2. Do any businesses function twenty-four hours a day?
3. Where and when should lighting be emphasized?
4. Are locking mechanisms adequate?
5. Is there a guard service? If yes, are they contract, proprietary, or off-duty police?
6. How does the office compare to similarly-situated buildings in area?
7. Were background checks done on maintenance, security, and other employees of the owner/manager with 24-hour access to occupants' offices?
8. Does the business have contract or proprietary maintenance service?
9. What were key factors in choosing contract services? Low bid? Good references? Documentation?
10. Is security training available for employees, contract services, and occupants?
11. What has been the owner/manager input into security?
12. What security policy exists? Supplied by whom?
13. Are incidents documented? Used as management tool?
14. Who do building occupants call if a problem arises?
15. Is uncontrollable and random discretion allowed in security decision-making?

The building owner or manager needs to be aware that office security is defined by planning and policy. If this is not the case, then the office building security has no foundation for consistency: 1) You cannot evaluate what has not been defined; 2) you cannot train what has not been evaluated; and 3) you cannot attempt to control an environment without understanding what needs to be secured.

Risks and criminal opportunities must be anticipated in order to be reduced. It is smart business for an owner/manager to include such anticipation as part of the profit center philosophy. Reduction of losses saves the same profit dollars that are gained through the acquisition of new business. *Security awareness is business presence.*

Consider twelve imperatives in the philosophy of office security that define and compartmentalize crime problems:

1. Has a complete security survey been completed?

2. Has there been a comparison of crime rates with similarly-situated areas and buildings?
3. Has the administration defined the role of security?
4. Have security policies and emergency procedures been formulated?
5. Is security policy updated through evaluation and documentation?
6. Is the administration familiar with security liability and litigation problems?
7. Do all employees receive preservice security training?
8. Are security awareness programs implemented?
9. What in-service training is available to both security and non-security personnel?
10. Is there accurate documentation of incidents?
11. Where is the security department within the organizational structure?
12. Who is charged within the complex to make security work effectively and who serves as backup?

Building Factors *was prepared by John Lombardi, Ph.D.*

Appendix I

Thirteen Steps You Should Be Aware of to Avoid Becoming a Victim

1. Report all suspicious activities immediately to police (suspicious-acting individuals; suspicious sounds like calls for help, screaming, breaking glass, a whistle being blown continuously; office doors ajar, broken windows, or individuals loitering near or in the doorways of your building.
2. Help deter property thefts—join Operation Identification—engrave all personal property with your social security number and the first two letters of your state, for example, GA 033-30-0799.
3. Lock your doors and pocket the keys—thefts only take seconds.
4. Do not lend a stranger your office key.
5. Request positive identification before opening a door to strangers. Use peepholes.
6. Leave a light on when you go out, even if only for a short time.
7. Select safe walking routes, preferably where there is the greatest light.
8. Walk in groups of two or more whenever possible.
9. Do not hitchhike.
10. Get a whistle and carry it in your hand when you walk alone.
11. Do not carry more money than necessary, or flash money or credit cards when making purchases—ideally, use travelers checks when large sums of cash are needed.
12. If it is necessary to carry a handbag, carry it with the opening toward your body and your arm through the strap.
13. Do not provoke arguments or confrontations—the other person could be carrying a weapon.

Stop and Think!

Most crimes can be prevented if we take a minute to *stop and think* about our own self-protection, safety, and the security of our possessions. Week after week make note of the various crimes that occur, such as bicycles stolen that had been secured by a poor-quality locking device, thefts from an office because a door was left unlocked, and thefts from a pocketbook that was left unattended. If you want to avoid being a victim of a crime, stop and think: most crimes can be prevented. Crime prevention is everyone's business. Help yourself... help your neighbor... help make your office and community a safer place!

Think Security
and
Think Prevention

Chapter 16

Management's Responsibility

Every office in the United States is faced with an ever-increasing danger of crime. Not only is the rate and cost of crime increasing at an alarming rate, but the nature of crime against the office is becoming more serious and more sophisticated. The situation has developed to a point where the business community has begun to look at the problem from a different perspective. Only a few years ago, the great majority of companies took only a few basic precautions in their daily conduct of business and wrote off the losses they suffered as the "cost of doing business." This attitude seems to be on its way out.

With increasing operating expenses, international competition, and tight money, the pressure is on management to maintain a profit ratio. It is no longer reasonable to assume that to merely stay ahead of operating expenses that a company will be in good shape. Not only have businesses become aware that losses from criminal activity are out of hand, but also that they cannot be accepted to any extent if businesses are to survive. A consistent statistic over the past twenty years, according to the U.S. Department of Commerce, is that one third of the businesses that go bankrupt do so because of employee theft and dishonesty. Consequently, businesses should be eager to implement any number of solutions to aid or protect profit margins.

In addition to the real concerns of employee theft and dishonesty, there is another major contributor to profit loss from external and internal thieves: liability. Liability and "foreseeability" in providing a safe and secure workplace for employees and the public who interact with the particular business.

Certainly, security or loss prevention techniques have come into greater focus as liability issues continue to negatively impact offices and businesses. Security, of course, exists in every office. The doors are locked at night and the cash is deposited in the bank, checks are countersigned, and so forth. But this kind of security is no more than the kind of routine precaution that any homeowner would take. Many offices have established systems whereby each department protects itself against assault—a step in the right direction, but it misses achieving the overall protection every company needs.

The job of security is a big one and getting bigger. Real security requires a specialized task force and a specific function within the company that deals with all matters pertaining to safety, crime prevention, and the protection of assets from fire, theft, or fraud. Industrial plants, universities, and large retail outlets have had security departments for many years, but offices have not. But that picture is changing and today businesses are recognizing, in increasing numbers, the need to establish a specific entity responsible for office security. This entity is incorporated into the organization in many different ways, but for better or for worse, it's a security department and its single mission is to provide security.

All this is a giant step in the right direction, but we still have a problem. The word *security*. We've talked about security all through this book and no one choked on it, so why is there a problem now?

Well, up to this point we've used the word security in its broadest sense, which is fine because that's exactly what we've been talking about. Unfortunately, most people think of the word "security" in a much more restricted way. The word frequently carries a stigma. It conjures up images of badges, clubs, handcuffs, jails, and whatever else is thought of as repressive and negative in today's society. The word *security* suggests to many uninformed persons that the department's goal is the apprehension of criminals and the detection of dishonest employees, which is only partially correct. The real goal is to prevent loss through the protection of all assets while providing a safe and secure place in which to conduct business, thereby contributing to profitability.

This is where one can make a strong case for a name change from security to loss control or asset protection. Such a change, in and of itself, would change the direction of a security department from that of an emergency response department to one that is implicitly challenged to operate on the belief that most losses can be prevented.

Obviously, the goals of this loss prevention function are a management decision that cannot be arrived at casually. In the decision to establish a loss prevention program, management must make an all-out commitment to make its effective operation possible—not an easy decision. It requires study. And to begin with, it boils down to a question of how much authority loss prevention requires to do the job.

Any evaluation of the scope of authority required by loss prevention must examine the organizational framework of the company and the proper role of loss prevention within that structure.

It must be recognized that in the concept of loss prevention we are talking about here, the department must cut across all departmental lines to enter into virtually every function of the company. Loss prevention should permeate the office—not as a repressive presence—but in the role of cooperative specialist. Even so, this role will inevitably lead to conflict.

On paper the relationship between loss prevention and other departments is ideal. They are working in concert to solve common problems. In practice, however, there is frequently some resentment and a feeling that loss prevention is interfering in the efficient performance of operational routine. In actual practice, good security controls enhance operational efficiency.

Loss prevention must have authority to accomplish its mission. It must have direct authority to establish or correct systems, audit system performance, and evaluate and reevaluate risks anywhere within the company. It must have direct authority to handle these and hundreds of other problems that fall within the scope of loss prevention.

Management must clearly establish the *degree* of authority the department may exercise in given situations. In increasing increments on the authority scale the department might exercise advisory authority, compulsory advisory authority, concurring authority, or final authority.

ADVISORY AUTHORITY

Depending on the nature of the business, voluntary acceptance of the advice of a security professional may be adequate to cover the needs of some companies. Even in companies where the security function operates at a high level of authority, the advisory approach is common, especially in matters concerning the employees' welfare. In other matters, the security executive should advise concerned supervisors of the situation and work with them (if the supervisors want) to develop corrective measures. Obviously, there will be many instances where the supervisor will reject the offered advice. In such a case, security executives must be able to take their case to a higher authority.

In an active company with a number of high-risk areas, a security function limited to advisory authority would be inadequate. Since security would have no motivating authority, it could neither implement nor adequately audit protective systems. There is the additional danger that security would be put in the position of having to constantly run to management to arbitrate matters that should be within security's scope to resolve.

COMPULSORY CONSULTATION

If consultation is compulsory, the security department must be called in before any action is taken by operating personnel. This plateau of authority at least keeps the loss prevention department advised about contemplated changes throughout the company. Because in most cases the contact between departments will be initiated outside of security, security's role in the discussion and in the eventual decisions will be strengthened. This level is still below the authority required, however, in companies with an appreciable number of high-risk areas.

CONCURRING AUTHORITY

In this situation, security has the authority to overrule any action that touches on its areas of responsibility. It may not necessarily motivate the action, but it can cancel it. This means, for example, that new file cabinets may not be ordered unless security approves of locks; Or that a new elevator system cannot be approved until security agrees that it satisfies certain safety standards. At the same time, security may disapprove the purchase of individual office shredders as unnecessary.

FINAL OR FUNCTIONAL AUTHORITY

This is the ultimate authority. In cases where this degree of authority is granted, the security official may exercise direct authority over any employee activities related to security in any way. This kind of authority could result in a directive from a security official ordering a revision in the receiving process or structural changes in certain offices for security reasons. Obviously, such authority should be used sparingly and with the greatest discretion. It is rare, indeed, that a security function has such authority, and when it does it must protect it with the greatest care. Management, too, must exercise judgment in granting this authority and should probably restrict its application to very specific areas.

It is likely that a well-run security department in a well-run company will have some combination of these authorities, but whatever the level in whatever circumstances, it is vital that management spell out this authority in the clearest possible language. With such an understanding, management can go a long way toward avoiding conflicts.

It is invariably the case that management turns its attention to security problems only after the office has been beset by a series of crimes. We can sagely observe that this is not very smart, however human a response it may be. High-salaried executives are not paid to be human in the sense of being subject to frailty and error; they are paid to administer company affairs in such a way to contribute to its growth, and to anticipate and forestall elements that might interfere with the essential health of the corporate body. Crime committed against a company is a most unhealthy and costly adversary. Proper security against such attack is a high-priority requisite. Security must be incorporated into a well-supported, effective loss prevention program.

Too few companies today show enough sustained interest in the never-ending problem of crime. Even after initiating an effective program in response to a wave of crime against the office, management often loses interest in security matters as crime declines. And, as management loses interest, procedures, systems, and controls erode and deteriorate. This situation is particularly dangerous because it engenders a false sense of security. In the belief that controls and anti-crime procedures are protecting company assets, management is lulled into unwarranted complacency.

It is imperative that top management demonstrably acknowledge that the security/loss prevention function has stature and is a dynamic force in the specific business's efforts to maintain a safe and secure workplace free of any crime. The function must be as creative and innovative as necessary because it is continually challenged by the ever-changing attacks on the business to rob it of its assets. The security department must be frequently reviewed and rejuvenated if it is to be successful in dealing with the enormity of its task. It must be adequately and continuously supervised. It must be managed and lead properly. It must be emphasized to be an important part of the organization.

It is curious—but true—that in security matters there is frequently a reluctance on the part of top executives to think past retaliation. They will commit elaborate funds to track down a thief and look for uncommon heroics in response to a fire, but they can find a lot of reasons not to spend money to prevent thefts or fires. Unless your company's management can be educated to a broader, more enlightened view you are doomed to a purely reactive security function and will certainly never make it to loss prevention.

If you do educate your management to the extent that you have been designated as the loss prevention department (or at least have the scope implicit in that name), you had better be sure that you are prepared for the job. Ask yourself if you are law enforcement–oriented. If you are, are you willing to broaden your base of expertise through additional training and study? Does your staff consist largely of uniformed guards whose duties are essentially access control? If so, you will need to take immediate steps to expand your departmental capabilities by hiring professionals with broad backgrounds in systems, accounting, training, administration, and research—a big step for a function that until recently was performed by a few door-rattling ex-cops. But if security is to serve the ever-growing needs of today's embattled companies, this step must be taken.

Finally, management cannot ignore the obvious threats and actual occurrence of workplace crime. It may be true that countermeasures addressing specific vulnerabilities can be seen as unattractive, restrictive, costly, and inconvenient, but the problem must be faced. A decisive attitude and cost-effective countermeasures fulfill the obligation that management owes its ownership, stockholders, employees and in the larger sense, society in general.

The business community's participation in the war against crime may be hastened by legislation that sets certain minimum security standards for all kinds of enterprises. If the notion sounds far out, think back a few years ago before there were codes specifying minimum construction and safety standards to combat fire and injury or death. In a way it is strange to realize that we had to enact legislation insisting that people protect themselves from the ravages of fire. Similar legislation could go a long way toward consolidating the business world in a united front against the destructive onslaught of criminals.

The situation should not be permitted to deteriorate to the point where inflexible regulations replace management's most efficient response to the dangers that threaten profits and assets.

Chapter 17

The Security Survey

A security survey is a critical on-site examination and analysis of an industrial plant, business, home, or public or private institution, to ascertain the present security status, identify deficiencies or excesses, determine the protection needed, and make recommendations to improve overall security.

It is interesting to note that a definition of crime prevention outlined by the British Home Office Crime Prevention Program—"the anticipation, recognition and appraisal of a crime risk and the initiation of action to remove or reduce it"—could, in fact, be an excellent definition of a security survey. The only difference, of course, is that a survey generally does not become the "action" as such, but rather a basis for recommendations for action.

Crime prevention can be divided into five component parts and analyzed so that its implications can be applied to the development of a working foundation for the security professional.

1. *Anticipation.* How does the anticipation of a crime risk become important to the security or crime prevention professional? Obviously, one primary objective of a survey is the anticipation or prevention aspects of a given situation—the pre-concept. Therefore, an individual who keeps anticipation in the proper perspective would be maintaining a proper balance in the total spectrum of security surveying. In other words, the anticipatory stage could be considered a prognosis of further action.

2. *Recognition.* What methods will best provide an individual conducting a survey with an understanding of the relationships between anticipation and appraisal? Primarily, the ability to recognize and interpret what seems to be a crime risk becomes one of the important skills a security surveyor acquires and develops.

3. *Appraisal.* The responsibility to develop, suggest, and communicate recommendations is certainly a hallmark of any security survey.

4. *Crime Risk.* This, as defined in this book, is the opportunity available to commit a crime. Total elimination of opportunity is difficult, if not improbable. Costs are measured in depth of protection and delay time. Obviously, the implementation of the recommendation should not exceed the total (original/replacement) cost of the item(s) to be protected. (An exception to this rule would be human life.)

5. *The Initiation of Action to Remove or Reduce a Crime Risk.* This section in-

dicates the survey phase at which the recipient of the recommendations will make a decision to act, based on the suggestions set forth by the surveyor. In some cases the identification of security risk is made early in a survey and it is advisable to act prior to survey completion.

The responsibility to initiate action based on recommendations is the sole duty of the survey recipient. The individual who receives the final evaluation and survey should be the individual who has commensurate responsibility and authority to act.

There are basically three types of surveys:

1. A building inspection advising an office manager in a large complex of his vulnerabilities as they pertain to the physical characteristics of the dwelling.
2. A security survey to be conducted either on the whole complex or only a portion of the site.
3. A more in-depth security analysis including a risk management study to analyze risk factors, environmental and physiological security measures, crime patterns, and levels of fraud and internal theft.

DEVELOPING YOUR SECURITY POINTS

Like most professionals, we need tools to do an effective job. The following items will assist you when conducting a survey: tape measure, floor plans, magnifying glass, flashlight, camera with flash, small tape recorder, screwdriver, penknife, pencil, and paper.

Your survey should be conducted systematically so the recipient can follow your recommendations in some kind of order. Start with the building perimeter. Once inside, start at the basement and work your way to the attic. Do not be afraid to be critical of areas that you are in. This is what the recipient wants.

After you have completed several surveys, putting them together will become easy.

DOS AND DON'TS IN DEVELOPING YOUR REPORT

Dos

1. Be honest in your recommendations. You are the expert.
2. Call the shots as you see them.
3. Be critical—physically review the property in detail.

Don'ts

1. Don't overexaggerate your reports. They are too important.

2. Don't inflate the report with maps and floor plans.
3. Don't repeat your statements.

The written report should include the following:

> Page One: Introduction or sample covering letter.
> Page Two: A. Identification of building
> B. Specific statement of the major problem.
> C. Alternative recommendations to the problems.
> D. List of further recommendations.

General statements such as the following also can be included in the report:

1. Physically inventory all property at least once a year. Your inventory should list the name of the item, the manufacturer, model, serial number, value, color, and purchase date.
2. Engrave all property in accordance with the established operation identification program.
3. All office equipment should be bolted down and all files, cabinets, and rooms containing valuable information or equipment should be locked when not in use.

Other Keys to Being an Effective Surveyor

Only when you have developed the ability to visualize the potential for criminal activity will you become an effective crime scene surveyor. This ability is an art. Nonetheless, it is important when you arrive on a survey site that you are prepared to give a property owner sound advice on the type of security precautions to consider.

In summary, to be a good crime prevention surveyor, you have to be a good investigator. You must understand criminal methods of operation and the limitations of standard security devices. In addition, you must be knowledgeable about the type of security hardware necessary to provide various degrees of protection.

NINE POINTS OF SECURITY CONCERN

1. General purpose of the building—residence, classroom, or office. Consider the hours of use, people who use the building, people who have access, key control, and maintenance schedule. Who is responsible for maintenance? Is the building used for public events? If so, what type and how often? Is the building normally open to the public? Identify the significant factors and make recommendations.
2. Hazards involving the building or its occupants. List and prioritize types of theft: office equipment, wallets, or stockroom inventory. Identify potential hazards that might exist in the future.

3. Police or security guard applications. What can they do to improve the response to the building and occupants from a patrol, investigation, or crime prevention standpoint? Would the application of guards be cost- and/or operationally effective?
4. Physical recommendation. Inspect doors, windows, lighting, access points. Recommend physical changes that would make the building more secure, such as pinning hinges on doors and fences.
5. Locks, equipment to be bolted down, potential application of card control and key control. Make specific recommendations.
6. Alarms. Would an alarm system be cost-effective? Does building function preclude the use of an alarm? Are the potential benefits of an alarm such that the building use should be changed to facilitate the use of an alarm? Consider all types of alarms, building-wide or office-specific. Consider closed-circuit television and applications for portable or temporary alarm devices.
7. Storage. Are there specific storage problems in the building such as expensive items that would be given special attention: petty cash, stamps, calculators, microscopes? Make specific recommendations.
8. Are there adequate "No Trespassing" signs posted? Are other signs needed?
9. Custodians. Can they be used in a manner that would be better from a security standpoint?

PERSONALITY OF THE COMPLEX
YOU ARE SURVEYING

Each complex you survey will have a distinctive personality. Take an average building that is open from 9 a.m. to 5 p.m. The traffic flow is heaviest during this period. During the span from 5 p.m. to 1 a.m. the building is closed to the public. Some staff members may work late. Who secures the building? At 1 a.m. the cleaning crew arrives and prepares the building for another day. The whole personality of the complex must be taken under consideration before your report is completed.

Let's take another example of building personality. The complex is 100-feet wide by 100-feet long and it has two solid core doors, one large window at the front of the building, and air conditioning.

Case #1: The complex is a credit union on a main street directly next to the local police department versus the same credit union on the edge of town.

Case #2: A large doctor's office. The doctor is an art buff and has half a million dollars in art in the office versus a doctor who has no art but has a small safe holding about $200 worth of Class A narcotics.

Case #3: A building housing a variety store that closes at 6 p.m. versus a liquor store that is open until 2 a.m.

In the three cases above, six examples are given of the personality of a complex. As stated, your recommendations must be tailored to fit the lifestyle and vulnerabilities of these buildings.[1]

SURVEY RESPONSIBILITY

In small offices already having a security program, the senior office responsible for security is usually either the treasurer, controller, head of administration, or the office manager.

In larger offices, where the security function necessarily covers a wider area and employs a staff whose sole function is security, there will usually be a security officer in charge of the operation. This person, in turn, will report to one of the company officers listed above.

As we have noted throughout this book, it is vital that the company officer having the ultimate responsibility for security be as highly placed as possible. Beyond the expression of management's commitment to security, a top-ranking executive to report to brings to the security task a broader base for evaluating decisions. The higher the executive, the greater the overview. If the executive security officer is to have the necessary access, the reporting level must be assigned to an executive having a company-wide overview, and one who regularly sits in on staff meetings with the chief executive officer.

Whether the executive security officer personally makes the survey on which planning is to be based, or whether an outside security consultant specializing in surveys is employed, depends upon the complexity and extent of the survey needed, and the time available to do such a job. Whatever the decision, the executive security officer must have the background and the special knowledge of your company necessary to evaluate the survey results and develop the best recommendations from it for your office security program.

THE SURVEY—GENERAL OUTLINE

If you hire a qualified consultant to conduct your security survey, your major decisions will be the degree to which the recommendations can or should be implemented. However, for your security evaluation, it would be wise to be familiar with the elements of a useful security survey in order to assess whether your consultant has adequately covered every base. On the other hand, if you plan to conduct the survey internally, the following outline will be equally helpful by enabling you to handle it in a systematic manner.

This survey guide is divided into three parts:

1. The building and parking area
2. Traffic within the complex
3. Departmental operations

Each part includes several areas that will require your attention. The extent to which you study each area will depend upon your potential for loss in that area and, therefore, your need to reduce that risk. As previously mentioned, the very small office will have fewer requirements, but as the office size increases the survey needs increase geometrically. If you have any doubts about the survey capabilities of your own personnel, or if you wish to be doubly reassured of their risk assessment, you would be well advised to call in a qualified security specialist.

THE BUILDING

Although most workers spend a third of their waking hours in the office, few of them are genuinely familiar with any part of the building other than their own work area. On the other hand, the thief who has picked your building as a target knows it well. He's gone over it from roof to basement to find all the security weaknesses. He may well be a professional in his business so you'd better be one in yours. You cannot afford to do less than a reasonably diligent thief would do in pursuit of his trade.

In evaluating your office space and the building in which it is located you must:

- Consider all building entrances and exits as security problems. This includes rooftop access, an important point frequently overlooked.
- Consider all building windows adjacent to, above, or below your windows, and other rooftops as security problems.
- Check all building receiving, shipping, basement, and lobby freight elevators and docks for accessibility (and the procedures followed in receiving and shipping).
- Check to determine if other tenants in your building have gate pass systems.
- Does your building have a properly supervised sign-in log for after-hours workers?
- Do elevators switch to manual or can floors be locked against access after normal business hours? When are they switched over? By whom can they be operated?
- Are there late night or early morning deliveries? (Often the case if there is a restaurant or employee cafeteria.)
- Who collects the trash? How and when is it removed from the building?
- Where are the fire hoses? What is their condition? How far into your office do they reach?
- Are there fire extinguishers in or near each of your offices? What type are they?
- Does the building have exterior fire escapes, enclosed fire stairs, or "smoke tower" firestairs? Can floors be reentered from the firestairs?
- In what direction do your firestair doors open? (While all codes appear to require that fire exits open out from the interior, a recent fire in New York City claimed the lives of several people trapped against a fire door that opened in, rather than out.)
- Are washrooms open to the public? Can a key system be arranged for tenant personnel? Are equipment rooms locked?

- Do firestairs open into the building lobby or outdoors? Can anyone exit unobserved by use of these stairs?
- Are hallways adequately lighted? What provision is made for emergency lighting?
- Is a master key system in use? Are issued keys cross-referenced? Have locks been changed when keys were lost? How are keys controlled and secured? (See Chapter 4, Key Control.)
- What type of alarms are used in the building—exit alarms, fire alarms, intrusion alarms?

These question checklists can be used to record the physical security of the office and building. The answers become a reference for future planning and a record that can be used to compare old locks, alarms, and doors to later installations.

THE TRAFFIC WITHIN A COMPLEX

A careful evaluation of traffic patterns within, to, and from your office is critical to establishing an effective security system. Depending on the type and volume of business your office does, this traffic can be very heavy or quite light in the course of a normal business day. You have no wish to reduce this traffic, but you probably should control or channel it. In any event you must be thoroughly familiar with it, its peak periods, who it consists of, and what its condition is at various times of the day. External traffic consisting of visitors, customers, vendors, servicepeople, messengers, and deliverymen will probably be of primary interest to you, but in the interest of personnel protection, as well as company security, you need to be familiar with established internal traffic as well.

External Traffic

- Who delivers the mail in the morning and at what time? What happens to empty mail sacks?
- If you or other tenants have a cafeteria, there will be night or early morning deliveries by a number of vendors. Who are they? What time do they arrive? How are they admitted? What equipment do they bring with them? Do they leave with the same equipment? Do they have access to other parts of your office or building? Are they inspected when they leave?
- Do you send records out for storage? How are they picked up? By whom? When? Is an inspection made of boxes picked up?
- Do you authorize certain people or organizations to sell or solicit contributions in your office? Who are these people? How do they carry material in? Are they inspected when they leave? Is their identification checked periodically?
- Who cleans the building and your offices? Are they given keys? Who is accountable for keys given cleaning personnel? Do they have access to master keys? Are cleaning personnel bonded?

- Who paints the building? How do they operate? Under whose supervision?
- What construction company does most of the interior work? How do they operate?
- Who are the servicepeople, the water cooler vendors, the machine maintenance repair personnel, the air conditioning people, the phone people, and the electricians? Are their tool cases inspected when they leave? How is their identification established? By the building? At the office? Are alarm company personnel allowed unlimited access?
- How is furniture moved in and out of the building? When is this done? What security is provided when moving occurs at night or on weekends?
- Do you or other tenants have substantial messenger traffic? Are messengers handled by a receptionist or other coordinating person? Or are they free to go directly to the person requesting or receiving the messenger service?
- How are job applicants handled? Is one person responsible for receiving all job applicants? Could someone posing as an applicant "case" or steal from your office?
- How are visitors received in your building? At the lobby? At the elevator? By your office receptionist? Are visitors met and escorted to your office? Are there precise, published instructions for handling all visitors?
- Which departments of the office (or which tenants) have the heaviest incoming traffic? What does this traffic consist of?
- Who uses the freight elevator? Does it operate automatically? Does it have an operator? When is it secured against operation? Does it open into your office space?
- Are people claiming official status, such as building inspector or fire inspector, permitted free access within your building or office or are they escorted? Are their IDs checked? By whom? Is there a policy for handling this type of visitor?

INTERNAL TRAFFIC

- Do building and office personnel use public stairs, firestairs, or elevators to go from floor to floor? Or only elevators?
- What comprises the heaviest traffic through your office or building? Where do they go? For what reason?
- Do you use messengers internally? Do they have access to offices that may be temporarily unoccupied? Are these messengers your employees?
- How is mail delivered throughout your office?
- Who is authorized to open your reception area doors in the morning? At what time? Who closes it at night? At what time? Who verifies this? What provision is made to ensure that this area is never unattended?
- Which floors have the heaviest traffic flow?
- If you have a cafeteria, who uses it besides your employees?
- Is office equipment moved from floor to floor or from office to office on the

same floor? Who authorizes such moves? Are office machines secured in place?

- Is someone selling drugs? (This should be seriously considered. Drugs are sold today in schoolyards and factories, and there isn't anything sacred about your office.)

An interesting point to keep in mind when making a security survey is the experience of the maintenance crew. Maintenance personnel (whether your own or the building's) have more firsthand knowledge about the personnel, building, and normal traffic than anyone else is apt to have. They are involved with every tenant and every department. They are aware of the movement of goods and materials into, through, and out of the premises, and probably hear as much behind-the-scenes gossip as any group in the building. They usually have keys to more areas than a tenant or office manager. Keep the maintenance people in mind when you evaluate your security needs; their cooperation can be a big help in your survey and in the security program itself.

WEEKEND TRAFFIC

It is essential to have a sign-in log—preferably in the lobby of the building but, failing that, at least on your own premises. Such a log will soon identify weekend traffic patterns. Authorized weekend workers normally prefer working on Saturdays, arriving around 10:00 a.m. and leaving by 3:00 p.m.

NIGHT TRAFFIC

There is necessarily a certain amount of traffic in every building after hours—cleaning, maintenance, elevator operators, watchmen, and alarm company servicemen, among others. Vendors also make deliveries in all buildings housing a cafeteria or restaurant.

The night traffic schedule should be analyzed, including a study of the sign-in log. A pattern will probably emerge from which you can predict events and possible nighttime trouble spots. Such records can be valuable in investigating crime in your building.

THE DEPARTMENT'S OPERATIONS

Each department within your organization should be evaluated separately in terms of its particular security risk. Consider each one from a potential loss viewpoint.

- What equipment can be stolen from the department?
- Are there any special problems relating to theft of personal belongings?

- Is the department function such that it is vulnerable to embezzlement?
- Can fraud or confidence routines be perpetrated against the department either from internal or external attack?
- Does the department have cash funds or negotiable instruments on hand—petty cash, customer accounts, or company safekeeping?
- Does the department house confidential records?
- Does the department house computer equipment and software?
- Does the department have attractive items in it, such as drugs and pharmaceuticals, jewelry samples, or valuable art?
- Does the department have heavy external traffic?
- Would a fire in this department cripple your operation? Is it near a fire hazard area?

VULNERABLE DEPARTMENTS

Discussed below are those office departments that are most exposed to crime. Also discussed are methods to evaluate their degree of vulnerability.

Personnel Department

- Can the department area be locked-off from the rest of the floor after hours?
- Are files kept locked when not in use?
- Who has the keys to doors and file cabinets? (Night access to the department can be tantamount to file access.)
- What systems are followed in the payroll department when adding new personnel? When terminating employees?
- What are the working relationships between the human resource and payroll departments?
- Does the department check applicants references? Are these checks done by letter, phone, or personal visit?

Security of personnel files are of extreme importance. Normally these files will contain information on every employee, past and present, from chairman of the board on down. This information is confidential and must be handled that way.

The Accounting Department

The accounting department has full functional supervision of your company's money and will almost always be the area most susceptible to major crime losses. Even through some protective systems undoubtedly are already in operation in this area, you will benefit from reexamination and reevaluation of the accounting operation's security procedures. For convenience, let's break it down into petty cash, accounts receivable, accounts payable, and company bank accounts.

Petty Cash, Cashier, and Check-Cashing

- How accessible is the cash operation to hallways, stairs, and elevators?
- Do posted signs clearly announce to everyone, including external traffic, where the cashier is located and what the operating hours are?
- Is cash on hand ever enough to tempt an employee to steal it? To attract an armed robbery?
- Has a study been made of the existing cash disbursement system to consider what constructive changes could be made in forms, controls, and audits?
- What procedures prevent the cashier from forging vouchers and pocketing the cash?
- Have you examined all the possibilities of collusion in the petty cash operation?
- If employees are paid in cash, or checks are cashed as a service to employees, is security provided equal to the risk?

Accounts Receivable

The accounts receivable section processes payments received. The most common fraud in this area consists of short-stopping these payments. In the event an account pays in cash, as when delivery is C.O.D., that payment is clearly subject to theft. More difficult, but nonetheless more common, is to destroy a billing record and cash the check. In evaluating this possibility you should:

- Consider billing procedures in accounts receivable, with particular attention paid to the forms used and the separate authorizations required.
- Try to determine how difficult it might be to cash a check payable to your company.
- Is it remotely possible for one or two people to destroy all records of billing while personally receiving and cashing incoming checks?
- Is it possible to alter invoices (and supporting documents, if any) to show a lesser amount payable? Or to destroy shipping receipts so that there is no billing?

Accounts Payable

This area is extremely susceptible to attack from within. The standard fraud is the phony invoice from a dummy corporation. A company check is mailed to a post office box or other drop, where it is collected by the embezzler or an accomplice. This fraud is difficult but not impossible to detect in a computerized operation, since payments are authorized by individuals.

- Reexamine the forms and the system of checks and balances on a careful step-by-step basis.
- Do you check the authenticity of new accounts? Are all receivers double-checked against their authorizing vouchers?

Payroll

Along with accounts payable this area has most often been attacked in today's office. The usual method has been to insert a fictitious name into payroll records and collect checks drawn for that employee. It is important here to review the entire procedure of making up the payroll, drawing checks, and distributing them.

- What are the procedures for introducing a new employee into the payroll system?
- Are there corresponding records in personnel and payroll that are cross-checked to verify employment?
- Is it possible to conceal fictitious employees by collusion between an employee in payroll and one in personnel?

Company Bank Accounts

- Can one person transfer unlimited company funds?
- Is there a ceiling which limits withdrawal of company funds?
- What instructions have been given to the bank? By whom?
- Are two signatures necessary for large single withdrawals or transfers? Can either or both be machine-written? Who controls the signature blocks?
- Who audits the company bank accounts? How often?
- Could the treasurer or controller suddenly disappear with all the money in your company's bank accounts?

If this last question is annoying, keep in mind that desire and opportunity comprise all the conditions necessary for embezzlement. If your financial officer could, in a moment of weakness she might. It is your responsibility to protect your company, but it is also axiomatic that no one person should bear the temptation of having all the company's funds at his or her disposal.

The Data Processing Department

- Check all your financial programs and determine if adequate audit procedures are used in conjunction with such programs.
- Check on the manner in which printouts of secret or confidential information are handled.
- Are there duplicate tapes or diskettes? Where are they stored? Are they up-to-date?
- Who can enter the computer operations center? Where can they go within the center? Can messengers enter the computer room?
- What are the fire prevention and fire protection procedures in the center? What training do employees receive in fire prevention, location of hoses and fire extinguishers, and fire extinguishing systems?

- How well can the computer area be physically secured against attack? Against unauthorized data acquisition or operating program access?
- Check all entrances to computer areas, including tape storage areas. Who has authorized keys, combinations, or other means of access? When was the list of authorizations last audited? Who has access after-hours and how is this recorded?
- Do you have a fail-safe indicator of actual computer use and a concurrent log of authorized use? Are these lists cross-checked?
- Re-study your program accessing controls.

Purchasing

In considering the purchasing function we will confine ourselves to the purchase of material for the office itself, such as supplies, equipment, furniture decorating, cleaning contracts, and the full range of business services from car leasing to computer maintenance. We are not concerned with the more sophisticated buyer of raw goods and materials in a fabricating operation, which presents somewhat similar problems with considerably more complex possibilities.

In today's office, the buyer of office materials is frequently the office manager, the service manager, or the administrative manager. Whatever the title, this person is frequently responsible for a number of areas in addition to the purchasing function. In larger offices, especially in highly volatile businesses, the volume of purchasing is usually such that a position or even a department is established to perform these duties.

Purchasing agents are faced with every possible temptation. If they are responsible for any appreciable volume of business, they will be catered to by unscrupulous vendors. Besides excessive entertainment, temptations in the form of kickbacks, trips to Europe, and other inducements are regularly offered by vendors seeking an advantage. While this is not a matter that should directly involve security, security may be called upon to investigate unexplained affluence. Certainly, purchasing should be carefully administered and management should be constantly aware of the potential for abuse.

There are areas in purchasing that must be evaluated from a security standpoint:

- Study the possibility of fraudulent invoices. This ruse is the same in purchasing as it is in accounts payable or payroll. What audit procedures check authenticity of vendors and receipts? How frequently?
- Can a system of competitive bids be established for all major office purchases?
- Check out forms used: authorizations to purchase, authorizations to pay, delivery receipts. Can copies be destroyed or altered without detection?
- How often do you inventory and audit office equipment, furniture, supplies, or other physical assets? Are there unexplained shortages?
- Selling is often a part of the purchasing function. Who negotiates for the sale

of wastepaper or other recyclables from your office? Do you verify the actual amount carted out? How are used furnishings or equipment sold or traded? How are they removed from the premises? What records are kept on the sale or trading of such material? Is the system audited?

Miscellaneous

- What guards against theft of stamps? Unauthorized use of the postage meter or theft of funds allocated to postage? What records do you keep of postage meter usage? Can it be cross-checked?
- What system do you use to control office supplies? Do you have a requisition form? Declining inventory? Sign-out record?
- Since certain documents may not be reproduced on your office copying machine, either for legal reasons or because of company policy, have you posted a list of these proscribed documents and company policy at the copying machine?
- If you have a large graphics department with platemakers and offset presses, have you taken steps to prevent its possible use for counterfeiting money or documents, or photographing confidential company documents?
- Do you exercise control over availability of all forms that can order merchandise, verify receipt of merchandise, or authorize payment in any way? Are these forms always numbered and their sequence maintained?

And More

This brief tour through areas of your office where you may be particularly vulnerable should serve as a guide to your own all-important survey. We cannot include, or even identify, every sensitive spot in your organization; only you can do that—by painstaking point-by-point inspection and consideration.

SET UP YOUR SECURITY FILES

As a result of your evaluation you now have records describing doors, windows, trouble spots, and other parts of the building. You have a description of both internal and external traffic. You have a thorough breakdown on the operations of each department. This should be a useful profile of the company's daily activities.

But don't stop there. To be effective these records must be accurate, reviewed, and updated on a regular basis. You should also subscribe to the latest information on drugs and drug distribution, demonstrations, criminal methods, arson and bomb threats, con games, and fire prevention and safety. You should develop a library of texts and files for relevant articles from newspapers and magazines.

In short, you must develop as much data as possible on crime as does, or might, relate to your office in order to keep up even with the ever more sophisticated crook.

As you accumulate these files they will become increasingly useful in your security operation. You will be able to determine and prepare for many kinds of assaults on your office, many of which are preventable if you have the proper data, for example:

- You will be able to predict which days and seasons will be the busiest for the security operation.
- You will soon see what areas attract the most criminal attention, and are therefore the greatest risk.
- You will have an overview of the type and number of crimes occurring.
- You will be forewarned by emerging patterns of crimes against personnel on payday, or the holiday weekends that seem to be most attractive to criminals, or the internal patterns which predict (or, perhaps, encourage) criminal activity.

The careful and thoughtful use of the data obtained is not only helpful in your defense against crime in the office, it is essential if you are to have any hope of success.

ENDNOTE

1. Lawrence J. Fennelly, *Handbook of Loss Prevention and Crime Prevention, Second Edition,* (Stoneham, Mass.: Butterworth-Heinemann, 1989), Chapter 4.

Chapter 18

Equipment for Security

As the crime rate and crime losses rise, so does the development of equipment for security applications. Almost daily we are offered new and more sophisticated devices to prevent or detect criminal activity. A similar but slower equipment explosion is occurring in the fire protection field. A dazzling array of equipment is spread before us, much of which if properly used and supported, could be invaluable in our security programs. But the essentials are the selection of the right equipment, its proper application, and its intelligent use and support.

TIMING IN EQUIPMENT SELECTION

Security equipment and fire prevention and detection devices installed in a five-year-old building are five years too late, since this equipment should have been included in the original plans and incorporated into the construction of the building. Not only does post-construction installation cost considerably more, but these costs may be prohibitive. Buildings on the drawing board or even under construction today should include provisions for fire and security equipment to specifications developed in consultations with *independent* (non-vendor) experts from the security and fire protection fields.

If necessary, walls, fences, gates, lights, locks, card access control, closed-circuit TV, and mirrors can be installed during construction and even during normal working hours. More and more prestigious high-rise buildings are incorporating proprietary central reception areas for fire and intrusion alarms throughout the building, as well as central closed-circuit TV surveillance of key areas.

FOLLOW-UP

Once equipment has been installed, tested, and in operation, it is important to ensure that it continues to work properly. Checking equipment requires physical inspections, regular maintenance, trouble reports, proper use, and on-going tests according to a prearranged schedule. Where equipment affects employees, their reaction to the equipment is important. Remember, every security point or zone must be completely checked and verified before signing off.

INNOVATE

Do not hesitate to be innovative in equipment usage. Professional thieves are familiar with many common hardware solutions and, unless you surprise them, they may evade or overcome your equipment.

Think for a moment of the suburban office building, the kind of commercial structure seen often outside of major cities. It's usually a low glass-and-steel structure surrounded by expertly contoured landscaping. The beautifully planted and meticulously cared-for grounds seem more suited to a country club or university setting than an office building. Hedges and trees outline the property and at night the lights accent the beauty of the surroundings. To the passing motorist it is a lovely scene. Thieves may or may not find it attractive. The hedges and trees may conceal a fence or a trip-wire alarm. At any rate, their vision will be substantially reduced by the glare barrier of lights while the inside security man have a clear view of the building's perimeter. But are the lights, fence, and pressure wire alarm useful only in applications such as this? Of course not. They are part of the security equipment arsenal and can be used wherever and however an imaginative security professional wishes.

Consider your own location. Wouldn't illuminating rooftops next to your building or the space between your building and your neighbors' eliminate the shadows so convenient for a thief? And suppose that chain-link fence was installed inside, floor to ceiling to encase the supply room or highly pilferable merchandise, and locked and alarmed? The trip-wire alarm stretched across a key office area at night is an effective alarm defense against the burglar who hides-in or evades the alarms on doors and windows.

The more unorthodox you are in the selection and placement of protective equipment, the more difficult you make it for the thief. On the other hand, equipment without competent personnel operating it is, of course, virtually useless. Innovation requires an above-average knowledge of equipment, its normal applications, and its special vulnerabilities.

THE EQUIPPED BUILDING

Imagine an office building equipped throughout with the latest and best security equipment. At night every door, except the main entrance, is doubly dead-locked, and checked periodically by guards. The main entrance is bathed in light. All the building's locks are highly pick-resistant. The interior corridors are "mined" with pressure-sensitive alarms. Hidden closed-circuit television cameras are scattered throughout. Most interior doors are locked. Consider, then, how all these devices were defeated in one masterful stroke by the thief who came into the building before closing time, and hid in a room closet where the company safe was located. That night his only obstacle was the unalarmed safe itself. He evaded all the other defenses. The next morning he strolled out of the office with his loot as the building prepared to begin another day. (This is an actual story of a crime committed against a major corporation's home office.)

In a comparable case, a New York firm placed expensive locks on the doors entering from the firestairs after a rash of office machinery thefts. The locks permitted exit to the stairwell from the inside office space, but once the door closed it locked behind you; there was no place to go except to leave the building. This was very effective in eliminating floor-to-floor movement except by elevator.

For a while, the thefts stopped, but then they started up again. Management could not fathom how the thefts were being perpetrated. Close observation revealed that the employees on the second and third floors preferred to walk down to the street level at lunch and quitting time—it was faster than waiting for the crowded elevators. The thieves caught on to this. They waited in the stairwell and, when employees opened the door from the interior, these well-dressed gentlemen thanked them and entered the office. After selecting a machine, they left by the same stairs.

The moral of both of these stories is that good security equipment alone is not the solution. In both cases a system was needed. In the first case, what was needed was a practice of checking all spaces before locking them for the night; in the second, an employee trained not to permit entry from the stairs would have balked at admitting strangers, however polite. Both are simple security systems that were overlooked. Many buildings have "traffic" alarms and closed-circuit TV observing the lower portions of stairwells. Such an arrangement would have spotted these thieves.

THE "PAPER WALL"

In today's modern office building, many private offices have metal doors with a three-hour "A" fire rating. Such a rating means the door will hold up against the pressures and temperatures of fire for approximately three hours. This door, fitted with tamper-resistant hinges and a reasonably pick-resistant deadlock with a one-inch bolt, would certainly stump any amateur bent upon forced entry, and might hold off a professional. Of course, if the attacker happens to be carrying a chisel, he could simply cut through the wall beside the door; it takes little effort to penetrate the type of wall construction found in today's office. To regard the expense of the door as wasted is to forget that the door is designed for fire-resistance, not security. No equipment can be totally effective so long as a weak link exists in the security chain.

FENCES

The majority of perimeter fences installed today are of the chain link type. By themselves, they can only prevent people from straying onto the property. Obviously, anyone intent on climbing the fence can do so. Installing supporting devices such as perimeter alarms and increased lighting will improve the security of the grounds, provided the fence is in good condition. Fences with holes, or those that can be pried up, simply are no fences at all.

METAL GATES

The accordion-type gate (and, less often, the roll-down grille) is used to protect storefronts, though it is seldom used to secure office building entrances where smash-and-grab attacks are much rarer. A freight entrance, on the other hand, may very well need such a device. These gates should have top and bottom slide tracks and be locked with a strong pick- and force-resistant lock; the hinge pins should be non-removable. Roll-down steel doors can be even more effectively secured, but if the freight entrance is not overlooked or frequently patrolled, it might be adequate to simply alarm the freight area at night and on holidays.

LIGHTING

The parking area and all entrance points should be well-lighted, especially rear and side alley doors. Shrubbery should be kept low and well-illuminated, so as not to conceal muggers and thieves. (For technical information on external lighting you should contact the Illuminating Engineering Society, which publishes the *American Standard Practice for Protective Lighting*.)

DOORS

Of the various types of doors, steel and solid-core wooden doors offer the greatest protection against forced entry. Unless lined with sheet metal, hollow-core doors are not recommended. Doors having glass panels should not be used in side or rear building entrances, where they can be quietly attacked. When doors with glass are used, they should be fitted with locks that are "keyed both sides," to use locksmith jargon; that is, doors that cannot be opened by breaking the glass, reaching in and operating a handle or a thumbturn.

While glass doors are often used at entrance locations, they are rarely broken to gain entry. Exterior door hinges on steel exit doors (which are necessarily exposed) should be nonremovable and preferably should not yield even when sawed. Where door frames are weak, as is true for glass door aluminum frames, special long-bolt, pry-resistant locks and cylinder guards should be used.

Overhead doors should be solid and the interior bolts secured with padlocks. Remember, the thief is as interested, or more interested, in an unhampered rapid exit as he is in getting into your building. Where elevators cannot be secured from operation, a second door requiring a key should be installed at the floor to be safeguarded against easy access.

Fire tower and firestair doors should be fitted with panic bars. These panic devices can sound an alarm when triggered and are used where fire doors are not to be opened except in a genuine emergency. If your firestairs are used as a convenience by personnel, door or stairwell alarms which can be activated at night and turned off during the day would be more appropriate.

WINDOWS

All ground floor windows should be secured with alarms, bars, or expanded steel mesh that cannot be removed with ordinary tools. Ground windows on an alleyway or in the rear of the building should be fitted with barrier protection and alarmed.

Windows opening onto fire escapes and rooftops should be considered emergency exits and should not be key-locked. Alarms should be installed in such windows. Air conditioners set into accessible windows should also be alarmed, since removing the unit creates access. Transoms are not features of newer buildings with central air conditioning, but where they do exist in older buildings they are a danger and should be permanently sealed.

Don't overlook other openings in the perimeter of the building which could pose security problems. Any opening greater than 64 square inches should be protected by grilles or bars. These openings include air and water intakes, exhaust tunnels, heating ducts, and culverts. Check all manholes within the area to see if they're a means of entering the building. These tunnels might require fences or alarms. Sidewalk elevator doors should be securely padlocked from the basement.

LOCKS

Lights burn electricity, personnel require salaries, dogs must be fed, and most equipment has maintenance expense, but once purchased, heavy-duty locks seldom require costly maintenance. Locks are by far the cheapest security investment you can make, and yet in an effort to save even more money, companies often buy—and architects even more often accept—cheap locks. This is sometimes justified by that tired old saw, "any lock can be picked by a pro." This is essentially true, but a top-quality six- or seven-pin lock cylinder can gain you time by stalling even a pro. (If surreptitious entry might be a problem, choose pick-resistant cylinders for critical doors.) Don't save pennies on locks; most attacks are direct jimmying efforts. The lock you buy should be top quality, deadlocking, and have at least a one-inch bolt. Locking hardware is usually a one-time expense and it could return your investment many times over.

The relative security factor of any locking device is measured in time; the purpose of the lock is to delay unauthorized access to an area or a container. Most locks (but not all) will buy you time, but they are simply delaying devices and should never be considered to be more than that. Of course, if the door is secured by a latch that can be pushed back (that is, nondeadlocking), there's little point in even closing the door.

In order to get the best protection from a lock, be sure that it is rated with a high resistance to jimmying, picking, and cylinder-pulling.

PADLOCKS

Padlocks should be case hardened and strong enough to resist prying. The shackle should be close enough to the body to prevent the insertion of a tool to force it. Lock cylinder inserts should have no less than five pins if they are to be used for security purposes. Padlocks should never be left unlocked because of the risk of substitution.

It is important to remember that the hasps or locking bar may be attacked to avoid the necessity of forcing the padlock; therefore, all the padlock hardware should be of hardened steel. The locking bar should have no external rivets and should be bolted through the door to the inside and through a backing plate with the bolt ends burred over.

SPECIAL DOOR LOCKS

Beside the standard door locks there are some which have special interest for security:

- Lock cylinder with multiple angled pins—operated by a nonreproducible key with indentations or varying angle cuts.
- Pushbutton—no key required, combination readily changed.
- Electronic locks—with computer links, record entrance and exit times of visitors. They are not highly secure unless alarmed, but offer other advantages such as code operation, rapid access, and remote operation.

Door lock cylinders should have beveled guards making it impossible to pull the cylinders out of the door. All locks should be of the deadbolt type, and spring latches without the deadlocking feature should never be used.

If your office has substantial personnel turnover, you may be faced with the need to change locks frequently. Obviously, you will make every effort to retrieve issued keys, but this is not always possible. In any event, most keys can be readily copied. You can be faced with the risk of having a key floating beyond your control and the cost involved in changing all locks the missing key opens. You may find that it will be cheaper in the long run to install removable-core locks or pushbutton combination locks. Code combinations can be changed almost instantly with any change of personnel or policy.

In reception areas, where doors are kept locked primarily to thwart unwelcome visitors, a remote control "electronic lock" is normally the most effective solution. With such a system, the receptionist can open a door by pressing a desk button.

Most pushbutton-operated "electronic locks" are actually standard locks released by activating an electric strike in the jamb of the door. Many of these strikes can be tampered with, and are only secure if electronically monitored to be certain the lock bolt is in the strike and the strike is in the closed position.

SAFES

If you occupy space in a building on more than one floor, your safe should be located as far from the core of the building as possible; force a thief to take greater risks to get to your cash. Remember, fire safes can be easily entered by burglars while burglary-resistant safes cannot protect your records against fire. Your best option is a fire-resistant vault containing a burglary-resistant safe.

KEYS

Key issuance and control should be the responsibility of your office security operation. This vital responsibility is frequently handled in a surprisingly off-handed manner and yet the potential losses resulting from key misuse are overwhelming.

In the dos and don'ts of key control you'll find a preponderance of don'ts, so we'll start with a few dos.

- *Do* keep your key cabinet and record files in order, current and cross-referenced. *Do* secure your key cabinet with a dial combination lock.
- *Do* make a visual inventory of all keys on hand or in the hands of employees from time to time. You'll not only find keys have been lost, but also keys that are not authorized to the holder.
- *Do* review your list of authorized keyholders regularly.
- *Don't* issue keys to anyone unless they absolutely must have one. For temporary access, have a keyholder or security professional admit them.
- *Don't* carelessly leave your keys lying around during the day; warn all keyholders against this. *Don't* leave your office keys in your car when parking at restaurants. (They are likely to make an impression on someone who is waiting for the opportunity to make an impression of them.) Professional thieves can identify the use of every key you have; to them keys are as readable as a book—especially master keys.

- *Don't* forget to change the key cylinder when an authorized key holder is discharged for cause.
- *Don't* use anything but highly pick-resistant key cylinders where surreptitious entry is a particular risk. Unfortunately, these cylinders are quite expensive to buy and replace.

PAPER SHREDDERS

There is a full line of paper shredders on the market today, ranging from wastebasket size to large industrial types. In the office they can be purchased and deployed according to need. A chief executive's secretary should make it a habit to use one constantly in place of a standard wastebasket. A centralized duplicating department could pass all day-end confidential waste paper through a large shredder. Smaller shredders should be placed beside decentralized copiers. Departments such as research, sales, advertising, personnel, and engineering, to name a few, should have shredders. Shred these documents before you recycle or dispose of them:

- personnel records and files
- insurance forms and reports
- marketing and sales data
- financial printouts
- blueprints and designs
- production schedules
- bills of material
- purchasing printouts
- vendor lists
- obsolete forms such as old checks and purchase orders

Remember, the Supreme Court has ruled that information in your trash is fair game to anyone, but privacy laws make you vulnerable to lawsuits when personnel records are disclosed to outsiders—even by accident.

MIRRORS

The threat of an attacker lurking around the next corner or out of sight in the elevator can be very real and a source of considerable anxiety to employees working late or on weekends. A mirror facing the turn of the corridor and other blind corners would alleviate this situation. These inexpensive reflectors pay off in increased protection for your workers. Additionally, they avert collisions where mail carts, hand trucks, and coffee carts are used. Mirrors can also be used in reception areas where one staff member can see a relatively large area while operating a switchboard.

SIGNS

Since office security is basically defensive in nature, we are constantly trying to prevent attacks from without. With that thought in mind we busily go about the task of creating traps and heavily fortified barriers to capture or deter thieves. If you consider the real function of office security, you realize you neither want to apprehend nor frighten away thieves—you simply want no part of them.

Having created a balance of power and perhaps a deterrent force, your next step is to make it public. Create and install signs that tell your adversaries, the thieves, that you have the means and determination to capture and prosecute them.

A word about signs. If you do put up informative security signs, keep them clean and, if possible, well-illuminated. All too often we have seen such burned-out signs caked with dust. A natural reaction to a well-kept security sign is that the company must have a well-organized security program. Put the signs where they will be read and have them say something forceful. They're not often put in expensive executive suites, reception areas, or even in the company cafeteria. But there are many places for them—by elevators and firestairs, on the back of doors, in loading docks, on perimeter fences and entrance gates.

LOCK-DOWN DEVICES FOR OFFICE EQUIPMENT

In an office having only a few computers, fax machines, typewriters, and calculators, it is definitely worthwhile locking those machines to the desk or the stand they are used on.

In larger organizations the problem takes on a different dimension. The cost of bolting down every machine is considerable and, in those cases where a machine is bolted to a desk or table, the mobility of the machine is decreased. On the other hand, experience has shown that where machines have been secured with lock-down devices, equipment theft has been drastically reduced and, in some cases, halted altogether.

Your job is to evaluate your current rate and risk of loss compared to the costs involved in securing the equipment. You may find that it's not worth the expense. But if it's close, or if certain equipment is more exposed to theft, then do it and eliminate one more lure for the criminal.

Inventory all office equipment, listing model and serial numbers. Consider advising your insurance company about any equipment that is bolted down. Premium rebates may be available.

TELEPHONES AND SCANNERS

Car phones and portable phones in coat pockets are common pieces of equipment. You should advise administrators that they can be monitored by individuals with the proper radio scanners. Corporate secrets can be easily lost by such forms of communication. Scanners can be modified to pick up ultra-high frequencies. A book like *Scanner Master* that lists your company's radio frequencies can be purchased for about $25.

FAX MACHINES

These machines transmit memos and confidential letters. Such letters may hang around and be read by unauthorized personnel. If you receive obscene faxes, the perpetrator can be caught by notifying your telephone company and having a trap placed on the fax number.

CLOSED-CIRCUIT TELEVISION

These cameras are usually hooked up to a monitor and a time-lapsed recorder that allows cassette playback. Cameras are generally placed in corridors, entrances and exits, parking lots, and sensitive areas.

FIRE AND INTRUSION ALARMS

Each of these alarms requires a response when they go off. All phone numbers for police, fire, management, and service companies must be listed. If a central station is monitoring your systems, they will provide notification. A policy and procedure for each emergency must be drafted and put into effect.

THE PSYCHOLOGY OF ALARMS
AND CLOSED-CIRCUIT TELEVISION

Office security is essentially a defensive operation, not primarily the detection and apprehension of criminals. True, it is important to root out the bad seeds in the organization, but security's real mission is to prevent the loss of company assets.

Since defense is the assignment, make every effort to keep intruders out of the office. Fit perimeter windows and doors with alarms that at least make loud, unpleasant sounds which frighten away all but the most dedicated criminal. Internally, take a different approach—use silent alarms that report to a central station or panel located where they will be seen by security personnel. If a burglar has entered the office, he may already have his loot by the time he trips an alarm. A loud alarm would send him running with company property. Although your role is not primarily apprehension, if an intruder manages to make it into the building, it is preferable to catch him before he starts making a habit of robbing you. Nevertheless, consider installing an audible local alarm (supported by central station or other remote back-up) installed at the exterior perimeter of the building or office to scare off intruders.

CONCLUSION

New, improved, and more sophisticated equipment is being manufactured and marketed each day. Deciding what is useful and where it might be employed in your company is a continuing function of office security. From time to time equipment will fail due to inadequate maintenance or accidents, raising the question of whether or not back-up equipment is needed. Many security people feel that it is difficult enough to justify basic equipment without endangering such proposals by including backups. In most normal offices, we agree. We think security must first show that it can walk before it attempts to run. If, by installing equipment, savings are realized by reduced losses, then perhaps back-up equipment expenditures can be justified. Even so, where company security personnel are employed, backups should not be necessary. Instead, security personnel should be deployed until the equipment is functioning again. Manpower should be as capable as the equipment it uses.

Finally, equipment can be best and most economically installed when a building is being constructed. If you are ever involved with new building construction, then that is the time to go for broke. You will never have a better opportunity to install proper security measures. Above all, remember to take special pains with your computer area, reinforcing walls, floors, and ceilings. You may one day sublease the floor above or below to a potential bomb blast victim, or your company itself could be the intended target.

Chapter 19

The Security Operation

With the results of your security survey in hand, you should have a thorough overview of your security problems and be able to identify most of the soft spots in your defense system.

You may be pleasantly surprised to discover that your physical and procedural defenses are already strong and that you need to install only a few new systems. But that probably won't be the case. If your concern is like most offices and office buildings, and if the survey has been carefully done, you are almost certain to have discovered that several new programs will be needed to achieve any real level of security. If this is the case, you have basic decisions to make.

IMPLEMENTATION METHODS

First you must decide whether to implement your entire security program or reformation at one time, over a short period of time, or whether you will set up systems, step-by-step, on a predetermined priority schedule.

THE GRADUAL APPROACH

The step-by-step approach is still the most widely used method of installing or upgrading a security program. It has its advantages. It allows you to get into programs on the installment plan, so to speak. You pick the trouble spot, develop your protective system for that problem, and implement it. In this way you can buy your systems one at a time. The initial costs are less, you can concentrate on the particular system, and you can devote more of your efforts to making the system operate smoothly.

On the other hand, this step-by-step approach has obvious flaws. It is essentially a reactive approach. It wards off criminal threats as they occur, or as you believe they will occur, guessing where the greatest dangers lie. If you are wrong, you may incur a catastrophic loss from an unexpected direction.

Another flaw inherent in the step-by-step method is management's waning interest in the security problem once the major hot spots have been cooled. It is a common management reaction to say "Why fix the roof when it's not raining?" This apathy frequently appears when the initial results of the first security systems were very successful. In these cases, a satisfied management team has frequently failed to support the installation of further systems, leaving the organization in some ways even more vulnerable than before because of the false sense of security generated by the partial success. Security personnel for such organizations, continuously frustrated in their efforts to fulfill their professional responsibility, often lose interest in their jobs. It is almost impossible to remain vigorous and creative in administering the security needs of a company that is plainly indifferent to security.

THE TOTAL APPROACH

The implementation of a complete security system—a total apparatus—on a short-term schedule is therefore the best way to move under most circumstances. Your decision, however, must consider the following:

- Total cost of the entire program.
- Availability of such sums.
- The existing degree of risks versus the cost of corrective measures to eliminate or reduce specific risks.
- A firm commitment from management.

The major problem in installing a total security system (assuming it is economically sensible and feasible) is that the administrative load in the early months of the system's development and implementation can be very heavy indeed. However, this difficulty can be largely overcome with proper planning.

Discussed on the following pages are some elementary systems used in office security today. Every security-conscious office has systems of its own making that work for that particular business, or in that particular place under its particular circumstances. You, too, will develop systems that suit your own needs; however, there are a few basic systems, like access, the most significant area in crime control, that should be incorporated into every security program.

Every organization, large or small, must have systems to control traffic into or within its building and/or office. This necessarily includes control over the movement of equipment or supplies, both for crime prevention and for after-the-fact crime detection.

KEY TO ENFORCEMENT SUCCESS

Before discussing these basic systems, let's once again emphasize the importance of vigorous management of each aspect of the security program. If, for example, five doors led into your office and one of them was regularly left unlocked and unattended, whatever you did with the other four doors would be irrelevant. You could lock them, alarm them, watch them via closed-circuit television cameras, and it would all be wasted effort as long as the other entrance was open; one entrance is all a thief needs.

Systems also must be maintained. If your security people fail to enforce sign-in and sign-out procedures or if they don't check passes for packages and boxes then you have no security for company property; an unenforced system is a useless system.

It is the security administrator's responsibility to see that systems are adhered to, and that security personnel carry out their responsibilities with due diligence. If you let up, then your people will let up, and their performance will soon become perfunctory and mechanical. This is the death-knell of any system. In fact, it's worse than death, because behind the illusion of security this indifference invites the thief to circumvent the minute degree of security remaining.

BASIC SYSTEMS

The following are basic systems in any security operation.

Building Package and Access Pass System

All office buildings should employ this system, but unfortunately many plead limited funds and do not implement this integral part of access control. Where it is used, it has proven highly effective in reducing office equipment theft. A properly administered pass system will go a long way toward defending against intruders and reducing the shrinkage in company property.

Policy

Before or after normal working hours or on weekends, visitors, vendors, and servicemen should not be allowed to enter a building without an authorizing building pass. No one, regardless of rank, should be permitted to leave the building with packages, boxes, or equipment without surrendering a pass describing the items and authorizing their removal.

Method

A list of tenant and company personnel authorized to issue access and package passes should be available in the security center. A specimen of each authorized signature, in alphabetical order, should be provided to building management guards at entrance checkpoints. The distribution of blank passes to these authorized persons should be controlled by office security, and a log used to record this distribution. Used passes should not be returned to the authorizing office, but instead held by security for comparison when questions arise. Employing a two-part consecutively numbered form protects the integrity of the system in the event a pass is not surrendered or is unused. Test transactions should be made periodically to verify the effective application of the system by entrance guards. Updating lists of authorizing personnel regularly is also essential.

Policy

Building and tenant employees, and emergency servicepeople (alarm service personnel, particularly) should be required to sign an entrance log when entering or leaving the building before or after normal working hours, including weekends and holidays. Periodic checks should be made with tenants and supervisors to verify their knowledge of the employees' and visitors' entries.

Method

The log should be placed in the lobby of the building at 6:00 p.m. and removed the following morning at 8:00 a.m. A uniformed guard or elevator operator must always be on duty to receive off-hours traffic, and witness the signing in and out of such individuals. All elevators should be taken off automatic, and the remaining elevator operated manually by the lobby attendant or a second employee. If secured firestairs restrict floor-to-floor movement to the elevator, visitors' access will be restricted to the floor they sign in to visit.

IDENTIFICATION CARD SYSTEM

In larger organizations and/or where security problems are prevalent, an identification card system can be employed. This system is far superior to the sign in/out log system alone. There are many kinds of ID cards. Some carry only the owner's name, affiliation, and signature, while others incorporate a photograph laminated into the card. If the card is properly designed, it will be difficult to alter undetectably. Taking photo ID's and maintaining a file of photographs is a highly effective system.

When integrating your identification card system with an automated encoded card-access system, you have implemented a huge labor saving device. Machine readable ID cards record not only entrances but also control access to internal restricted areas. Further secondary values are realized such as clocking employees in and out for payroll purposes, and recording the names and times of those entering an unattended doorway. Individuals joining or leaving the company can be immediately added to or deleted from automatic systems, whether or not the access card is surrendered upon termination. This has particular value for an office having a high turnover rate and irregular hours—the system is extremely flexible and easily up-dated.

Don't be confused by the numerous types of access-control technologies available. The encoding methods all provide the same function, which is to send a message to your computer to allow some action to occur. The types of card encoding technologies available are listed below, but we suggest that you engage a security consultant to help determine which system best suits your specific needs.

Access-Card Control Systems[1]

Time and technology have increased the sophistication of access-control systems. Today's popular systems are microprocessor-based; the majority use a variety of encoding techniques on an access-control card about the size of a standard credit card. All systems do not take the same size card—there is little interchangeability where the different encoding methods are concerned. This is also true of card readers. While one card may be used in several variations of a card reader, there is little commonality among readers.

In a typical access-card system, the individual inserts a card in a card reader at a controlled location. The sensor extracts information from the card and the reader translates that information into a code number which is then sent to the system's local processing unit or remote terminal unit (RTU). The number is compared with the user's programmed access criteria and either grants or denies entry. In the latter case, an alarm may or may not sound, depending upon the system. There may also be a printed record of each alarm or, if desired, a recording of each access granted by the system for a permanent history of individual card activity.

Magnetic Strip Cards

Of the variety of magnetic cards available, probably the most popular are magnetic strip cards that are similar to typical credit cards. They can be used in a card reader that is relatively inexpensive and has few or no moving parts. With this type of card a digital data pattern is encoded on the magnetic strip. When the card is withdrawn from the reader, it moves across a magnetic head, similar to a tape recorder head, that reads the data and sends it to the system RTU for verification. If entry at that point is validated for that time, the RTU sends a signal to release the door.

These cards are relatively inexpensive, and an exceptionally large amount of data can be stored on the magnetic strip as compared to other types of cards. The cards can be made of standard vinyl plastic; however, they tend to chip and break with prolonged use. The magnetic strip on this card will usually be a single-layer, three-track, high coercivity, American Banking Association standard track two encoding.

A superior medium for the magnetic strip card is a Mylar/polyester core material that maintains its properties and flexibility over temperatures ranging from -50°F to over 350°F without cracking or breaking. Mylar cards are also available with a single layer high-coercivity strip of 4,000 Oersteds and a Teflon coating to protect the magnetic strip from flaking or wear. Also available is an insert that is pre-diecut with a recessed aperture in the top layer of the dual My-lar center core. This allows for consistent registration of miscellaneous bits of information on each card. Mylar cards are only slightly more expensive, but have an active life more than ten times greater than the standard plastic card. It also causes fewer malfunctions. For long-term applications this type of card is highly recommended.

MAGNETIC DOT CARDS

In magnetic dot cards, very small dots or pieces of magnetic material, often barium ferrite, are laminated between plastic layers. These dots are positively or negatively charged in a variety of configurations. When the card is inserted into the reader, internal sensors are activated by the magnetically encoded areas on the card.

Disadvantages of this type of card include its vulnerability to deciphering, vandalism, and wear and tear. A major factor in the selection of the magnetic dot card might be lower cost, but it is still more expensive than the standard magnetic strip card. This type of card and reader are less durable than others and may require more frequent replacement.

WEIGAND CARDS

Weigand effect access-control cards, also known as embedded-wire cards, use a coded pattern on the magnetized wire within the card to generate a code number. When the card is passed through a slot containing a sensing device, the wire pattern is retrieved and forwarded to the reader for decoding.

The reader technology makes it less vulnerable to weather and vandalism than readers with more conventional slots. The cards are moderately priced and can contain a modest amount of information. A major drawback is wear and tear on the card as it passes through the tracklike slot. The card must also be properly oriented when it is passed through the slot to achieve a correct reading. Weigand cards can effectively handle large volumes of traffic during opening and closing time surges of card reader activity.

Proximity Cards

Proximity card readers work on the basis of a number of passively tuned circuits that have been embedded in a high-grade fiberglass-epoxy card. To gain access, the cardbearer holds it within 2–4 inches of a concealed device that senses the pattern of the resonant frequencies contained in the card. This pattern is then transmitted to a remote card reader that deciphers the pattern and unlocks the door.

A major asset of the proximity system is the durability of the sensing element. It is encased in a weatherproof, vandal-proof, dust-proof, and shock-resistant enclosure. The sensing element can be concealed within walls, mounted behind glass, or simply attached to a surface, providing considerable installation flexibility and higher sensor security.

Since the cards can be read through most materials, they do not generally need to be removed from a pocket or purse for the cardholder to gain entry. A primary disadvantage of the proximity card system is higher cost.

OTHER TYPES OF ACCESS-CARD SYSTEMS

- Capacitance cards. Capacitor material is enclosed within the card and the coding is achieved by connecting selected plates to provide a specific coded identification.
- Optical cards. These cards have a pattern of light spots that can be read or illuminated by a specific light source, usually infrared.
- Smart cards. The card itself actually contains an integrated circuit chip embedded in the plastic. This type of card has both a coded memory and an intelligent microprocessor. The card acts as a superminiature computer as it records and stores information and personal identification codes in its memory. Smart cards have a nominal data storage capacity of about 4KB, comparing favorably with the 1.7KB capacity on the magnetic strip card. All other cards fall far below these two in data storage volume.

CARD READERS

Before selecting an access-control system, the user should be familiar with access-control readers and their operation to avoid buying a system incapable of providing the necessary mix of access-control functions.

The wall-mount swipe card reader mounts on the wall and the user simply swipes the card through the slot to obtain access to the controlled point.

The turnstile card reader is similar to the swipe card reader. The card is run through the reader from front to rear and releases a turnstile after reading the information. These are commonly used at high-volume and shift-change checkpoints.

Various models of the common insertion card reader are available. They are not normally interchangeable with each other, so a thorough understanding of the total access-control system's capability is required. There are also insertion card readers with keypads for more sophisticated applications. A valid card is inserted at the proper place and time and the cardholder enters a personal four-digit number on the keypad and removes the card. If all information and requirements have been met, the door will open. A duress feature should be part of any keypad card reader installation. Vendors and manufacturers can supply information on the specifications of keypad card readers.

The key-type reader is almost in a class of its own. In this access-control function, a rigid plastic key is inserted into the reader slot and withdrawn for access.

BIOMETRIC ACCESS CONTROL

Going beyond card reader systems, there is a new generation of personal identification and verification that may or may not be used in conjunction with card readers. These sophisticated systems are specifically personalized and are sometimes referred to as *biometric systems*. Among the various biometric access-control systems are the following:

- Hand geometry systems electronically scan an individual's hand and store the image in the system's repository for future comparison. On future system activations, the present image is measured and compared with the initial stored reference version. A positive match between the current image and the stored version allows access.
- Fingerprints are unique to an individual. A fingerprint from one finger is taken and stored by the system. The fingerprint file may also be generated manually, but this calls for a trained operator to compare the prints on a card. A computerized system uses an electro-optical recognition technique to establish a positive comparison from stored data before permitting access.
- Palm prints are as individual as fingerprints. A biometric system based on palm prints works much the same as the fingerprint technique. Palm print measurements are taken, digitized, processed, and stored. The large amount of computer memory required for this method prevents broad use of this approach.
- Retinal patterns can be captured by a device that recognizes the retinal vessel pattern of an individual's eye. A scanned picture of the back of the eye is converted to analog signals that are then converted into digital data for storage. This digital data is stored in the system's computer as a standard for later comparison and matching.
- Signature verification requires that the individual make a minimum of three copies of his or her signature. The average of these signatures is retained and stored in memory. The system's signature verification system is based on the dynamics of the individual's pen motion and also is related to time. These measurements are taken using a specially wired pen or, in some cases, a sensitized pad. Future signatures made to gain access are compared with the original or averaged signatures; when a match is made, access is granted. Early versions of this system suffered from a series of pen malfunctions and breakdowns, but later versions seem to have overcome this problem.
- Voiceprints are taken by the system and recorded in an analog signal that, like the retinal pattern technique, is converted to digital data. Measurements are derived and stored in the host computer. Future references are based on

an individual voice pattern of a few single words. The system may require the individual to speak three or four words from a reference file of seven or so words. A match of the voice patterns from the reference file permits access.

Closed-Circuit Television (CCTV) Access Control

Closed-circuit television together with the security guard officer or receptionist remotely monitoring and granting access must rely upon current knowledge and personal recognition of specific individuals. Closed-circuit television is very compatible with the identification card system of access and is capable of operating from a video picture file for granting access, adding a higher degree of security than card-only systems. The additional cost of dual-camera systems with videotape recording abilities should be weighed against your needs, as should computer-linked time recording access card systems.

Policy

Ideally, personnel should not be permitted to enter or leave the office or building outside of regular hours without producing an identification card. Where additional security is needed, this requirement should be in force at all times. Personnel who do not have their cards could be escorted to the personnel department for a temporary ID card. Such a system requires employees to cooperate in what is often considered an annoying and time-consuming routine at least twice a day. It requires all of management's skills to convince employees that this security system is necessary and is in their and the company's best interest. Security personnel must make every effort to avoid any implication of undignified treatment and harassment of employees while still maintaining the integrity of the card system.

Method

Access methods vary depending on the type of system installed, but the essential choice is between visual, remote, and electronic card inspection and acceptance.

CRIME INFORMATION SYSTEMS

Reports

In spite of all precautions, some incidence of crime is inevitable. When such incidents occur every effort must be made to catch the criminal and record the event in such a way that data is developed that may help improve security procedures to prevent reoccurrence. To this end, a crime or missing property reporting procedure is essential. Over a period of time, loss profiles and circumstances will be of considerable value in risk analysis, procedural evaluation, and security program updates.

Security reports and records may be input directly into an automated or computer-controlled system. When more advanced methods are not used or the security staff's knowledge prohibits their use, then consecutively numbered, preprinted security forms should be used. In either instance, data must be treated as confidential and appropriate safeguards provided to maintain their security. In instances where insurance claims could result, it may be necessary to use specific forms; expanded distribution advisories may be required. Please note that for insurance purposes missing items are just that—missing—until proven stolen.

INFORMATION GATHERING

To support information gathering and collection, the experience of other tenants and neighboring companies and buildings with similar security problems can be most valuable. Maintain contacts with them in order to exchange information, discuss new techniques, and work out mutual safeguards.

It is also important to establish active lines of communication with local law enforcement and fire authorities. You should know, preferably from actual test runs, their response time and capabilities in various situations. Most police departments are understaffed and are necessarily perfunctory in investigating what they must classify as petty crimes. On the other hand, police will appreciate prompt, thorough, and accurate crime reports from you. When new criminal operations develop in your area, your local police will know about it and, if your lines of communication are open, you will know. As long as you are able to anticipate a criminal's moves, you are a long way toward preventing attacks against your company or building.

IMPLEMENTATION OF SECURITY SYSTEMS

The more complicated a security program, or a system within the program, the more difficult it will be to implement. Advance testing—"dry runs"—give a strong indication of applications and can help debug any new system. All equipment involved should be tested completely over substantial periods of time, in order to ensure it is functioning properly. When a system is activated, sufficient supporting supplies should be on hand for continuing system operation, such as receipts and record forms for keys or identification card systems. As part of the program's inception, security personnel must be thoroughly trained in, and completely conversant with, the systems they will administer. Supporting systems and procedures should be equipped and supplied to work with the main system. A target date should be chosen. While every effort should be made to meet the target date once it is set, no system should be activated until everything is ready—a blundering introduction may permanently hamper system or program acceptance.

Notification

Since systems almost always involve people, indoctrination is necessary to ensure success, not only before, but also during and after systems implementation. Where a system has been pretested, you will be further along because at least some employees will have seen the system in operation. Even the simplest system such as a sign in/out log in the lobby will require some personal supervision for its introduction. A memo to all employees is necessary, but insufficient by itself. An extra person temporarily stationed with your lobby or elevator guard can help remind people of the need to sign in and out. Within days the system should be operating smoothly. On the other hand, the introduction of ID cards to be used with access-control and identification equipment will require more preparation. Here pretesting is particularly important. The test should be of a part of the program; for example, in a small area where access is limited and the number of people involved is small enough to be readily managed. A staff memo should be issued well in advance, a second reminder shortly before implementing the system, and another on the day it is activated. Follow-up memos should be sent as needed to correct misapprehensions or to reaffirm the need for cooperation.

Temporary signs or instruction posters are helpful as additional reminders of new procedures. Support personnel should be deployed and used freely to help explain where necessary. Department heads should be asked to help by reminding their people of the need and reason for such a system. Conspicuous senior security management helps to impress upon employees the importance given to the new system. When introducing an identification card system involving equipment, a senior manager should be present at various key locations during heavy traffic periods in the initial phases and until both the procedure and the equipment are working smoothly.

Modifications

In the testing and follow-up process, you will discover bugs in your program. Every system will need some alterations or adjustments; even if it is an exact duplicate of one used by another office, it will still need tailoring to fit your company's needs.

When necessary, modifications should be made as quickly as possible. Explanatory memos should be precise as to changes being made and whenever possible, as to the reasons why. Retraining may be necessary and new equipment may have to be installed. This should be done on a crash basis, if possible. Speed is essential in any system modification, since any interruption means more retraining, more explanations, and more resistance.

Follow-up

Follow-up of any new system is an absolute necessity. Without it weeks or months of planning may be wasted. Follow-up consists of checking all operations and procedures. Operational personnel should also get reactions from each group affected by the system—employees are less candid in responding to management inquiries. Pay particular attention to equipment performance and system efficiency at peak periods.

Demonstration

To demonstrate how a system works is both the simplest and the most effective teaching method. When an on-site physical demonstration is not possible, a visual presentation in an auditorium or conference room is an almost equally effective alternative. Slides, films, boards, or a blackboard can all be useful to clearly present the basics of a security system.

Keep the meetings small, short, and informative to encourage discussion. Train enough security personnel to conduct such meetings so that your entire organization can be reached quickly by scheduling a number of small groups simultaneously. Be sure each speaker is well prepared for questions; nothing can be more discouraging to listeners than a speaker who doesn't seem to understand a subject fully. Any speaker, however, is bound to get an unforeseeable question or two. In that case, don't fake it. Tell the group you don't know, but you'll find out. And then follow through. Find the answer and be sure each member of the group is notified.

Even if the question and the answer are inconsequential, it is important to show that you care, and that you are willing and capable of researching your subject as much as necessary.

Maintenance

Equipment is faulty or becomes obsolete. Systems are streamlined or short-circuited. Personnel can become lazy and enforcement complacent. Unless your program is dynamically managed, all of this security erosion can take place. You must inject a daily challenge—an atmosphere of innovation—from the top down. As we know, security requires active, minute-by-minute participation to be effective, and it is your job to keep that participation alive in your organization.

Maintenance and renewal of equipment and systems is vital. New equipment should be evaluated and considered as potential replacements in the event current equipment becomes obsolete. It is important that you keep abreast of the latest security techniques, trade publications, and vendors. While you may find that a great deal of the material doesn't apply to your situation, if you find only one new technique or one effective piece of crime prevention equipment a year, your continuing attention to the security field will have been worthwhile.

Security system erosion can begin with forms being bypassed or improperly filled out. If this continues without immediate and firm remedial action, personnel will lose confidence and respect for the system. While system modifications are frequently necessary, you must be flexible enough to make them whenever and wherever necessary; these changes must be made by management in response to need, not by employees for reasons of convenience or indifference.

Of all departments, security can least afford the luxury of low standards. To be the guardian of the office, security must always be on guard—even of itself.

SECURITY PERSONNEL

All of the diverse elements of an efficient and effective security program are designed to function within a specific environment. Each element is important to the operation of the whole, but if all factors were rated in the order of their importance, the majority of security experts would agree that the most important element in any security program is good security personnel. Machines, equipment, techniques, and systems—some enormously sophisticated—are available, but it is the security professional who selects and—even more important—operates them. It is essential, then, that security personnel at every level be given support, cooperation, and all possible help to increase their understanding and skills in a difficult and, all too often, thankless job. It is equally important to seek out the best young people interested in security as a career, rather than recruiting only retired police or military personnel. We need balanced teams of veterans and rookies backed by an educated pool of applicants in order to phase in new guards in an orderly fashion.

In order to create and operate an effective security department, personnel must be your first concern. Since security presents unique problems in terms of employment, management will be very much involved in the security personnel function. Our discussion here is limited to the special needs of security personnel and does not apply to the broader personnel needs of the company as a whole. Let's take a brief look at some elements of security personnel management: procurement, development, advancement, integration, and maintenance.

Procurement

When seeking applicants for a proprietary security force, management frequently has settled for the "guard" mentality and filled its ranks with low-wage retired persons, college students, and/or moonlighters. Emphasis should be placed on education and experience; however, we should be alert to the degree of interest an applicant demonstrates. We must look for applicants who show signs of innovative thinking, flexible approaches, and firm principles. Candidates should be active performers, not passive automatons. They must be capable of following orders, but at the same time be self-motivating. They should be familiar with general company policies, especially in regard to crime prevention, detection, apprehension, and prosecution, without any reservation. Finally, their backgrounds must be thoroughly investigated.

It is particularly important that reference checks be made as far back and as completely as possible for security job applicants Where it is at all possible, these checks should be made in personal interviews with past employers. Phone calls should be made only if personal interviews are not possible. If you do not make thorough, multiple reference checks of potential security personnel you might as well close this book—you cannot possibly have a dependable security program.

The initial procurement process should be handled by the human resource or personnel department, with security management entering the picture when a prime candidate has been discovered. A sample process is outlined below:

Human Resources/Personnel Department

1. Recruitment through newspaper and trade magazine advertising, employment agencies, recommendations of present employees, labor unions, schools, and colleges.
2. Application review
3. Preliminary interview
4. Testing
5. Reference checks
6. Refer to security management

Security Department

7. Final interview
8. Physical examination and substance-abuse screening
9. Further reference checks
10. Offer of employment

Development

Development and training of security personnel must be a continuing concern of management. Career development in security is largely accomplished by regular training to improve skills and knowledge and to stay abreast with the latest advances in the field. The merits of such training will be reflected in each person's attitude toward the job. In almost all cases, the result is a positive attitude, better morale, and increased incentive. Naturally, each individual's background will determine the amount of training required. Above all, never believe that a former law officer does not need training—they definitely do. In order for them to be successful in security, they must develop new skills and overcome some of their previous training. Your training program should consist of some of the following:

- Company indoctrination
- Company and security department policies, systems, and procedures
- Basic operation of departments
- Training in applicable basic laws (individual rights, citizen's arrests, rights of search and seizure)

- First aid, cardiopulmonary resuscitation (CPR), OSHA's Bloodborne Standard 1910.1030
- Self-defense, including weapon use, if armed
- Methods of surveillance
- Fingerprinting and photography
- Indoctrination in security equipment
- Professional standards, including attitudes toward fellow employees and other departments

Security personnel must be cheerful, cooperative, and tolerant in all their dealings within the company, for they—and the company—need every employee's cooperation. They must be patient when faced with excessive inquisitiveness, flip remarks, or irritable attitudes from their fellow workers. They must understand that they are not members of a law enforcement agency, but employees who have the job of helping to provide office security. If they are good-humored, patient, tactful, and professional, fellow employees will soon come to hold them in the highest respect. It won't happen overnight. They may have to hang in there for a while. But it will happen.

Security personnel should be reminded that they are professionals in an ever-changing field. They should be encouraged to keep themselves informed by reading security texts and publications, joining security associations, and taking formal security courses where these are available.

Advancement

In the process of career development, an individual expects to be told how they are progressing. Individuals demonstrating an interest or motivation in advancement need to see a path or career ladder in order to progress. Recognition of talent and accomplishments as well as seniority must exist.

Titles and Ranks

Most companies use military or police designations to delineate rank and authority of security personnel: corporal, sergeant, lieutenant, captain, chief of staff, security manager, director of security.

Military ranks may be appropriate for industrial guard and security forces, but in the office environment they are not suitable; they tend to create a barrier between security and the rest of the company—the very barrier that security must break down. Titles should be created without military connotations since we cannot afford to have a security force considered a paramilitary operation distinct from the business of the office. Security must be considered as much a part of the organization as accounting or sales. Possible titles that blend in with business titles in general use might be:

Top management: security executive, security operations analyst, executive security director, vice president.

Middle management: security manager, security supervisor, associate director, assistant vice president.

Operational level: senior security agent, security agent, operations officer

Because office security is different, it has the opportunity of establishing an original image rather than being saddled with inappropriate stereotypes. It is important that this be a positive image, rather than one that creates an almost instinctive resistance.

Salary

It is poor economy indeed to skimp on the wages paid to your security personnel. A poorly paid security person is a poor operative—and a resentful security person can be doubly dangerous. Better to have a smaller staff adequately—even generously—paid, than a larger staff of undercompensated personnel who feel, with some justice, that they are being asked for more loyalty than they are given in return.

Salaries should be kept above the average for your area and periodically reviewed. Each position should have a sufficiently wide salary range to allow considerable flexibility in your management of the department. Periodic performance appraisals will often dictate salary increases when promotion is either not indicated or possible because of your organizational structure. A wide salary range for each position will make this possible.

Integration

The integration of a security person into the security organization is more involved than the integration of new employees in other departments. Where other employees simply receive the personnel department indoctrination and are introduced to their nearest neighbors in their new department, the security person must be familiar with the workings of each department in the formal organization and conversant with the informal organization.

By way of review, the organization chart shows the formal organization of a company—lines of authority, reporting, responsibility, and control. An informal organization is created by friendships and association, and crosses and bypasses the formal lines.

Both types of organization are real and operate concurrently in every company. Good management uses both. It is part of the security person's job to know both intimately.

Obviously a tour of the building from roof to basement, including every setback and crawlspace, must be included as part of the integration program. Personnel should be given or have access to simplified and reduced floor plans as part of their on-the-job training.

Evaluation

The new person should be closely supervised and evaluated on the basis of how he or she reacts to different situations as well as on their overall performance.

Suggestions and changes in approaches should be made as soon as possible because it will be more difficult to break habits later. At the very least, all new security employees should be on a 90-day probation or trial basis.

Follow-up

After the new person has been on the job for a few weeks, and at intervals thereafter, you should check with them to see that their training, indoctrination, and equipment have been provided as scheduled. Without this follow-up, you can't be sure that they have been properly integrated into your operation. They also will be impressed by your concern and will usually react with increased confidence.

Morale

We need to be more concerned with morale in the security force than in many other areas of the company. Security personnel deal constantly with daily visitors and vendors, as well as fellow employees. What they do and how they do it has a negative or positive effect on the image of your company and on your security force.

Morale, of course, is more than just helping to solve employees' problems. It involves dignity, respect, and considerate treatment. The harmony you create among your people and, as an extension, that they create among the people they deal with, is a playback of your actions and attitudes in working with them.

Maintenance Uniforms

There are many different schools of thought on this subject. Uniforms, business attire, or a combination of both? Because in your office it might be inappropriate to project a uniformed image, it will be necessary to provide some method of identifying the security force to employees and others. Lapel pins, visible color-coded ID cards, pocket medallions, or name/function plates may be considered.

In outfitting the security force in a recognizable uniform, whether formal or informal, the appearance of the staff should be smart looking, functional, and properly fitted.

All too often we see people in obvious hand-me-downs that were cheaply made to begin with, and clearly don't come close to fitting. A guard so uniformed looks ridiculous and projects the same image. Once you put a person in uniform you identify him or her as a professional—which is the reason for doing it. It should follow that you will want to identify your force as neat and carefully dressed. A spit-and-polish appearance suggests a competent and efficient operation, and furthers their sense of confidence and strength.

The company should bear the cost of uniforms and accessories as well as the cost of having uniforms dry-cleaned on a regular basis. If this is not possible, a less desirable way of handling cleaning is to provide a cleaning allowance for each guard.

Minimum Equipment

Since security personnel wear uniforms or street clothes as need dictates, a locker should be assigned to each person to secure equipment and personal items.

Watch: We live in a clock-oriented world. Security guards must know when to report and when an incident occurred. This is a personal item not provided by the company.

Flashlight: A necessity for night patrol and emergency situations. Company-provided.

Pocket pager or two-way radio: Can be vital to any coordinated effort. In emergency situations, managers must be able to round up their people and instruct them immediately. Company-provided.

Communication equipment: Walkie-talkies, portable telephones, beepers, and car phones. Company-provided.

Pen and pad: For taking notes for later transcription. Company-provided.

Basics such as these are necessary and depending on the location and/or type of business, other considerations such as restraining devices, personal protection, and firearms may be considered. The justification for any of these items, and in particular firearms, require a detailed analysis and liability study.

Routines

Make it a practice to change assignments and vary routines. Movement and change will keep your people mentally active and interested. As your force becomes more effective and the rate of incidents is reduced, such changes may be the only exciting events that occur. You should also alter your routines frequently enough to make them unpredictable to a thief. Building rounds, for example, should never be made on an exact schedule.

Communications

Security, like so many special fields, uses its own language, a language derived from police usage. A sentence like "the perpetrator of the aforementioned act was apprehended while he was intent on escaping from the scene of the crime" might be considered proper securityese, but it won't enthrall management. Since management must be enthusiastic if security is to succeed, it is best that security learn to communicate in the manner management prefers.

Management is not fond of bombast or oratory. The simple stuff makes it. Management likes concise and positive answers—even a quick *no.* In writing reports, use the 5 "W's" and 1 "H": Where, When, What, Who, Why, and How. Be simple, direct, and positive about what you know and what you don't know. Don't try to fake an aura of professionalism by the use of specialized language.

SELL YOUR PROGRAM

Now that you have evaluated your security requirements and decided what your needs are, your next step is implementing the program. This means committing your company to what could be substantial expenditures. In order to get management approval for this commitment, you must submit a budget and a specific plan of attack. Most managers need little selling to accept security; they recognize the need and want it. They are, however, frequently ignorant of the elements and costs that go into an effective program. They are also, as we have mentioned, frequently unaware of the potential costs of an inadequate security program. It is important to recognize that although management rarely needs to be sold on the need for security, it very often must be sold on your security program. Management's blessing for a considerable cash outlay is not easy to get. Additionally, many companies, especially highly competitive sales-oriented firms, find it difficult to generate any enthusiasm for expenditures that cannot be directly related to income. Remember that a company's energies are largely directed toward maintaining or improving the level of net income, and not on the reduction of losses. Your job is to refocus some of your company's attention to this aspect of profit-making. You will have to sell your proposal using every tool at your disposal—slide projectors, charts, graphs, films—any device that supports and dramatizes your presentation. Be brief, but above all be accurate. You are in a business that is effective insofar as it is direct, specific, efficient, and accurate. Your presentation must reflect these qualities throughout.

The Budget

Certainly the bottom line in any presentation that touches on basic company policy is budget. Its preparation separates the professionals from the amateurs; once you've made your basic decisions you are on the firing line. Every management sharpshooter will take a shot at it, and you will need a strong will and a cool head to stand up for it. It can be a tough job to create a virgin budget. But it's your job to do, and do accurately. Many department managers overbudget to protect themselves against unforeseen contingencies and the cost-cutting attack of a sharp-eyed controller. Don't get into this game. Of all departments, security must make every effort to remain aloof from this kind of gamesmanship. Be accurate. In your budget include:

- equipment costs, including maintenance
- system costs, including supplies
- personnel cost, including miscellaneous expenses and projected increases
- a designated contingency figure

ENDNOTE

1. Don T. Cherry, *Total Facility Control*, (Stoneham, Mass.: Butterworth-Heinemann, 1986), pp. 159–69.

Chapter 20

Strikes

STRIKES AND PICKETING [1]

The following is excerpted from Russell Colling's book, *Hospital Security:*

> A real test of a facility's protection plan comes when the facility faces a strike
> or picketing situation. A *strike* occurs when some of the organization's em-
> ployees, represented by one or more unions, refuse to work as a protest against
> a serious grievance or a failure to negotiate a mutually acceptable contract.
> Picketing refers to the placement of people around the exterior of the facility
> for the dual purposes of informing the public of alleged problems and curtail-
> ing deliveries of supplies and equipment. This discussion is restricted to
> strikes and picketing related to organized labor.
>
> The primary purpose of a strike is to create hardships for the hospital,
> weaken its bargaining position, and resolve the dispute in favor of the union.
> The hardships may include disruption of patient care, intimidation of non-
> striking staff, loss of revenue, damaged or stolen property, and negative com-
> munity reaction to the institution.
>
> An organization need not be unionized to become the focus of a picket
> line. Picketing may be set up as a result of a strike or for the purpose of at-
> tempting to force the organization to recognize a collective bargaining unit.
> The immediate effect of a picket line is that union drivers will refuse to cross
> the line to make deliveries. In the initial stages, nonunion drivers will often
> cross the picket line until threats are made or physical violence is directed at
> the company, the vehicle, or the driver.

THE UNION

Reasons why a white-collar worker joins a union seem to go beyond general mo-
tivations such as salary protection and job security. Some of these attractions
might be:

- White-collar workers fear mergers and subsequent layoffs.
- Unions are now more acceptable to white-collar workers, who see teachers,
  firemen, and policemen bargaining through unions.

- Recent recessions and job losses have highlighted the insecurity of non-union work, where layoffs can be an arbitrary management decision.
- White-collar workers believe unionization can stamp out nepotism and cut down on office politicking.
- White-collar workers are being approached by more sophisticated organizers.

There is little doubt that you can look forward to attempts to unionize your office if it hasn't already happened. This is not necessarily a source of trepidation—especially if you have done your homework.

UNIONIZATION AND THE LAW

Laws governing union activities have evolved over the years and are designed to curb excesses by both unions and management and to protect the rights of individual workers. They also establish ground rules for that difficult and delicate time when a union attempts to organize an office. Legally, a company cannot:

- Intimidate, coerce, or punish personnel in their attempt to unionize.
- Spy on personnel for the purpose of determining who is actively engaged in unionization.
- Discriminate against employees who are engaged in unionization.
- Change company policy to terminate a union employee.
- Change working environments to eliminate unified groups from expanding the union concept.
- Ask potential employees about their position on unions.
- Imply operations will shut down or current benefits will be reduced because of unionization.
- Stop union personnel from soliciting members outside of business hours.
- Give preferential treatment to employees opposing unionization.
- Go to the homes of employees to solicit their opposition to the union.
- Create a petition against the union.

On the other hand, you can take certain steps to prevent unionization of your office. Legally, you can:

- Prevent the soliciting of membership during working hours.
- Campaign against unionization by stating your position.
- Air opinions, even derogatory ones, concerning unions and union officials.
- Apply all company rules regardless of the employee's position on unionization.
- Defend company policy under union attack.
- Prevent unauthorized intrusion into company space by union organizers.
- Allow your employees to talk to you about the unions.

STRIKES

In any dispute with management, the union's ultimate weapon in any dispute with management is the strike. This can take many forms, but is usually the final response to a stalemate in contract negotiations.

Strikes are unpleasant situations. Even where there is no violence and a satisfactory solution to the differences between the two parties is found, there is an aftermath of bitterness, lost wages, and division within the company. Obviously strikes are best avoided, but when it cannot, the conduct of management—and security as representatives of management—plays an important role in reconciliation.

PICKETING

Picketing is both legal and permissible as long as it is not violent and those wishing to cross picket lines are allowed to do so. The number of pickets can be limited by a court injunction to prevent mass picketing or to reduce the risk of violence where there is a bitter dispute. The real danger in picketing or demonstrating is the very real possibility of a flare-up that could lead to general violence.

Security's Role

Because any strike situation is potentially explosive, it is important that management develop contingency plans for the handling of strikes and other labor-management confrontations. Basic policy must be a diplomatic and restrained approach.

Overall, security's role should be a firm neutrality that does not hinder lawful union efforts to picket or to unionize. Security's main function is to anticipate and prevent problems, and to protect the premises, personnel, and assets of the company. Beyond these responsibilities security must not take or even imply a position in any labor-management matter. Contingency planning for strike situations includes:

- A routine for closing affected operations: Checking unoccupied areas thoroughly to see that all is in order, machines turned off, water and electricity secured, chemicals and glues properly stored, and doors and windows locked.
- Removing all strikers from the payroll.
- Notification to vendors and customers.
- Adjusting security routines for the situation.
- Employment of private contract security personnel where the possibility of sabotage exists. These supplementary guards should take over posts and patrols not seen by strikers, if possible.

- Prestrike planning.
- Determining what operations will remain active during a strike.
- Preparing a statement to the newspapers for release when a strike is called.
- Issuing a statement of position to employees.
- Advance notification to authorities of probable picketing, and determining what standby help will be available in the event of trouble.
- Evaluation of key control. Are key-holding employees among the strikers?
- Having photographic equipment available in case of mass picketing or violence, for use in seeking injunctive relief. Visible cameras can help to cool a situation or they can provoke violence, depending on the temper of the picketers. A remote television camera with a telephoto lens and videotape recorder is probably the best solution.
- Establishing a schedule of designated company spokespersons who can be reached or on hand to provide constructive replies to the press, and on the premises in the event of trouble.
- Reminding all non-striking personnel before, during, and after that the strikers are fellow employees having a dispute with company management that will be resolved shortly, and that today's strikers are yesterday's and tomorrow's coworkers.

CONSISTENT STEPS

Security plans against bomb threats, bombing, arson, demonstrations, riots, and strikes have many similarities. At the top of the list in each category is the ability to establish firm and efficient access control. Knowing and controlling who goes in and out is basic defense. Just remember, "the majority of office security problems come through the front door."

ENDNOTE

1. Russell L. Colling, *Hospital Security*, (Stoneham, Mass.: Butterworth-Heinemann, 1992), pp. 450–51.

Appendix I

Internal Relations[1]

Too often, in security/loss prevention books and in practice, attention is given to external or public relations while internal relations are ignored. A loss prevention program is wise to focus on internal and external relations, especially since many experts state that the greatest threat to business or an organization is from within. Furthermore, employees throughout an organization can be recruited to aid loss-prevention efforts.

Benefits of Good Relations

In regards to a loss prevention program, the following list will help readers understand the importance of good internal and external relations:

1. Builds respect for loss prevention department, its objectives, and personnel.
2. Reinforces compliance with policies and procedures to prevent losses.
3. Fosters assistance with loss prevention activities (e.g., programs and investigations).
4. Presents a united front against vulnerabilities to lessen losses and extend the impact of strategies. Money is saved.
5. Educates employees, community residents, and others.
6. Improves understanding of complex problems.
7. Reduces rumors and false information.
8. Improves understanding of loss-prevention program.
9. Stimulates consciousness-raising relevant to loss prevention.
10. Makes the loss prevention job easier.

Human Relations on the Job

Getting along with others is a major part of almost everyone's job. Many say it is half the job. Frequently, good human relations are a difficult objective to reach. The result, however, is increased cooperation and a smoother working environment. These policies can assist a security professional in developing human relations:

1. Get along with all employees as well as possible.

2. Say "hello" to as many employees as possible, even if you do not know them.
3. Smile.
4. Think before you speak.
5. Nonverbal messages (e.g., body language, facial expressions, and tone of voice) may be more accurate than verbal messages.
6. Listen carefully.
7. Maintain a sense of humor.
8. Try to look at each person as an individual. Avoid stereotyping (an inaccurate image of an individual or group).
9. Accept that personalities vary.
10. Don't interpret shyness as aloofness.
11. Carefully consider rumors and those who gossip.
12. Remember that when you speak about another person your comments are often repeated.
13. If possible, avoid negative people.
14. Don't flaunt your background.
15. Everyone makes mistakes. Maintain a positive attitude and learn from mistakes.
16. A positive attitude increases the quality of human relations and has an impact on many other activities (such as opportunities for advancement).
17. Cooperation increases productivity.

ENDNOTE

1. Philip P. Purpura, *Security and Loss Prevention*, (Stoneham, Mass.: Butterworth-Heinemann, 1984), pp. 71–73.

Chapter 21

Domestic Violence, Rape, and Sexual Harassment

Domestic violence—spousal abuse, child abuse, and elder abuse—continues to pervade every socioeconomic, racial, and ethnic group in our society. Public attention has been closely focused on domestic violence in Massachusetts, for example, in the past several months as a result of an alarming increase in the frequency and seriousness of domestic assaults. Recently, there have been increased efforts by the legislature, courts, and criminal justice system to coordinate an effective systemwide response to the problem of domestic violence. Other states are also addressing the problem. No business office is immune to domestic violence, abuse, stalking, and harassing phone calls.

The following material was provided by the Ryka Rose Foundation.

Domestic Abuse

If You Are a Victim of Domestic Abuse

The most difficult step for you to take is to actually admit that you are being abused by your husband or boyfriend. Yet admission is the first step necessary in finding your way out of an abusive relationship. How can you tell if you are being abused? Just ask yourself these questions:

- Does your partner prevent you from seeing family or friends?
- Does he constantly criticize you and your abilities?
- Does he intimidate or threaten you?
- Does he hit, punch, slap, or kick you?
- If you have a gun in your house, has your partner ever threatened to use it when he was angry?
- Has he ever prevented you from leaving the house, getting a job, or continuing your education?
- Has he ever destroyed things you cared about?
- Has he ever forced you to have sex or forced you to engage in sex that makes you feel uncomfortable?

If you answered "yes" to any of these questions, you should seek professional help because you may indeed be in an abusive relationship. Millions of women are struggling with similar difficulties. Perhaps you and your partner can work through these problems. But if you feel you are in danger, you owe it to yourself to seek help and support.

How to Help a Friend

One out of every two women will be in an abusive relationship at some point during their lifetime. Therefore, it is likely that you will know someone who needs help. You *can* make a difference.

- *Learn as much as you can about domestic violence.* The greatest difficulties domestic violence victims face are overcoming the emotional, physical, legal and financial hurdles that are consequences of their victimization. For further information and suggested readings, contact the National Victim Center at 1-800-FYI-CALL.
- *Never underestimate a friend's fear of danger.* Domestic violence increases in severity. Believe what your friend says, and try to help her find a safe place by calling local hotlines and shelters.
- *Contact local shelters and support groups to see how you can help.* Many crisis hotlines need volunteers to help staff the phone lines. Shelters and support groups for survivors of domestic violence need volunteers to help women rebuild their lives. You can make a difference simply by driving someone to the grocery store, accompanying her to court, or by donating basic household goods.

Rape

If You or Someone You Know Is Raped

The most important immediate steps you can take are:

- Get to a safe place or call someone you trust.
- Call a rape crisis center or your local hospital.
- Don't take a shower; preserve the clothes worn at the time of the attack.
- Get a medical exam to ensure medical aid and prompt collection of physical evidence.
- Inquire about tests for possible pregnancy, HIV, and sexually transmitted diseases.

If You Are a Rape Survivor

Friends and family may think you are "okay" if you were not otherwise physically harmed in the attack. Many people do not understand the extent of the trauma endured by rape victims and even victims of attempted rape. Your body may look fine, but you still need time to recover emotionally and spiritually. As time goes on, you may undergo all or some of the following steps toward recovery:

- Guilt, shock, and denial
- Anger and depression
- Understanding and acceptance

Fortunately, there are many community-based programs to assist you, your partner, and your family through these stages of recovery. By seeking early intervention, you may be able to prevent future problems which are common among rape survivors, such as:

- Eating disorders (anorexia, bulimia, and overeating)
- Substance abuse
- Sleep disturbances, nightmares, flashbacks
- Loss of self-esteem, trust of others, and the capacity for intimacy
- Chronic stress, self-blame, unshakable sense of irretrievable loss
- Memory impairment, trouble concentrating
- Phobic reactions to events, places, activities which trigger recollection of the trauma
- Intense startle reactions (hypervigilance)
- Abdominal and gastrointestinal complaints
- Palpitations, dizziness, paresthesia
- Chronic headaches
- Fatigue and sexual dysfunction

Facts About Rape

- Rape by someone you know is still rape.
- Even if you submit, it's still rape.
- Victims almost always feel guilty.

Violence Against Women:
Why You Should Get Involved

Most of us think, "It can't happen to me." Well, it can. The truth is that domestic abuse and rape can happen to anyone, regardless of age, race, creed, sexual orientation, or financial status—and regardless of what we might or might not do. The statistics can no longer be ignored.

1. One in eight women will be raped at some point during her lifetime. (National Victim Center)
2. More than six out of ten rape victims are under the age of 18, and three out of ten are under 11 years old. (National Victim Center)
3. Rape has a devastating impact on the mental health of the victims, with almost one third of all rape victims developing post-traumatic stress disorder

(PTSD). These women are thirteen times more likely to have serious alcohol problems and twenty-six times more likely to have major drug abuse problems. (National Victim Center)
4. Domestic violence is the number one cause of injury to women—more than rape, auto accidents, and muggings combined. (National Woman Abuse Prevention Project)
5. There are only 1,500 battered women's shelters in America, compared to 3,800 animal shelters. (*New York Times*, March 18, 1992)

Violence against women is illegal, and it will not end unless society speaks out in unison, condemns such behavior, protects its citizens' rights and safety, and supports its victims.

How to Get Help

Most communities offer a variety of services, including counseling, support groups, shelters, and referrals for legal services. Most states have toll-free hotlines available, but they are often hard to find in the phone books. Here are a few suggestions:

- Call the National Victim Center at 1-800-FYI-CALL
- Call the National Council on Child Abuse and Family Violence at 1-800-222-2000
- Call your state Coalition of Battered Women Services Groups (usually listed in the white pages beginning with the name of the state)
- Check both the White and Yellow pages for a Rape Crisis Center, Rape Hotline, or Battered Women's Hotline
- Check the "Self Help" section of the White pages for crisis phone numbers

National Victim Center
555 Madison Avenue
Suite 2001
New York, NY 10022
212-753-6880

309 West Seventh Street
Suite 705
Fort Worth, TX 76102
817-877-3355

2111 Wilson Boulevard
Suite 300
Arlington, VA 22201
703-276-2880

© 1992, Ryka Rose Foundation. Permission granted to reproduce by Ryka Rose Foundation

Violence

Have you ever sat in a room full of survivors of rape or domestic abuse? Believe us, it can be quite an experience. We feel that if a book such as this will be read by thousands of people, it would be incomplete if we didn't address this topic and give some advice so you, the professional, can pass this information on to coworkers.

Sexual Harassment

Media coverage always raises awareness of issues. Laws have been passed to protect the victim from offensive behaviors, and sexual harassment should not be allowed to continue in any office surroundings. If, as a manager, you allow it, an employee will have no other alternative but to seek a complaint in the courts.

Legally, What is Sexual Assault?

Under Massachusetts law, as well as that of several other states, there are two major categories of sexual assault against adults: rape and indecent assault and battery.

Rape occurs when the offender "has sexual intercourse or unnatural sexual intercourse with a person and compels such person to submit by force and against her will, or compels such person to submit by threat of bodily injury." Rape and attempted rape are punishable by up to twenty years imprisonment.

Heavier penalties may apply if the rape causes serious bodily injury, is the result of group attack, or occurs during the commission of certain specified crimes, such as robbery.

Both men and women may be the victims and perpetrators of rape under Massachusetts law. Rape may occur when the victim is unable to give consent because he or she is unconscious. Rape may occur between people who know each other, and between people who have previously had consensual sexual relations.

The crime of indecent assault and battery occurs when the offender, without the victim's consent, intentionally has physical contact of a sexual nature with the victim. This type of contact may include touching a woman's breasts or buttocks, or the genital area of a man or woman. Indecent assault and battery may be punished by up to five years imprisonment.

Acquaintance Rape

Acquaintance rape is a rape committed by someone known to the victim—a friend, classmate, coworker, instructor, relative, or casual acquaintance such as a clerk in a store. It is important to remember that acquaintance rape is not a separately defined crime. Any person, whether an acquaintance or not, who compels a person to submit to sexual intercourse against his or her will, by force or by threat of bodily injury, commits the crime of rape.

One recent study concluded that women are more likely to be sexually assaulted by a person known to them than by a stranger. In one survey, most of the college women who had been raped knew their attacker, and the attacker was the woman's date in more than one-half of the rapes.

Victims of acquaintance rape are often involved in situations where they trust their acquaintance not to be an assailant. Some assailants foster a false sense of friendliness in order to sustain a level of trust in their intended victim. They use this technique to gain their victim's initial cooperation in going to an apartment or vehicle where the aggressor can more easily exert force or threat of force on the victim.

Preventing Sexual Assaults in Social Situations

Certain contributing factors repeatedly surface in acquaintance rape situations: ineffective communication, the use of drugs and alcohol, and sex-role stereotypes. Understanding some of these factors can help prevent sexual assault.

Men and women will want to understand their right to be free from harm, and the legal consequences that increasingly fall upon persons who compel sexual relations by force or threat of force.

For Men

If, by force or threats, you compel a person to have sex against his or her will, even if you know the person or have had sex with him or her before, you are committing a rape—even if you think the other person has been teasing and leading you on, even if you've heard that women say "no" but mean "yes," even if you think it's manly to use force to get your way.

1. Avoid excessive use of alcohol and drugs. They interfere with clear thinking, effective communication, and your ability to respond in your own best interest.
2. Being turned down for sexual relations is not necessarily a rejection of you personally. A person who says "no" to sexual relations is expressing his or her unwillingness to participate in a specific act at a specific time.
3. Accept the other person's decision. "No" means no. Don't read in other meanings. Don't continue after the person says "no."
4. Don't assume that just because a person flirts or dresses in a manner you consider sexy that he or she wants to engage in sexual relations.
5. Don't assume that previous permission for sexual relations means a person is under a continuing obligation to have sex with you. Don't assume your date wants the same degree of intimacy that you do.
6. Rape is a crime of violence. It is motivated by the desire to control and dominate, not solely by sexual desire.
7. Don't assume spending money on a date entitles you to sex.

8. Don't make statements that imply forced sexual demands.
9. Don't allow others to attempt forced sex with another person.

Remember that people who have been sexually traumatized carry this pain with them for a long time.

For Women

1. Say "no" when you mean no. Communicate your limits clearly. Say "yes" only when you mean yes. Know what you are feeling, and express yourself clearly.
2. Be assertive. Submissive behavior can encourage sexual aggression. Passivity might be misinterpreted as permission. Be direct and firm with someone who is pressuring you sexually. If someone starts to offend you, respond promptly and firmly. Overly polite approaches might be misunderstood or ignored.
3. Pay attention to what is happening around you. If you feel threatened, don't be embarrassed to ask for help or to leave.
4. Trust your intuition. If you feel you are being pressured into unwanted sexual relations, don't hesitate to express your unwillingness, even if it might appear rude.
5. Be cautious of or avoid dating men who push you around or display extreme hostility, anger, jealousy, and possessiveness.
6. Carry enough money so that you can leave a situation, if necessary.

Index